# Hope Remains

## The journey through the first year after my son's suicide

*Lori Boarman*

RED
PENGUIN
Books

Red Penguin Books

www.RedPenguinBooks.com

Special discounts are available on quantity purchases by corporations, associations, educational groups and others. For details, contact Red Penguin Books at 516-448-4993 or Stephanie@RedPenguinBooks.com.

ISBN

Print 978-1-952859-01-4

Digital 978-1-952859-00-7

# CONTENTS

Unqualified.

I never, ever, saw myself writing. It was the one thing I loathed in school and it's probably the one thing that has kept me from pursuing my masters degree. In high school, I used to ask my dad for help and I would speed abbreviate so that I could capture every piece of the sentence he was saying while telling him, "No, no I'm not writing what you say word for word." I never thought I was creative, and I always struggled to find the words; but sometimes we are called to do things we feel we are unqualified to do. God often uses "broken people" (scripture has an abundance of examples) and now I'm very much one of them as my second son, Logan Ray Boarman, unexpectedly took his life with a single gunshot to his head on December 15, 2017 at the age of 23.

You see, I'm a NICU nurse and my husband is a detective for the Sheriff's office. We had 4 amazing children (one adopted) and we have a great marriage with little to no disfunction (everyone has some though, right?). We had married young as we started a family earlier than expected, but a mom was the reason I felt I had been put on earth to be. My husband, Glenn, helped me get through nursing school with a total of 3 kids at graduation. We had made it nearly debt free, moved to Colorado Springs to be closer to family, and found a house in a great school district that by definition made us a middle-class family. Glenn resisted faith initially, but in the last 15 years had found it to be "truth" and therefore gave me everything I had ever wanted: a loving intact family, a great job, my favorite dogs to love on, a community full of love, an ample lifestyle, and a family that did faith together. But now, everything changed as my single most important identity on earth—a mother—was put on trial (if only in my mind).

And I became a writer. Without regards to how it would taint our family name, I began to heave info. I didn't wait for people to ask the questions, I love the details and just assumed they wanted them, too. I felt like I was 'saving' those from the agony of their thoughts and awkwardness of asking. Without fear of contaminating thoughts of how we had previously been perceived, I acknowledged Logan's death was by suicide and that he likely suffered from severe clinical depression. Many praised this stating the stigma surrounding both, but that only cheered me on.

We learn so much about someone when they're gone, and without realizing it, I became the preserver of Logan's legacy. I recognize he probably wouldn't have liked me sharing intimate details, but it's now about the needs of the living. It has been therapeutic for me to talk through the journey, but it was also a *hope* that I could somehow bring awareness and not only helps others feel less alone, but maybe change one life.

I never felt qualified to write, but I did continue to pray about where God wanted me throughout this experience. I wondered if it was speaking in schools, working with non-profits, changing jobs to something mental health, what?? And in the meantime, I put words through the keyboard when prompted and wasn't even realizing I was writing a book. Thinking out loud seems to give me the freedom to release those thoughts, feelings, or topics, at least for a little while. By being raw, vulnerable, and honest, I hoped to offer insight and help others sympathize with a mother's grief and for those hurting throughout the same torment of mental health, offer relief from isolation. Severe trauma changes us and my goal was always to use it to change myself for the better. Although there are definite weeks, days, or minutes I have aimed more for the pity party, unable to evict all my regrets and deal with the word forever, somehow the tiniest light has continued to show me hope—that the sun always shines in the morning and a new day and feelings will occur.

So as time passed, the plea's and encouragement to write a book didn't cease, although it continued to be daunting to me. "Can I do this?" I was a good communicator, but not a good writer. "I don't have the skillset or ability to do this task." But reflection revealed I was drawing my confidence from the wrong place, and not realizing that God calls the unqualified so that there exists the gap that He can fill. He wants us to trust that He will cover us with his strength and power, otherwise we would think we have done the job ourselves. When our skillset doesn't measure up, we often put aside and wait for things we're qualified to undertake, but then we are missing out on some incredible opportunities to see God working. When I really asked, "Is God calling me to do this?" I got my answer when I was reading back over my posts and realizing I hadn't even remembered composing most of them and they didn't appear to be things "I" would produce. I had followed His prompting each time, and there has been no confusion on if this was my work or His. I had the most important requirement: I had an experience others could benefit from learning from, and I had a desire to follow the verse I had tattooed on my foot last year: Not my will but yours be done Luke 22:42. Everything fell into place as a coworker prompted by a post introduced me to my amazing editor, who appreciated my vision and reassured me the book had already been written; it's my story.

Clearly, I could have a hundred conversations with you about how my life has been forever changed, how I'm not the same as before and even offer my advice, but this book is a synopsis of how we actually reacted in real time, through the first year of the most horrific unimaginable journey we would endure. This book is about the end, but also a beginning and all the what ifs in between. It's composed of those day to day posts I made on Facebook. While nearly all entries were extracted from Facebook in real time, a couple have been inserted, some not originally published due to the sensitivity of others at the accompanying time. Will I regret some of my decision about what I wrote when I see things differently? Perhaps, but you get the raw, genuine feelings of that coexistent time. I may apologize at some of my hasty actions, my explanations of suicide and even analyzations, but this is grief, and it's not pretty much of the time. I had actually hoped to have this finished and produced much sooner, but I never imagined how demanding it would be to sift through the very difficult details and accounts of our lives since Logan died; many which would have better to some, forgotten.

There are ways I know I'm getting better, moving through this process: a friend announces a baby and I don't automatically feel jealous (well, most of the time at least), I don't log into Logan's email account everyday hoping to find another tactile presence, and some mornings I can be awake for 20 seconds before it hits me like a thud that he's no longer here. But suicide is like no other kind of death and being gentle and forgiving of myself has been an immense struggle. Suicide is one of the most confusing experiences. In my research, there are times I sympathize, times I'm angry, times I feel sorry for him, times I blame him, times I'm so sad for him, times I feel it's so irrational, and times I actually empathize with the pain I'm feeling and want it to all go away like his did. Every emotion as I walk this journey is wrapped in this multidimensional and complex state. The hardest part is the entire part. There's no arriving, it's a never ending journey. What ifs wrapped in hope.

---

Don't worry, this book isn't *all* about faith. It's about my furry friends and glimpses of how those #painsuckers warm my inner being and keep me laughing. It's about family and how they sustained my essential purpose. It's about experience and struggling while #findingjoy, but realizing it can be found. It's about #mentalhealthawareness and #suicideawareness and #whatifs. It's about strangers, it's about friends. It's about my son, Logan, and how he left extreme sadness, anger, contrite feelings, depression, and lots and lots of tears. But it's also about a testament of *Hope* despite those tears.

---

To my fellow suicide grievers, I am so sorry. There is a definite difference between grieving a suicide than another kind of death. It takes such a toll on the body emotionally, spiritually, and physically. Seize all the experts advice and take care of yourself first. I hope you can find joy in your journey. Grieve and some days, grieve harder. I've learned that you can still hurt and be able to smile at cute fur babies and celebrate other's accomplishments. It's exhausting being okay, but it's also okay to not be okay. You will likely have an inflated view of your role so be gentle, identifying how you would treat a friend. Have the same compassion for yourself. When you have what ifs, deviate them to what you hope for now. It will facilitate your survival.

To everyone else, just be still. Don't try to fix anything, it can't be. Just be present and don't say, "I can't imagine." Try to instead. Keep educating yourself on mental health, suicide, and then go implement it out there.

I am not a writer, *He is*. He is writing my story, I'm simply putting it out there for others to see. I am admitting my weakness, and in that, I get to see the power of God at work; when I am weak, He is strong. God is glorified when I am unqualified. I hope you have a story like this. If one doesn't come to mind, maybe you are just asking if *you* can?

---

My aunt sent me this and I think it's so perfect. She wrote:

"Read this verse and thought of you and the project in front of you.

*The Father is a merciful God, who always gives us comfort. He comforts us when we are in trouble, so that we can share that same comfort with others in trouble.*

- 2 Corinthians 1:3-4"

# PROLOGUE: A NEW BEGINNING?

My son, Logan Ray Boarman, took his life on December 17, 2017, one week after quitting his job. He was barely 23, his birthday only days before...

He was the second born, following in order to another brother, Bryce, who was 4 years older and 2 miscarriages. The happiest baby most had ever seen, literally smiling at everyone who would even give him a glance. A sister we named Savannah followed only 19 months later and although I worried about this close gap and how that would impact Logans attention, he was always a character gaining notice, and they both shared much of their play they would become best friends and hardly notice me! I had always wanted little blond locked babies full of personalities, and so I loved showing them off and was constantly so incredibly grateful my house was full of life (and with so much cuteness was the icing on the cake). While we joked that Logan was the most planned because I was merely 17 with Bryce and Savannah preceded my graduation from nursing school (born after we attempted a birth control study to earn some extra money for bills), my heart was so full. The only thing I truly ever wished for was to be a mother. It was innate in me and I clung to the hope that I would somehow be lucky enough to have this dream come true.

As a very young child, we could see his love of books emerging. His "stack" by his pillow was an ever so important bedtime ritual. If even one fell, he would get frustrated and fix them immediately. I quickly realized he had many memorized after only a reading or two, and long before he could distinguish letters. As time went on, we discovered his picture perfect memory, imagination, and intelligence was a gift. He could ever so quickly recite full minute commercials on TV, explain the exact toxins in cigarettes he had learned about once to the unsuspecting smoker, and use words in arguments that both we and his teachers had to look up! He was a connoisseur of conversation and engaged easily. Although his imagination took over frequently, including vivid memories of him conquering all the evil power rangers on the soccer field in the middle of the game, he was also very matter of fact and would like to correct those that weren't following the rules, or if you left out pertinent particulars of information. Being honest, he would often tell his friends, "I'm done playing now and would like to go home and rest". Although he was not shy in any way, I believe he was introverted and needed his quiet time and a book to recover.

Logan grew up in a snug middle class neighborhood. He had all the makings of a well rounded kid; boy scouts, sports, pets, guitar lessons, church-VBS, camps and youth group, fun city events, family gatherings, and learning to be independent with me working part time. Being so close in age, he often shared in sport events with his sister. He had everything to do with video games, which was a shared loved between his dad and brother. He made everything exciting, whether it was wanting to always win the best costume on Halloween, or being the goofiest, loudest at any given event. He was known for his smile and friendliness, but we often heard, "there is something special about that kid". I'll never forget one teacher conference when she told me, "I really believe Logan is going to do big things, he is so unique and gifted". While some teachers would take offense to Logan's intellectual corrections, she saw his brain clicking and the potential it had. There's no doubt as he aged we discovered he was a different kind of thinker. Sometimes being so frustrated as we were stumped in our parental arguments, we attempted to make it not be the elephant in the room. We all knew he was different and we willing acknowledged it and tried to embrace it.

Everything came easy for Logan, and with that came a little bit of laziness. He could do the hardest of math problems without showing his work, so why should he? He could draw his family tree acknowledging each person by simple changes in the stick figures, so why give us fancy bows or full outlined clothes? He scored a few goals in soccer games, so why practice? He could pass his AP physics class by getting the grade reflected on his final, so why do any homework along the way?

He reinvented himself during late middle school attaining new friends that were more in line with his ethics and intelligence. We adopted 5 year old Amaya, from Africa, after a sit down family meeting where everyone consented with excitement. Logan took to her more than the others, spending hours watching movies and over time frequently assisting with her homework when it became difficult. He would often intervene between us when he thought our parenting was unfair or our emotions were spent.

Freshman and sophomore year came and went without much incidence, but then somewhere around his Junior year, Logan began to withdraw from the family. He no longer wanted to participate in family events without solicitation, he came straight home from school to his retreat of a bedroom arising only for dinner, and even discussed his doubts about faith and arguments for pulling out of youth group. My fears, which I expressed often in words and time limitations, were of video game addiction. At the time, there was little documentation to the attributes of this diagnosis, and therefore I had no arguments in his book.

When he was accepted at School of Mines, a prestigious engineering school he automatically qualified for because of his academic achievements, we thought this would be his new beginning. A brilliant HS student scoring one point away from perfect on his ACT's and having nearly a years AP credits going into college, this school had all the promise of him fitting in and excelling. But after tucking him into a dorm filled with large TV consoles and gaming set ups, I was discouraged. And then subsequently it was extremely disappointing when he decided to come home at semester struggling with grades and having physical issues I attributed to anxiety (although he didn't agree). I then became convinced of his computer addiction. Not knowing which came first...the anxiety/depression from gaming or the gaming pulling him away from reality, we struggled to know how to parent a now adult. We knew he was struggling and we, ourselves, could call it addiction, depression, etc., but he was never diagnosed and we never realized the seriousness of it. We were immune to the world of clinical depression, a disease, and the dangers if left untreated. Despite our ignorance, we still pursued helping him in every way we could. Him and I went to counseling a couple times only to my disappointment at his denial of behaviors, therefore little forward implementation on his part. I wished now that I had found another therapist, as really neither of us connected to the young girl in any way.

For nearly 3 years Logan worked as a Pizza Hut driver, and attempted college locally at UCCS to pursue a degree in Engineering, wanting to help people by creating orthotics and devices to better their lives. He somewhat transformed himself again after being home just a few months, when he met a girl we later found out he had wanted to marry. I could see the hope in his eyes and he would often tell me he loved me again. They dated for about 2 years and although he had perked up a bit during this time (even taking a family vacation with us), we could see the step back after the breakup when he once again was drawn for extended periods of time to his dark, cold room in the basement. When confronted on the D that was consistent in at least one class a semester, he acknowledged difficulty sleeping, frequent headaches, and focusing in class, but would never acknowledge that he might need professional help. The end of the semester of December 2016, was an all time low as he refused to finish out the last week of school. I'll never know what talks actually took place between the dean and him, but I'm still a little bitter they (or Mines) didn't address the root cause of weak performance in an otherwise bright and promising kid. Although we were not surprised, were deeply saddened for him when he announced his desire for a different path than school. We nevertheless supported him, even helping research what it would entail to pursue different interests.

His demeanor that spring remained fairly stable and attempts to exercise, eat better, be present, and find a career, although were not ideal, were noticed. When he so excitedly accepted a position as a call taker (911) with the city in August of 2017, we thought this was another new beginning (see a trend here?). He appeared the happiest we'd seen him in years in those first few weeks; bonding with his nurse mom and police man dad with both funny, and tragic stories. Then, in early December, despite sensing he was a little more down in the last week or so, discovering he had resigned, we were angry, confused, disappointed and scared. Although Glenn found out through a co-worker he had left, we were waiting for him to come to us about it. That moment never came and on December 15, 2017 at approximately 0300 in the morning, we got the news that would cause never-ending pain: our sweet Logan, who was not violent and hadn't even ever cussed at me in the heat of the moment, had defied the rules of life and taken his with a single gunshot wound to his head. He had applied for and purchased a gun, written letters, and driven to a familiar parking lot. One last call to dispatch with directions on how to find him. I only wish he had found himself...

**Lori Logan Boarman** is with **Mowgli Mia St. Bernard** and **2 others**.

Posted by Lori Logan Boarman

December 15, 2017 · 🌐

I'm not really sure how I'm supposed to share this news, but Logan Boarman took his life late last night.

We loved him so much and as best as we knew how.

Please, if you think ending your life is the only answer, get help. There is always hope. Call me. Jesus loves you this I know. And He is always good. We will only get through this because God is bigger. He will carry us through this awful time too.

 Write a comment...

# DECEMBER 2017

**DECEMBER 15, 2017**

*(Shared from Bryce's post)*

*Logan, what I wouldn't give to spend 1 more day with you! I love you and*

*will cherish the memories forever, like our shared love for Barney!*

*Today has been one of the hardest days imaginable but my comfort comes from my god. "God will wipe away every tear from their eyes; there shall be no more death, nor sorrow, nor crying. There shall be no more pain, for the former things have passed away" (Revelation 21:4)*

*If you or someone you know is struggling please seek help! National Suicide Prevention Hotline: 1-800-273-8255*

*(Shared from Savannah's post)*

*I wish I could hug you, I wish I could hear your voice and that deep laugh one last time, I wish I could listen to more random facts you had stored in that brilliant mind of yours, I wish I could've taken the pain away..there's a million things I could wish for right now, but most importantly I wish you knew how loved you were. This has been the hardest day, but the love and support we have received from family and friends just shows how much you were loved and cared about.*

*We miss you like crazy and we love you even more. "The Lord is near to the brokenhearted and saves the crushed in spirit."Psalm 34:18 Rest easy big brother* 🤍

*Please don't let your pain and suffering go unheard before it's too late. National Suicide Prevention Hotline: 1-800-273-8255*

## DECEMBER 16, 2017

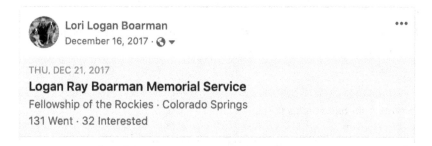

## DECEMBER 17, 2017

Friends. I have not been able to be on FB and read your messages but I'm told there are so many sweet people that have left them. I am having glimpses of peace, and despite how short those are, I'm feeling your prayers.

When everyone asks what they can do, please, don't just say you will pray for us, take time and actually do it. We need it. And if you don't actually believe in prayer, reach out to me. Despite my pain, *nothing* could give me more peace than to know that Logan's death could lead even just one to knowing Christ.

I promise, in time I will read through each one of your messages, posts, etc. I just want you to know I appreciate them even though I haven't responded or acknowledged them.

I love you all.

## DECEMBER 19, 2017

Animals sure know…

**Lori Logan Boarman** is with Mowgli Mia St. Bernard.
December 19, 2017 · Colorado Springs · 🌐 ▾

Is this a hug?

## DECEMBER 19, 2017

It's so so hard. This notice is not perfect. Our brains are still in a fog and it's something you have to get done, even when you are still not ready. So many things I already wish I could change in it. But I know it's just a piece.

I'm sharing, hoping you understand how hard it is to sum up Logan's life in a few sentences.

National Suicide Hotline 1-800-273-8254

Logan Ray Boarman

Dec. 11, 1994 - Dec. 15, 2017

Logan Ray Boarman; son, brother, and friend died on December 15, 2017 in Colorado Springs, Colorado at the age of 23.

Logan is survived by his parents, Glenn and Lori Boarman of Colorado Springs; older brother, Bryce; younger sisters, Savannah and Amaya.

Logan was born on December 11, 1994 in Aurora, Colorado to Glenn and Lori. He graduated from Cheyenne Mountain High School in 2013. Logan continued his studies at Colorado School of Mines and University of Colorado, Colorado Springs. Logan most recently worked as a dispatcher for the Colorado Springs Police Department.

Logan's family remembers him as a kind and brilliant young man who could recite both encyclopedic knowledge as well as useless facts. Winning multiple state science Olympiad awards and scoring a near perfect on his ACTs were some of his proudest accomplishments.

Logan attended Fellowship of the Rockies and during his youth group years he played guitar and served on several Juarez Mission trips. Attending church camp each summer and acting in church plays was something he was very passionate about, even returning as a counselor.

Boy Scouts, soccer, distributing Bertie Botts, and certainly his creative Halloween costumes will most be remembered from his younger years.

He always loved reading, particularly Harry Potter and Lord of the Rings.

He grew into an avid gamer and certainly those friendships surrounding that were important to him.

Memorial Service, 4:00pm, Thursday, December 21, 2017, Fellowship of the Rockies, 1625 South 8th Street, 80905.

All are welcome to attend and celebrate Logan's life.

In lieu of flowers, memorial contributions may be made to Fellowship of the Rockies in Logan's name.

---

# DECEMBER 20, 2017

So proud of my youngest daughter. There are no rules on how to do this, but she's doing it well.

Pick up any book and you will learn quickly that we don't all grieve the same. But what about children? As adults, can we have any understanding of what they comprehend?

Amaya knows what death is and, by definition, that means she knows Logan is not coming back. But doesn't she understand that? What exactly does that mean in an 11-year-old mind? How would I know because I don't even know what that means in a 45-year-old mind.

Of course, it's hard to be her mom right now as I want to question and analyze her every move making sure she is okay. But I'm realizing she has a more maturing mind than most her age. She has learned to articulate what she wants, what she is thinking and is okay with everyone not agreeing. Her counselor and teachers say she is as healthy as she can be because she is able to say what she needs, even if it's that she doesn't know.

Last Friday, she was awoken just as we were in the early hours of the morning and the day began long. She was fairly stoic all morning, crying only rarely and only a few tears. Was she thinking of all the things she could have done, just like we were? Was she thinking of the movie she watched with Logan on Sunday? Was she happy, or sad, that she was the last one to get a good-bye and a hug? Was she already worrying about the math he wasn't going to be able to help her with? Was she wondering what forever looks like? Or was she just trying to figure out why she wasn't crying, sobbing like we were?

Just before lunchtime, she asked if she could go to school. Of course, we wanted to give her whatever she thought she needed and my Aunt offered to take her (only a block away). Her one request was that she didn't want anyone to approach her about it. She knew some would already know but just didn't want to talk about it. Fair enough.

School seemed to go okay for her and she came home asking if she could still go to the Christmas party she had been invited to. What? I couldn't comprehend...but she said, I don't know what else to do. I don't want to just sit around here while everyone is just crying. For me, it was a relief that she would be gone for a few more hours and I didn't have to play the mom role and figure out how to include her in, well, in the nothing that we were doing. She went to the party and a friend's mom posted this picture. Hard to see. And I wondered as people were finding out would they think it was crazy she was at a party? I almost removed my name from the tagging. I don't usually care what people think, but was this weird? I didn't understand it. How could she be happy? How could she be having a good time? Does she really get it? Or is this just how 11-year-olds process...

With Monday approaching, Amaya made it known she wanted to continue going to school. It was the same response when I asked why. "I don't really want to just sit around here all day while everyone just cries." She did request once again to not have to talk about the situation though. However, I'm a realist and know some kids already knew, some will be curious and the rumors will be flying. I pointed out to her that if it were one of her friends, she would be wondering and she would want to ask. Not to be mean or rude or even invasive, but it was just human nature to be curious. So we discussed it and she agreed that the teachers could tell all the kids what happened, but to please let them know that she wasn't ready to talk about details. If they wanted to say they were sorry, that was okay, but to please not ask questions. Walking to school she looked at me and said, "Mom, I feel bad that I want to go to school. I feel bad that I'm not crying like everyone." It was true, I had only seen a couple of tears in as many days. Oh her heart; my heart. I did the mom comforting thing and let her know it was okay. That we all do things differently and that in time, she might cry a lot, or that she may never cry at all. How can I know? How can she know?

(A year later we are driving in the car and she looks at me and says, "Mom, do you ever just cry and you don't even know why? Like last night I just cried in bed as I was trying to go to sleep and I don't even know why?!" I responded, "Yes, and it's probably hormonal for you." But in fact, I really lied, although just a partial lie? Sometimes, I find myself crying and I'm not sure what triggered it, but every tear has Logan's name on it. It ends up being about Logan despite where it starts. It's like I can't waste a tear on something else that wouldn't be as important as my son...so I always go there...)

## DECEMBER 21, 2017

Today will be hard. But today I'm hanging on to this:

For I know the plans I have for you, declares the LORD, plans to prosper you and not to harm you, plans to give you hope and a future. Jeremiah 29:11

I know there will be good things that come out of today. Look for them with me.

## DECEMBER 22, 2017

Generations, families, are supposed to look up to and cherish those that were before us; contributing and tending to our legacy. We hope we gain character traits from those we respect so much and even pass on our favorite physical attributes to those to come; like my blue eyes and blond, natural highlighted hair. We like to dream of how our flicker of life will be presented to those looking for reasons to identify with our family name.

Suicide voids so much of that. It makes so many things final.

He won't get to contribute to the next generation and I wonder how he will be remembered by those that one day talk about him in past tense terms: "My uncle took his life, I wonder if I get my depression from him?" Will he be regarded and remembered for his fun, uninhibited personality with useless facts? or will people just think about his last act of a one-sided goodbye.

I can remember the time our beloved first Saint died very unexpectedly at age 4, arresting upon arrival at the vet. Logan was 11 years old and at soccer practice. Because I would have wanted to, I thought he should see her before she was cremated and so without giving an option, I pulled him and let him in on the news of our direction of travel. This would be a one-sided goodbye. And he wasn't happy about it. I have since learned that not everyone needs closure in this way and hoped he didn't hold a certain bitterness towards me regarding our Bosco's death. He later chose to be with Zippy, our Wheaton Terrier of 12 years as we allowed her to part this world in comfort just a year ago. He was more mature, but Zippy was also alive so it was an active goodbye. And it's weird how in certain moments I had an omen and had wanted Logan to be close to death hoping that would engage him more to his faith. This was one of those moments I remember being thankful he was there for.

Would he have wanted to say goodbye to his sibling? Dead or alive or it would have mattered?

Logan died in an instant and so there was no visiting him at the hospital. However, there was that chance at the funeral home.

His siblings said no.

His dad said no.

It was just me that needed a goodbye, one-sided or not.

Now don't get me wrong. I am not much of a believer in getting much out of a box of ashes. His spirit is not there and I just don't consider that him anymore, but will I regret not running my fingers through his blond hair one more time? Decisions are so difficult after suicide because you doubt all you've made and question the what-ifs and frankly don't trust yourself. But I made the resolution to go see Logan before my sweet baby would be downsized to a box we keep on an undecided shelf.

My cousin, Collin, who was one of the adults that knew Logan better than most and an important piece of Logan's life (mostly through camps Collin ran each summer, not only a kid attending, but then as a counselor, but also from our families being so close) was around much of the first days after the horrific incident. He was in contact with the funeral home and was guiding me in every situation. Initially, we weren't sure if they would even allow us to view his body but Collin had requested to go with me should we get the privilege of seeing my own baby boy. I was told it was their decision which gave me the feeling they had already confiscated my parental rights. I felt yet another part of the crime scene. Thankfully the word came in that he could be…and my mind turned to better versions of his appearance. He died of a single bullet to head, but does this mean he did a good, clean job? Your mind can only wonder…

When the subject came up early on, a few people had offered to accompany me. In anticipation, my dear friend Kristi, who was also very present both in our past and current lives, had offered first and so I declined all subsequent sweet requests. "You aren't going by yourself, right?" Because my immediate family abandoned their rights to go, I didn't think it was fair to allow a general viewing. But then there were my parents…they had assertively told me on the phone (they were in Kauai catching a flight) they wanted to see him. Greedily, I wanted to tell them no; but I had to remember Logan was not just my son, but their grandson and he didn't tell them goodbye. Even if they wanted a one-sided one, they deserved that choice, unlike I had given Logan with the dog all those years ago.

It was Tuesday, and what a mind experience I went through preparing myself for that hour. My parents would be coming straight from the airport so we would just meet them there. I selfishly was dreading seeing them. I didn't want to comfort anyone else this day as I was ready to fully embrace my weakness and emotions. I was already feeling like I owed people explanations and apologies for what my son had done. His betrayal had taken my strength and on this day, I had nothing else to give.

Kristi picked me and Collin up. I honestly don't remember what we talked about on the way there, but once there my parents arrived in the parking lot just a minute later. After the agony of my reluctant hugs, we said not much else and walked inside. "Are you ready?" Mmm, whatever does this mean but ya, take me inside. I did ask my parents to wait to join me. I needed time to release a few things before feeling like I had to reel them back in. I wanted to focus on this time, but I was so distracted by everything stupid. The funeral director followed us in.

Guess he had to make sure we were going to be respectful? I kept thinking about his job, how much it sucked. What was he thinking about me? About us? What had he thought about who Logan was? Was he seriously going to stay the entire time because I didn't find that very private. I didn't like the color of the couches, they should have been colorful and not brown and somber. Because we weren't burying Logan but cremating instead, they had him in a white box that was disposable in nature. I was annoyed at the colors of the markers sitting there for our use to write on the last thing he would lay in. We had brought clothes the day before when we came to sign everything. I couldn't risk the emotions of going in his room so Glenn had grabbed them. I knew they didn't match and the bottoms were a favorite pair of his PJs. Maybe I wanted to keep them forever? The moment before seeing him I changed my mind and asked for his jacket (we previously had told them we didn't want any attire he had been wearing returned) only to be told it was too late. I don't really know what one is supposed to be thinking in these moments. I know there are no rules, but shouldn't I be reminiscing on his baby face and laugh instead of fixating on the stupid?

I approached the makeshift casket. When you are handed your child for the first time after birth, you touch their face and study everything about them. I was being presented my child again, insanely to be examined in a similar way. Now his identity is not life. It's dead. Gone.

My first thoughts were how much he looked like my cousin's son. Ugh. Would he notice that too? Would that bring it even closer to reality? I vividly remembered thinking just days before I needed to cut his hair, noticing its length was beyond where he had been keeping it in the last year. As much as it secretly cut into 'my time,' I always did it happily. Now, I had all the time in the world to struggle with regret that maybe, just maybe if I would have offered that week to cut it, we would have chatted about life-changing things. The way he was laying, his locks looked so flowing, and his bold jawline, youthful appearance, and lips gave way to centering my focus back to my cousin's son again and again.

Both Kristi and Collin remember noticing my hands first coming to rest just below his ears. The undertakers had done a great job attempting to mask the holes that began the creation of the biggest one; that which now resided in my heart. Details...I needed them all. Looking back, maybe it was also a disbelief like the disciples had with Jesus after he was crucified, and arose. Some might think it was the nurse in me. I think it was just the mom. Or maybe it was instinctively both.

I wanted to touch every appropriate area of his body I could, even giving way to a kiss knowing he would never feel it. I finally crumbled to the ground in a fetal position. I often felt a very out of body experience, and in that moment it was as if I was watching myself as if I was the character in a movie. I think sometimes people do that in the movies? Am I doing it just because I've seen it? Or am I just letting my body take over my mind and allowing it to navigate?

It's hard to know how much time is enough? To a serious fault, I often consider others and figured this guy had other things to prepare and so I allowed my parents in probably before I was ready, but it was okay. Collin prayed and they took their pictures promising only to show my sister, who couldn't be there and wanted to be. Details... while my norm is to want them all, I actually didn't want those to clarify my future clouded visuals of this day. But I was already comparing my NICU experience with parents who had lost a baby and knew that sometimes they later regretted not having photographs. Maybe someday I would ask for them, but definitely not feeling that way right now.

After writing "I love you" (and probably more but in my oblivion I can't even remember what) I scribbled a pizza. I knew it wasn't a good drawing, but I had wanted to be last with the markers and didn't care if the workers noticed it; they would be tossing it only to be melted away along with every bone in his body. Anticipating saying goodbye for the very last time gave way to the biggest anxiety. Leaving that room knowing I would never be able to touch my son again was really something I can't put into words. I had, of course, thought about how much time would be adequate coming up empty; As if there was such a thing. Eventually, you just have to do it and get on with the day.

Retracing, self-pity, rejection, abandoned. These all filled my thoughts as I walked away.

In the car on the way home, we talked about the obvious. My emotions had been released to the max but as I was saturated in numb now, it was interjected by an overwhelming feeling of wanting to break things. Glass really. I just wanted to take drinking glasses and throw them as hard as I could. Being a realist, I imagined a dumpster so that no one would have to clean it up. Collin said he's heard of such places, maybe one day I'll go. Arriving home it was just more of before: an aggregation of people and hugs and how are you's…God, I hate that question now.

I so badly wanted to reach Logan, but he decisively refused and violently ended all hope of that. And now I found myself remembering all those times I felt our relationship was one-sided. I know many parents feel this way, at least at certain times, but this was definitely a one-sided goodbye.

I hope you never have one.

## DECEMBER 23, 2017

Everyone keeps saying they don't have words. Well, I don't either really, but I will say that we are truly overwhelmed with the love we have been shown. I feel like that is such a cliche statement, but I just don't know another way right now to say it.

I still have not been able to be on FB hardly at all. I will go back in the next week and read all of your kind words. They will comfort me as my house becomes empty from friends and family visiting from afar.

I promise. If you have messaged me, I will get back to you.

I will say, we have truly felt your prayers. I, particularly. While I am usually so critical and have a hard time being satisfied, putting together Logan's day just really flowed easily. I truly loved the service and I am not second-guessing any part of it.

I thought it was beautiful.

I am forever grateful for those that made it happen but particularly for those that spoke (and Alec, we heard your words). The words were perfect and I know they have made an impact. I have already heard good that has come from it.

For the Lord is good

And His love endures forever

And His mercies will not fail us

They are new each day

## DECEMBER 25, 2017

Last year's and this year.....

Our hearts will forever be missing such a huge piece and I can't stand the thought of not having another picture of my 4 beautiful children together. When families celebrate together on Christmas, for us, it's going to be so hard since ours is no longer complete. We never missed a Christmas without one of us. Logan was always the one that would go find empty tubs for everyone to put their stash in and loved to help do the handing out. Even though it's not about the number of presents, it was for me. The more we had, the more time we all spent together sitting closely in the living room. Today was so very different. So many "presents" were not exchanged. Instead cards with where we would direct money to help the less fortunate. It was quick, but we are here and together.

Although it was a sad day, and not easy, we did make it. We had to. To celebrate—Jesus' birthday 🎉 —the real reason for today. The only reason we have HOPE today that tomorrow can be a little bit better. Thank you, Jesus, for giving us Peace. Peace that passes all understanding. Because it's hard to understand.

Merry Christmas. I hope you found some Peace in today, too.

## DECEMBER 28, 2017

Here is my note that my dear cousin read for me at Logan's service:

*I'm exhausted from the pain mentally. I'm exhausted physically. I keep wanting to start a letter to Logan, but it's too much right now.*

*As a mom, your biggest sadness is having your child forgotten too soon. So I decided to use this time to give you a few memories of mine, to help you keep my Logan Boy in your heart for as long as possible.*

*When you see a baby that smiles just because you look at them, think of*

*Logan. To this day, I have never seen a baby with a more beautiful smile that was so easily handed out.*

*When you have a young kid tell you your hair cut is bad, think of Logan. Man, he could be blunt sometimes,*

*Matter of fact,*

*Even so black and white.*

*But he never meant to be mean.*

*People didn't understand that about him. I often struggled to understand that about him.*

*If you see a pink power ranger, think of him and know my Savannah is wishing he would chase her one more time, using his "powers" on her.*

*When you eat beets, think of Logan. He was such a picky eater, but he loved those!*

*When a kid tells you jokes that you have heard a million times before, but you can't remember the ending, think of Logan. Amaya tried to stump him all the time but he knew them all.*

*When you see a girl holding tightly to a yellow my little pony, think about how much Logan loved Amaya. That was a gift he gave her. He was so good to her, more patient than any of us with her homework. You could often find them going to the movies together, or just watching one downstairs. Last Sunday they watched a movie together and she was the last one to get a hug from him.*

*When someone is talking about Harry Potter, think of my boy, who has read each of those books at least 10 times. Each. And of course, he was one of those waiting at midnight to pick up the latest one. His daddy took him, and he would get that book read within hours. And then read it again. And then go back and start the series over again.*

*When you are taken back because a boy in his late teens/early twenties says he loves classical music, Logan probably would have been friends with him.*

*When you hear the song, Separate Ways*

*by Journey, know that was his favorite song.*

*When you hear any Barney song, know that I can sing it with you. I can still see Logan, sitting in his Barney chair, with his stack of Barney books (that you better not knock over by the way), holding his little Barney figurine, wearing his Barney PJs and Barney slippers, reciting every word, and singing every song.*

*...and when you sit down with your family or friends to play a board game, just know that was Logan's biggest love and I will forever regret not taking more time to play them with him.*

*Please don't stop talking about him to me, I want to hear your memories.*

*And if you get to Heaven before I do, please tell him I love him so very much and can't wait to see him again.*

## DECEMBER 30, 2017

Walking Estes Park we found this ornament and it was the last one left. Although it brought instant grief, I'm glad we found it. And soon after I was able to smile again.

At many times lately, I have felt guilty. Guilty about a lot. I even felt guilty for enjoying a milkshake.

But then a friend reminded me of something that made so much sense —God says He came so that we could have life, and to live it to the fullest, John 10:10. This tells me it's ok to have Joy, even in your sorrows. So this weekend I am working hard at trying to find Joy, AND to not feel bad about it.

Do you wonder how some people ever muster the strength to continue, much less thrive? (A joyful heart is good medicine. Proverbs 17:22). We want to be those people. Joy is how we get there.

I refuse to see myself as the victim. I want to do just what Andy Dufresne did in *Shawshank Redemption:* "You either get busy livin', or get busy dying."

"I could never be that strong," you think. You're right. You couldn't ever be that strong. But neither can I. If I have shown strength, it is only because I have admitted my weakness and claimed God's strength as my own. (My grace is sufficient for you, for my power is made perfect in weakness, 2 Corinthians 12:9-10.)

This is the only reason I am able to find a smile at this terrible time in my life. Without Him, I might be still be putting one step in front of the other, but I know it would not be with a smile, with some sense of Joy, and certainly not without hope.

# JANUARY 2018

## JANUARY 3, 2018

This was obviously taken at Logan's service. The number of friends (and I believe some had left before we took this picture) was amazing. I am SO very thankful for all of them and I loved hearing so much about him—things we didn't know.

Please—as you see how many friends Logan had, and know that he was loved and he also loved— see that all people who are hurting are not necessarily alone or lonely...

#suicideawareness #misshimsomuch

## JANUARY 4, 2018

I'd like to share some of what Logan's best friends said about him over the next couple days. Love the new bond I'm forming with so many of them💕. Thank you all for sharing so many of your memories.

This was a post that Jared made on FB but also similar to what he said at the service:

*Logan has been my best friend for about the past 7-8 years since I've known him, and I've loved every moment of it. When I heard the news, it was from waking up to a call from Mitchee saying he got the text from his sister on what had happened and asked me "Jared, is Logan ok? Please tell me he is." I was in disbelief thinking there's no way he's not fine, he was a fantastic driver so there shouldn't have been anything with that, he might have gotten sick or something but I never could have imagined this severe as I had just seen him 2 days earlier and he seemed to be doing great. As I sat on the news that morning I was in complete denial of what happened but it ate at me more and more as I wanted to wait for more confirmation. I couldn't sit still and remembered Mitchee saying it was at the UCCS parking lot. So I went and checked every parking spot on campus for his car. But I didn't want to find his car because if I found it then I knew it was true. I didn't find it, however, the act was only going to give me results that I didn't want as it didn't prove that he was still with us. The meal I ate after the search was as hard to swallow as the truth told to me that morning that I didn't want to believe.*

*The best times and fondest memories I have with Logan are playing games together with him. Video games, board games, or anything else like going out to eat at great restaurants or watching good and terrible movies. I owe him so much to be the friend to help me experience all of these wonderful times and memories. The guy was so smart, developing strategies for any game we played that really challenged our friend group so much we pretty much had to focus on him to stand a chance at winning otherwise he would wipe the floor with us. The guy was so good he even made as high as #2 in all of North America in Hearthstone, an online card game that he adored playing and talking about. I learned a lot from playing those games with him, I think a lot of my analytical and strategic thinking skills developed with his help as he explained his thought process on things, but he wasn't always strictly strategic to win, he also had strategies that were funny and hype that would give all of us the best times of the countless nights we all spent together. While he enjoyed winning those games, he had a much better time making sure everyone would be having fun and that they felt included. This part of him came out the most I think whenever he played smash bros. It's a game that Mitchee, Galen, Logan and I would play all the time and that part of him grew as we got into the competitive scene where he was my training partner to develop and have fun with as well as a rival for me to overcome, we have met so many amazing friends making the greatest connections, an opportunity I wouldn't trade for anything. Every tournament I would see him playing or talking with people having a great time, if he wasn't a part of my life then those things might not have happened, or at least not to the extent that they are now. Which to that I am deeply grateful for.*

*Logan was a guy that you could always look to for a solid foundation. He was willing to help you out with any problem you came to him with, whether it was for something like games or life advice, he was there for me. He may not*

*have been always the best with getting out his own emotions but he was always there to help you think things out logically and come to the conclusion that you probably needed to hear even if you didn't always want to.*

*No longer will I be able to play games with my best friend. No longer will I be able to debate and discuss with him about silly things, go get delicious food, watch movies with, learn more perspectives on how to tackle something, have great drives in his pizza scented car or have the talks I needed to get through a rough patch in my life or to try and help him get through his. No longer will I be able to make these memories with him. And though I may not be able to create more of those memories, I will be able to cherish them for years to come. I will be able to celebrate his life by continuing to find happiness in all of these things in the future thinking of him.*

*I'll miss you, buddy.*

## JANUARY 5, 2018

My very good friend and angel Maggie Frey was a huge part of Logan's life. My kids spent many overnights and even days with her as Glenn and I both worked night shift and I would then help her out as well. The kids were in many activities together including camp each summer. All kids being blond and blue-eyed with similar features, people often thought we had 5 kids—that they were all related. We were—I consider them family. ☺

Erich spoke at Logan's service and I wanted to share that:

*Logan and I became friends through playing on the same soccer team when we were 8 years old. Logan is my oldest friend who I experienced many formative years with. When I think back to when I was younger, there are few memories that will make me stop in my tracks and laugh and I was fortunate enough to experience many of these memories with Logan. One of these memories includes being in a two-man band named the "Sting of Rock." Our parents always laughed and said we should name the band "Two Skinny Dudes" and maybe that was more fitting. But the memories that I cherish and miss the most were the times when we were bored and nothing to do. That's when we had the most fun we came up with these elaborate storylines where we were the heroes and there was always a town needed saving. We would always talk about how excited we were to grow up and now all I want to go back to those days when I had my friend, my elaborate imagination and not a single worry in the world. When I think of my childhood and the friends I had, I think of movies like The Sandlot or Stand By Me. Just like in these movies, we were the weird kids. We weren't the popular kids, but man we had a great time. We scuffed up our knees and elbows, made our parents crazy, and had the times of our lives.*

*As I remember Logan and all the fun we had growing up, there is a quote from the film Stand By Me that really hits me hard and makes me remember how great of a person he was—"I never had any friends later on like the ones I had when I was twelve. Jesus, does anyone?" I will always remember Logan for who he was. He was the goofy, funny, nerdy kid who was my best friend. He was better than the best friend any boy could ask for.*

*I will always remember and cherish all those times we played video games until the sun came up, all those hours we spent playing air soft, all the shenanigans we got into running around the neighborhood, all the debates we got into over which Lord of the Rings character was the most badass, and just all the dumb fun stupid things kids do when they are growing up.*

*Thank you for allowing me to be your friend Logan. It was an honor, you will live on in my memories forever.*

*Rest in Peace brother, it was a pleasure growing up with you, thank you for being part of my story and allowing me to be in yours,*

*Good Bye Old Friend.*

## JANUARY 6, 2018

The night we found out Logan took his life, both of my older kids posted amazing words on FB. I was so proud, so heartbroken. No one wants to see your kids hurt the way they have. Another component of suicide...your children's hearts breaking and knowing they are going through the same questioning and regrets as you are. But I am also so thankful they have held to their faith so tightly and have been able to find joy in their sadness.

I did share those posts (Dec. 15) for those of you that missed them, but I also wanted to share what they wrote for Logan Boarman service.

Here is what Randy read for Savannah Boarman:

*Logan,*

*Growing up you were my best friend and I'm so thankful for that. You taught me how to have an imagination, showed me what a caring heart looked like, and always gave me someone to look up to. Going through home videos and all your pictures I laughed more than cried and was reminded of just a few of those amazing qualities you had. I can still remember you taking me into your world of power rangers and fighting the bad guys in living room...you not only showing up to my princess birthday party but wore a snow-white costume just to make me happy, and you trying to convince me to read harry potter because it's just THAT good (and it must be since you read the whole series 10 times). I have a million wishes right now, including to re-live those days, but most importantly I wish you knew how loved you were. You meant more to us than you will ever know and the love and support we have received shows how loved and cared about you were.*

*You weren't like a lot of people; you were an intellect and had such a brilliant mind. Not many people understood you, I wish we could have, but you were so complex in your own way. Even though we had a hard time relating to you at times, you gave us a different perspective and we were always intrigued by your thoughts, and appreciated your knowledge...I, for one, was always jealous about how smart you were, and thought you were gonna be the next Einstein... It's a shame we won't get to see where that big brain of yours would've taken you.*

*As I stand up here continuously asking myself "why", I just remind myself that God Is Good and he has a plan, and I need to trust in that.*

*Words truly can't express how much I love you and miss you, and I will forever cherish the memories we had, rest easy big brother.*

## JANUARY 7, 2018

Here is what Jon Anders read for Bryce Boarman at Logan Boarman's service. I just love the way he put some of these memories into words:

*Dear Logan,*

*This past week has been so tough for me. I have gone through just about every emotion imaginable. The pain and sadness are real, but as time passes the negative emotions will grow weaker as the memories grow stronger. Over the last week, my mind has wandered through the 23 years we spent together. There are countless things I will remember and admire about you, but there are 2 qualities that seem to be most prevalent throughout my memories.*

*The first is your incredible imagination. I can say with supreme confidence, I will never meet someone with a bigger imagination than you. I will never forget; I was the blue ranger and you were the red as we tore apart the house and jumped from couch to couch battling any bad guy who dared oppose the power rangers. You would even break out into full battle mode in the middle of your soccer games if there happened to be villains up to no good. Who cares if the other team scored a goal when the fate of humanity was at stake.*

*When you were not fighting evil, you could often be found in a quiet place reading a book. I know you loved reading because it allowed your imagination to run wild. Last I knew, you had read each of the Harry Potter books at least 4 times. I remember our conversations about the Harry Potter movies since I would never read the books. You always told me that the movies were just ok, but they could never live up to the books. Another outlet for your imagination was the fantasy worlds of video and board games. I remember playing the Lord of the Rings games for hours on end because we had to beat co-op mode on the hardest difficulty. I also remember playing Risk, Settlers of Catan, and other strategy board games with you. It was no secret that being able to outwit and outmaneuver your friends and family in any board game brought you great joy.*

*The second quality that has been evident throughout your life is your caring nature and desire to put others before yourself. I will always remember when we went to Mexico with the youth group to build homes for families in need. The video of your prolific hammering display is legendary, but I also* remember watching you give the rest of your ice-cold coke to a random little boy. You have always been able to connect with kids and had a knack for helping them learn. Although I was never a camp counselor with you at Camp Elim, I have heard from so many people that you were a favorite amongst the kids and counselors. When Amaya joined our family, it was clear that she extra special to you. You loved to teach her new things but still showed her no mercy when you played Wii Sports. You were the first person she looked for when she needed help with homework, and you demonstrated over and over again that you had more patience than the rest of us when she struggled to understand things. Even when you went to college to become a mechanical engineer, your goal was to help people by creating better prosthetics. When you got the job as a 9-1-1 call taker, it was clear by all the stories you shared how much you loved what you were doing…helping other people.

Logan, I am forever grateful for the time we shared. I love you!

To everyone here today, words cannot describe how thankful I am for the support you have shown me and my family. My heart has been shattered but your love and prayers have helped to start the healing process. My life will *never be the same because Logan is no longer here, but I am comforted by the fact that my brother is waiting for me in heaven. I Love you all — Bryce"*

## JANUARY 8, 2018

**Amaya Boarman** has sent a message on TeamSnap.

View Message

Hi all,

I should have sent this out before now, but just realized with practice today, I should probably clarify some things.

As you are all probably aware, Amaya's 23 year old brother took his life on December 15th. He did still live with us and was very close to Amaya. We were and are devastated. He shot himself in his car and let the police know where to find him. Just like in the movies, they knocked on our door in the middle of the night to tell us. We are comforted as he did leave letters of which he stated that he knew he was loved, loved us, and knew he was being selfish. He was a brilliant kid with lots of friends, but unfortunately had an underlying depression for the last few years that likely caught up with him. He denied the depression and wouldn't agree to getting help. On the outside, his friends and co-workers had no idea what was going on in the inside, as he seemed happy. He had recently started a job that he loved, and wasn't meeting "his expectations" on how well he should be performing. In his letter, he stated that he had never "failed" at something he really wanted, and he just couldn't handle "being a failure". He knew others wouldn't see it that way, but that his opinion is what mattered most. Of course, we are left with more questions than answers and I am open, at some point, to talking about it. We don't have secrets in our family and if it can help someone, I'm all for having open communication. We very much believe in Jesus Christ and have vigorously held on to His promises. Because of this, we are focusing on what good can come of this and trying not to focus on regrets, etc.

Now that you have some background info and hopefully most questions answered, I will let you choose how much you want to share with your girls. With that being said, please talk to your girls and let them know it's okay to approach Amaya. Hugs and "I'm so sorry about your brother" is fine, but please let them know Amaya DOES NOT want to talk about the incident or why he did it. Asking about Logan and what he was like is fine, but just have them ask their questions regarding what happened to you or me, please.

Thank you all for your support, we are so blessed to be surrounded by so many people that care.

Lori

## JANUARY 9, 2018

As I sit here writing thank you notes, I am amazed and in awe at all the ones I get to write to our church family (Fellowship of the Rockies). It got me thinking...

...People don't think to be Believers, they need church. While to live eternally with Jesus in Heaven that is true, I would beg for you to consider this aspect:

Our youth pastor was a HUGE part of my kids' upbringing and faith. It's very apparent to me that my kids have a good foundation they are leaning on right now and I attribute that to church youth group. Randy Unruh was at our house holding them so tightly within the hour that we let him know what was going on. A familiar hug, a longtime friend, a spiritual comfort.

Our pastor, Stewart, was also praying with us in our living room within an hour. His wife, is one of my best friends and I can't tell you in all the ways she has helped me. Stewart went to Sams that morning and flooded us with necessities and food, on behalf of the church. Within that morning, I'm sure we had hundreds praying over us.

Within the next couple of days, many from our church family sent messages, dropped off cards, and provided food. Many I don't even know. For this, I'm struggling at knowing where to send thank you cards. 😇

Our church family helped with the service in so many ways; providing food, music, helping put together the program, slide show, and so many other things I'm sure we don't even know about.

They are our ROCK. They continue to reach out, to love on us, and to pray.

Yes, there are other reasons to belong to a church family, but if no other reason seems good enough for you, let me tell you, that having a solid support system when you're going through the worst experience of your life is so important and can keep you afloat. I needed the church this month. We needed the church this month.

Yes! We do have amazing friends outside the church that went above and beyond. However, the feeling of belonging to a bigger family and for those points mentioned above is a great reason to find a church family for yourself right now.

You can never have too much support.

- Church is not just for people that know and understand this God thing. It's a place to learn. So many people are afraid to go to a service because they think others will realize what they don't know. This is so not true. Most churches have all the words on the screen, don't ask you to raise your hand, and definitely aren't going to quiz you walking in the door. Our church even has all levels of classes and studies outside of service so that you can feel comfortable wherever you are at in your journey.
- Not all people within a church are going to be people you want to be around. I get it. People, Christians are not perfect. And some are hypocritical. But, look beyond and know there are places with great people. And some of those "bad" people might need God more than anyone. Pray for them.
- Not all churches are the same. If you have tried one and didn't like it, find another. There is one out there for you, I'm sure if it. I would encourage you...start looking for one that fits your needs. If you don't like the first 5, don't give up. I bet you've tried at least 5 desserts, watched 5 movies, or been to 5 different restaurants— that weren't good, or even awful—you didn't give up and stop eating dessert, watching movies, or eating out. Don't give up on church.

The church is not a building,

the church is not a steeple,

open the door,

the church is the people.

These past few weeks, I am beyond thankful for those people.

## JANUARY 12, 2018

After much and careful thought, our family has decided to use the money collected in honor of Logan to help support our church's youth mission trip to Juarez, Mexico. Logan went on this trip over spring break numerous times. As a mission team, we partner with Casas por Cristo to built houses from the ground up in 5 days. At the end of the trip, we get to hand the keys of a new house to a family that had been living in structures made with whatever scraps they could find.

Although Logan could often be found taking a break while everyone else was working, it was because he was using his Spanish with the local kids, playing soccer, other random neighborhood games, and even (like Bryce mentioned in his letter) sharing his Coke with them. Here, he found joy.

It has been a super common theme from his friends and co-workers how much Logan loved and wanted to help people. We think he would be smiling and nodding in agreement knowing youth would get to participate in something meaningful on behalf of him, but also that families' lives are changed forever in the process.

He was so practical, this would make sense to him! Thank you to everyone that gave in his name. 🩶

PS. This year all ages are welcome on the trip. Message me about details if you or your family are interested.

## JANUARY 14, 2018

One of Logan's best friends, Mitchee Costelo, posted this on his timeline on Dec. 17th. Mitchee also spoke at the service. He had recently moved to California and we were honored he flew in (as did others) to celebrate Logan's life.

*I have so many thoughts swirling in my head, and I wish I could say it all but I just can't seem to form the words correctly.*

*Last Thursday night, my best friend for 9 years took his life. I was one of the first people to be informed by his family Friday morning, so I've had a bit of time dealing with it all. I am still struggling coming to terms with it though, and I have so many regrets now.*

*- I miss going to Five Guys with him*

*- I miss making fun of him for being so White, he thought ketchup was too spicy*

*- I miss arguing about Clean Plate stickers at King Chef and how he never got any*

*- I miss talking about the most recent anime I made him watch and what he thought about it*

*- I miss reading a manga chapter and instantly wanting to talk to Logan about it*

*- I miss getting excited whenever I saw "toothpic is online"*

*- I miss him shotcalling the team in League of Legends and him complaining about us not listening to the call*

*- I miss getting chain grabbed to death in Super Smash Bros by him*

*- I miss getting frustrated every time he'd beat all of us at board games*

*- I miss talking about what new genre at betterfap we found and how weird it's getting*

*- I miss knowing if a date went well for him strictly based off of if the girl got a Coke or Pepsi product*

*- I miss the bro talks whenever one of us were down*

*- I miss laughing with him*

*I really miss my best friend*

## JANUARY 16, 2018

Do you believe in signs?

I do, and I look for them but often I think they are way overrated. I mean, I feel like people find the craziest, weirdest things that they turn into a "sign." Sometimes I think it's way exaggerated and made up,

and then other times I think,

if someone sees it then it's still a sign by definition!

Think on that…

I guess for me, it just has to be pretty obvious. I'm not going to stretch hard to create it to be what it's not. And I don't see them like 'all the time.' But I will say, I think we who are hurting, we are looking for signs more than anytime before. Probably because we want comfort? We want to think all the best things and we have that hope. We are struggling more than ever for reassurance that everything will be okay.

So a dear friend of mine offered to take me with her on her monthly massage appointment. It's hard for me to accept things like that, but she did a great job of selling me.

Remember the sympathetic nervous system, the fight or flight response? Tense muscles, releasing of stress hormones, etc. that can cause some serious physical discomfort. Grief triggers this all the time (multiple times daily at first) when you are reminded of what was lost and acts as a threat. A massage can stimulate the parasympathetic nervous system that helps rest and restore a response that occurs once a perceived threat is past.

Anyway, I have been praying diligently for days for some comfort, for some peace, for a sign that Jesus is holding Logan so closely.

....and then I had a moment in that massage chair....with my head down, eyes closed, I slowly opened them ever so slightly. Not sure why I was lead to do this, perhaps to just reassure myself it wasn't totally dark in the room. But then it appeared, with the minuscule amount of light that was shining through, I could see the exact outline of a cross. I tried again... thinking I was making this up...I closed my eyes and peaked so that I could reassure myself this *was* a silly moment.

The same cross.

Appearing just like when the sun is peaking through the clouds, with all the brightness and rays/beams shooting out.

I never said anything to anyone, and the interesting thing is that I argued with my soul. I saw it and I know I did, but then I kept rationalizing that I somehow 'created' this in my hopes. Perhaps I had been able to creatively squint? as to see just the right symbol or thing I wanted to?

Even days later it's popping up in my thoughts and I'm trying to decipher if it was just me wanting to see it so I somehow made it happen?

But just like we stumble upon faith sometimes, I wasn't looking for a 'CROSS' per se, and there is no doubt that is what it was.

Is that you? Do you know God has grabbed your attention? You saw exactly how He did it, but you keep sensibly passing it off as a coincidence?

Maybe you're not looking, but I promise you God is chasing.

And maybe that wasn't God answering my particular plea regarding his hugs for Logan? But the more I reflect, I'd like to think that God was giving me lots of hugs that day (using the therapist's hands) and... the cross...well, call it what you want, but I believe it was one of those peace 'signs' I had been asking for ✝ ☀.

And when you have peace... you don't 'worry' about the other stuff.

#suicideawareness #findingjoy #misshimsomuch

## JANUARY 18, 2018

A perspective on Logan's memorial service day, which was Dec. 21, by his friend Merrick:

*"Hey I'm super bad with words but here's what I wrote. (I tried to put this into words without being a \*\*\*\*)*

*5 years ago today was supposed to be the end of the world. I remember posting the title cards from Majora's Mask leading up to it:*

*"Dawn of the Third Day..."*

*"Dawn of the Second Day..."*

*"Dawn of the Final Day..."*

*Of course, the world didn't end, so just as in Majora's Mask, I posted the title card, "Dawn of a New Day." that memory greeted me in the morning as I got ready to head out for the memorial service.*

*Today is also the winter solstice, the shortest day of the year. In correlation it is also the darkest day, the longest night of the year, so long in fact that the tradition is to light a candle through the night so that the sun may find it's way back into the sky.*

*Robin Williams was a great man. He made me laugh, made me smile, and I didn't even know him. I, like many, didn't even know that he was masking a sadness that would inevitably overwhelm him, compelling him to take his own life. It's wild to think that someone I didn't even know would make me feel heartbroken with his passing, But Today I feel it even stronger. One of his last roles was as Teddy Roosevelt, in Night At The Museum, where his last line was, "smile my boy, it's sunrise."*

*Today we paid our respects to a friend who lost his own battle with that same sadness, but like Robin Williams, he cared more about making people smile than showing his pain. He was loved by many, and his absence will always be felt. Today is truly fitting of the title, "darkest day." this past week has been so surreal. It's felt like the world is ending, but just as in Majora's Mask, there will be a Dawn of a New Day.*

*It's hard to put into words how I feel about all of this, but I know that this darkest day will end. Just as every dark day we have ever had, there will be a sunrise, another day to make it better. Tomorrow will be the dawn of a new day, one without him. We will get through it, and we will return to the way things were, but we will never forget him. I hope that the future will treat us all well. As for now, I will do my part to guide the light back to us. I will light my candle through the night, and in the morning, remember those words, "smile my boy, it's sunrise."*

*We will meet again, Logan Boarman."*

## JANUARY 19, 2018

Although I don't enjoy knowing how many people are grieving with us, I do love hearing the good that is coming out. It's my main hope these days. It gives me genuine smiles at a time so many are forced.

If 150 people:

reflect on their family for even an extra day,

if they go home and hug their kids a little tighter,

if they tell someone they love them when they normally wouldn't have...

I can smile. A real.genuine.smile.

Thinking of you 💙 just wanted to share with you Jim's work day.
He is in San Diego with his new team, leaders and bosses. He had 10 minutes to prepare a speech in front of 150 people regarding the approval of this new drug... and how the experience was for him.
He broke down in tears... he shared that when he was informed of the approval of this new drug... he did not care... he was at a young mans celebration of life... and told them how strong you and Glenn are and your faith..... and that we all need to focus on each day and count our blessings each day.
Your family touches all of us 💙 in so many ways

## JANUARY 20, 2018

So I completely recognize that most people don't want to watch a memorial service. How depressing right?

Well, I'm posting the link to Logan Boarman's service because you might just need to watch it.

Are you feeling like there is no hope right now?

Are you living a double life? Those around you see you as happy and enjoying life when in reality you are in physical pain, in your head telling yourself you're not good enough, or something similar?

You might want to skip the singing, you might want to fast forward the video of Logan's life, and you might even want to fast forward the statements/letters...

but what you SHOULD listen to is Randy Unruh (beginning) and Collin Grant(towards the end) messages. Both of these men are dear to our family. One is even blood family. They loved Logan and Logan loved them. I was so amazed at what they had to say.

It was so raw. So real. So honest. And it was TRUTH.

You just might need to hear this. Right. Now.

https://www.youtube.com/watch?v=uIpWfvMigzM&feature=youtu.be&fbclid=IwAR2_uPMwWEor6W4YZtohaEWHwoIJb6W1-hrdZnpgLrzhlddgqz4ofp6Xc_s

## JANUARY 21, 2018

So I've been told a lot lately that I'm strong. I'm still trying to figure out exactly what that means, and I suppose it might mean something different to the person that says it.

I honestly feel weak much of the time because I break down so often, but most of what I'm reading tells me crying is not a sign of "weakness." But our twisted society somehow makes us feel that way. One minute I don't want to cry because I want to feel 'strong' and/or I need to push through to get things done, and then the next moment I can go into the guilt thoughts of if I'm not crying then I'm somehow moving on or don't miss Logan as much.

It's a struggle for me every day even though I can know there is no right way or wrong way to grieve. And I know these thoughts don't make sense. Thankfully, I can tell myself the reality at some point in those moments.

But I do know this: if people are saying I'm being strong because I still have my faith, then that makes me think...do circumstances really determine if you have genuine faith in God?

## JANUARY 22, 2018

This letter is probably the most special letter I'll receive. It comes from pain, it comes from love. And it comes from someone super special in my life.

So many tears when I received it, but it did help me feel a little less lonely, a little more like someone understood my pain, and reminded me that we are not the only ones really hurting here. I think overall it's a good perspective for us parents, to talk about the hard things. Kids have perceptive and...know. And never stop needing support.

You're never alone in your pain despite feeling that way.

#suicideawareness

Dear Glenn, Lori, Bryce, Savanah, and Amaya,

I wanted to write you this letter and express a few things to you and with you. My hope is that you'll find solace in my experience… I want you to know that you are not alone.

I'm so sad about the death of Logan, it was hard for me to express my complete sadness at his funeral but I've sat in my home office on multiple occasions crying about him and also thinking about my dad. Logan's passing has made me face my own pain and sadness which is something I've pretty much avoided for 30 years. Every time I cry about this it releases a little more pain.

This letter is to tell you what I have gone through in hopes that it will help you find a little peace today and in the days to come.

The pain never goes away. I know, that's a great way to start the letter right? But it's true. Time will pass and the memories will become dream-like but never go away.

My biggest sadness for you is the sadness to come. I hope you can direct the sadness into something more productive than I had done.

My father, ████████████████, was only a part of my life for about 4.5 years. He was my father, I looked up to him for love and guidance and he was an integral part of who I have become (for better or worse).

The night he took his life, we had set up a little trap for him when he came into our room to say goodnight to us. He never came back. When we woke up in the morning we didn't know why our little trap didn't go off. Then later the police showed up to our door in the morning with the bad news.

After they came to our door I didn't even really know what was fully going on. Everyone else was crying so I felt like I needed to show sorrow and cried too, but at the time was unaware of why I was really crying. I fully expected him to walk through the door at any minute. I almost think that may still happen now. How weird is that?

After his death, I felt guilty. I was 10 years old and I felt GUILTY. Was it something I said, was it something I did? Why would he do this TO me? Why would he do this TO our family? Did he not love me? Did he not care about me? Did he not want to be around me? Why would he do this TO me? I believe it has more to do with them and their pain than it has to do with any one of us. But these are the brain-rotting questions that will never be answered but your mind will figure out a way to keep asking these questions. Your mind (deep down) knows there is no answer but it's trying to figure it out. It never will. These questions will never be (fully) answered.

One memory I have is that everyone in our family went to see his body for a final viewing (2nd viewing) before the funeral and I didn't go. I stayed home and played Nintendo. I didn't want to see him again, it scared me and it was beyond what I could comprehend. I never told anyone that. I have felt guilt about that decision too, what kind of son wouldn't go see his father before he could never look at him again? Another brain-rotting question that does not serve me. ████ and I talked briefly about that moment and I cried talking about it because I still carry pain over that decision. Why? I don't know. I almost look at it from my adult perspective of what my 10 year old self should have done but my 10 year old self was just scared and didn't understand. My guilt comes from my adult self almost scolding my younger self for not doing the "right thing" even though it wasn't even possible for me to comprehend that at 10 years old.

As I grew up without a father I felt alone. I felt very alone. At that time I couldn't see that anyone else could understand not having a father. I had nobody to show me the things that fathers teach their sons. I didn't have an example of a father to show me how to be a man. I've struggled with this my whole life. I still struggle with this today.

The ▬▬ family doesn't ever talk about it... ever. It sucks, we all know we need to talk about and I've tried to open dialogue about it without a real response of any substance. This is a mistake, this is the worst mistake that I think could be made. Please talk about, talk about your feelings, be vulnerable, be loving, be weak, be strong, be whatever you feel you are at the moment when you talk about. I pray you don't hide from this pain because this pain will grow unless you talk about it. I hope you allow the pain to make you better instead of bitter. It's been 30 years since my dad died and I still have to work on this and feel the pain of it.

I had no outlet, I never spoke about it. It made me ANGRY but that was how I expressed my sadness. It wasn't really anger, it was masked sadness that came out as anger because I didn't have a healthy way to show my sadness to anyone. I can't recall a single conversation that allowed me to express my sadness about the situation. Not one. This kept the sadness inside of me which became anger. I still have anger issues today that hang over me like a black cloud. I've been really working on myself and with some new tools I've discovered I have been able to make more progress in the past 12 months than I had the previous 30 years regarding my father's suicide.

I have always felt ashamed about his death, I thought my dad was weak and because of his weakness that I would be weak as a man. This messes with the psyche of man. I had to reframe his death in a way that empowered me. The "story" that I had been telling myself for 30 years was bullshit. It wasn't until I could step back and realize without him I wouldn't be here today. He gave me life, he made a commitment to me and our family, but he was in so much pain he made the ultimate sacrifice. I had blamed him for most of the bad things that happened in my life but I never blamed him for the good things too. If you blame someone for the bad, you have to blame them for the good too. That's something I've learned recently. I've come to realize there are two types of pain men experience: the type of pain they want everyone else to feel (expressed as anger) and the type of pain they don't want anyone else to feel (felt by them as depression).

I look back at my late teens and pretty much all of my twenties into a place that was very dark for me. Everyone else saw "happy ▬▬" when mostly what I felt was loneliness and darkness. Men are very good at hiding their feelings of unworthiness, their feelings of sadness, and their feelings of inadequacy. But hiding these feelings create angry and sad men. I couldn't find the light because I was covered in darkness. I was scared of my darkness. This was made worse by the alcohol-fueled lifestyle I lived. I never tried to kill myself but would have been completely OK dying at the time and did things that probably should have killed me. I took physical and mental risks that nobody knows about, I took risks that would shock my family if they knew. Hiding in the darkness was made worse by the fact I didn't share it with anyone. I couldn't share it with anyone, too much guilt and shame. It's different now...

I want you all to know that YOU ARE NOT ALONE. I love you. Please reach out to me if you just want to talk or share your joy or your pain. I want you to know that your pain has helped my pain. Pain shared is pain divided. Much love.

My niece was unable to attend the service for Logan Boarman, but she wrote a letter that was read:

*I can still hear your super-low voice and see your Adam's apple wiggle as you say "Hello, how are you, Aspen?"*

*I can feel your small body on mine as we awkwardly hug.*

*I can still smell those pizza boxes throughout your Honda.*

*I can hear Queen playing in the background as we take Amaya home.*

*I remember wondering why you had so many CDs of Queen.*

*I admire your superfan self!*

*Logan, I look up to you.*

*You had the coolest collection of army figurines and Grandpa Ray's army memorabilia.*

*You were always the most creative when it can to Halloween Costumes.*

*My Favorite was the half girl and half boy.*

*I remember the yellow, blue, and red blanket as well as all those sleeping bags on the floor downstairs.*

*The half-eaten ramen, the cold couches next to you.*

*I miss sitting and watching you play Xbox.*

*All these memories are burning in my head and becoming more vivid then I expected.*

*I never even thought I would remember things like that.*

*I wanted to wish you a happy birthday.*

*I am so sorry, Logan.*

*No one is better off alone.*

*Just remember... you are loved, and you will never be forgotten.*

*I love you and I hope you are having a good time up there.*

*Love, Aspen*

## JANUARY 24, 2018

Hey, Lori, it's for you.

"Who is it?"

It's Jesus, says he wants Logan.

"My son? I'm not ready for him to be taken from me."

He says he's not your son, he's His. He just let you borrow him for some time. Logan wants to come home and He is allowing it. Jesus said He has other plans, good plans, and is taking him now.

"Ok. I trust Him.

......But can you tell him to be patient with me, I wasn't ready...."

#suicideawareness

## JANUARY 25, 2018

People often say, "I can't imagine."

I know I can't exactly convey...and certainly we all know everyone is different, but here is a piece of what it was like for me today to run into Ross for just a few minutes for some dog stuff...

I walk in wondering, "Do they know? Can they tell I've been crying? I don't really care, but I still wonder..." (I don't even wear mascara on my bottom lashes anymore. This helps some, so at least I don't have noticeable black running down my face.)

A young, polite security guard greets me. His noticeable Adam's apple reminds me of Logan's. Wish I could see Logan's move as he talks, even just one more time. I answer this guy's greeting...that, "How are you?" question... and say, "Okay." Wonder if he caught I didn't answer good.

I see dorm stuff and wonder why it's up front and think about what it was like when we dropped Logan off at School of Mines a few years ago. I remember how much I thought that was his answer to a new beginning. I keep walking and my thoughts get interrupted quickly by seeing shoes.

Seeing men's shoes reminds me of Logan. I used to buy his shoes, even as he got older. And I usually got them at Ross.

I see they have inserts today; Dr. Scholls and other kinds too. Logan complained a lot about foot pain. I should have bought more of these for him. Tried different kinds maybe.

I see the socks at the same time and move on to thinking about how often I bought socks from here...Logan was always losing one and then would wear mismatched sets. It drove me nuts and I would just buy new ones.

I still have a few of those mismatched ones in the laundry basket right now. I wonder when I'll be ready to toss them.

I continue walking and see all the men's clothes...I think about how thankful I am for the time I spent with Logan at Kohl's in August, helping him choose outfits for his new job. I was excited to see him in something other than a t-shirt and shorts after all. He had asked me to go and I was happy to get to spend time with him. This trip had been just him and me. I especially loved helping pick out shirts. He likes simple. I kept trying to get him to do some patterns. I helped him sign up for a Kohl's card so he could get a hefty discount. Now I have to make sure that card is closed...ugh.

Do people know I'm not focused on shopping?... My thoughts are totally elsewhere.

I see decor...all those happy signs. My eyes fall on the one that says "happiness is a long, hot bubble bath." Are you freaking kidding me?

Finally, get to the pet stuff. They don't have what I even wanted/need.

...But at least I haven't seen someone I know.

(I'm still fearful of seeing someone that might NOT know. Especially a mom of someone Logan knew. They might ask how he's doing. I see one of these moms at the gym and for now, I am avoiding her. I don't think she knows and I haven't actually had to TELL anyone yet. Well...that's not true, I've had to tell a few strangers, like the bank lady when I was closing his account. But not anyone I "know.")

I hear a couple of guys talking. Throwing out the F-bomb every other word and I'm annoyed. I think about how Logan would be annoyed, too. (He was such a rule follower and I can't say that I ever heard him cuss.)

I'm walking so slow...I want to get out of here, but my tired body just strolls slowly, so slowly.

I see the pillow aisle and remember buying Logan at least 2 pillows in the past year. He didn't sleep well. Why didn't I piece that together more? That even though he was so happy in his new job, I would ask him how he slept and he often would say, "not very good." I think about how for Christmas I was going to buy him a new mattress. His was very old...he needed a new one and I should have bought one long ago.

More so, why didn't I see that his poor sleep was a sign of ongoing depression?

I'm almost out of here but have to go by all the candy. Logan loved candy. His favorite was Skittles. There were some still in his drawer in the kitchen that I had bought him after the Halloween sale. I remember him asking, "Who kindly filled our drawers with delicious treats?" I was happy to say, "Me." Now I think about that drawer. I cleaned that drawer yesterday. Moved his stuff to a box that will likely remain on the dining room table for an unforeseeable amount of time. We haven't had an extra drawer and Amaya has been asking for one. Now she has one. I'm thinking I'm not sure if I was ready to move his stuff, but Amaya is important too. And it's just a drawer, right?

I open the door to leave...okay, I made it and thankfully I parked really close. Moving faster now I get in my car and turn it on. Not sure why, but my car is a safe place to shed tears. Again. But I'm thankful I have a stockpile of Starbucks napkins to the rescue. I hear a familiar song on my Christian radio station that reminds me, again, that "hope can be found." Thankful for these words. I need to be reminded of them so much lately.

PS...I wrote this a bit earlier, but I picked this picture just now. I chose it because it's one of him in his clothes I helped pick out. As I'm getting ready to post it, I see the words on our wall in the background, "great hope comes from great faith, in God". More true than ever.

It's also the last picture I took of him.

## JANUARY 26, 2018

Some people are genuinely worried about me. My pain seems too much. They want me to see that it won't always be this bad and I'll make it through. They want to fix me.

Maybe my writing hasn't conveyed enough that I am "ok?"

What is ok?

Well, I'm (we) getting dressed each day. While I admit I care a little less about doing my hair, makeup or even that I'm wearing similar outfits every day; I am showering and doing laundry.

I dread appointments, grocery shopping and driving in the car alone, but I am going to them, eating, and I blast my music, crying or not I sing to worship music. Sometimes it's comforting and sometimes it's painful.

I'm going to lunch, coffee, and soccer games. Even went on a hike today. I still see God's beauty. Beauty in the present, but also beauty in the ashes.

I am wandering through the hallway and doors are opening. Still figuring out which ones to take. But I'm hopeful.

My writing is not to worry people about how bad I'm hurting. It is bad. I do hurt. But it's how I am processing. It helps me to get it down on paper. My intentions are not for you to feel sorry for me, but to give people an inside peek into what's it's like. And maybe to even allow that one that is thinking of ending their life, to experience what the survivors go through?

Every grieving mom feels many of these same things, they just don't write about it or express it the same. You can't fix it. It's here and not leaving anytime soon.

So let me talk. And tell me you are thinking about me. Tell me it's hard for you to read, or that your heart hurts for me. But don't try and tell me what to do to make it better. Don't offer commercialized suggestions. Just listen and acknowledge. I'm a fixer so I know it's hard, but this one....just let it be.

#hopeful #suicideawareness

## JANUARY 28, 2018

I am Grateful. I am Thankful.

Really.

I was always taught to be grateful and to give thanks. My mom was that mom that "always" made me write thank-you notes for every gift I received. Ugh, right? But what a valuable lesson. We also prayed before every meal thanking God for it, even if we were at a restaurant and people would see. And one of my favorite memories is being on the ski lift many many times with my dad, singing "Climb, climb up sunshine mountain...." and talking about how beautiful His creation was and how grateful he was to be able to enjoy it.

I remember years ago a Neonatal Practitioner I work with said, "Think about if you only received tomorrow what you thanked God for today" (thank you, Mimi Stilson). That really had an impact on me and ever since I always start my mornings by thanking God for those most important things...my family, my extended family, my health, my job, warm water 😉 ...and then sometimes I move to the less important ones...even Starbucks coffee that I love so much. It's something I enjoy, why not thank him for it? Those people in Ghana don't get to enjoy a drink like this.

So when the police knocked on our door in the wee hour on Dec. 15, asked to come inside, and told us the most terrible, horrible news that I will EVER hear, I am so GRATEFUL my mind could automatically think of some things to be THANKFUL for;

I was thankful first that Logan didn't take other lives before his. (No, I didn't think for a second that he was ever capable of this, but lots of families that this has happened to didn't think that either.)

I was thankful he didn't choose for his last breath to be here. (I choose not to imagine how much worse that would have made it.)

I was thankful he called law enforcement just before and told them where to find him. (I assume that was so we wouldn't spend hours or days wondering where he was, and also so another innocent person wouldn't find him.)

I was thankful he didn't use one of Glenn's guns.

I was thankful he left letters. (We were unable to get them at that time.)

I was thankful we had each other and that we were all home together.

Not immediately, but a little later that same day.

I was thankful for the 23 years I did get.

I was thankful for the amazing family and friends that, upon learning of our loss, were immediately there to support us.

I was thankful for his amazing friends that somehow were able to come by.

Once we were able to read the letters;

I was thankful for some explanation even if it was something we couldn't fully understand. That he knew he was loved. He knew he was liked. He knew he was being selfish. He knew he was blessed with good friends.

He knew I cared.

Most of all, I was thankful he wrote, "I love you all."

I know many survivors of suicide don't get these affirmations.

No... I'm not saying I have "rejoiced in thanksgiving" (maybe that's to come, but honestly I'm not there yet) over this terrible loss of my son. Or even that I'm not just plain angry at times.

But there is some comfort in being grateful. A peek into hope? I feel the very nature of being grateful gives Hope. Hope that I can survive. That my life will not rest in this pain. That the hallways I'm walking down and doorways I'm looking through do contain things that I will be able to be grateful for.

And if my human self is going to blame Him for the bad, I have to blame Him for the good, too. (Thanks Taylor Grant 😊.)

At the end of the day, I don't believe God wanted Logan to take his life, but I do believe he could have stopped it and didn't.... God is not punishing us, but somehow, for our joy and His glory, He's letting us endure this and walking us through. I'm so thankful His promise is to never leave me, just like He never left Logan.

# FEBRUARY 2018

## FEBRUARY 2, 2018

If loving and being loved kept people from ending their life, there would be very few suicides. Love has little to do with suicide.

Emotional pain perceived by the sufferer as intolerable, irresolvable, and unending has everything to do with it.

#suicideawareness #mentalhealthawareness

## FEBRUARY 6, 2018

This one is for my mom (Wendy Logan).

*Grandma Wendy holding Logan right after he came home*

Yes, today I made myself cry by going back through some of Logan's scrapbooks I had put together (not to be confused with his photo albums 😊).

How it started: I was actually just moving some things around (trading some things in certain cabinets in the living room to help my older female child have easier access to her school supplies....interpretation: to make my life easier by having a more convenient cabinet to throw her books, papers, etc., etc., in after she leaves or goes to bed and they still lay amongst the rest of my picked-up house).

Upon moving items, I realized these scrapbooks were staring me down. It was 1:00 and no one was home. I could cry without making a scene or feeling guilty causing others, too. So, I decided to do one of the things I've been dreading (only because I knew how much it would hurt), I went through some of these memories.

I'm not gonna lie, I couldn't handle it all. But I know there will be more days for that.

Yup, I was "that" mom you see in the movies, that just wept at the very first pages I saw. (Really? I like to be different. Not do it the way they show...but) I couldn't help myself as I pulled the pages out of the sleeves so that I could actually place my fingers on and touch the scribbles Logan made. There were coloring book pages where he only colored with one color for the entire picture, and then there were hearts for Mother's Day that were mostly made by the teacher, but he managed to print out his name and I could read it. Preschool, then kindergarten, then he started writing sentences and I felt the need to touch the pencil marks. I guess for one second it made me feel like I could touch him. Yup, I was making a scene from a movie, only no one got to watch.

Ok, back to the part regarding my mom.

I came across this sweet, sweet essay written when he was 10. I was overwhelmed to read these words, that he described his most prized possession as "my grandma's blanket she made for me."

The other day when I was looking at his photo albums, I actually posted on his wall for his friends to see, just how much he was already talking about video games....and it was years before this was written. They were what he wanted for Christmas, what he loves to do, what he did when spending time with his friends, etc.

So I fully expected this essay to claim his most prized possession as, 'my video games.'

I know this essay might be hard to read, and you don't have to attempt it (although it's pretty good), but please know how much Logan loved his blanket. The one that was made with love from Grandma (and Savannah has a matching one!).

👁 What you don't know, is that my mom very much wanted Logan's blanket to be displayed at his service, along with some of the other items we took. With the chaos and brain fog, it got left behind and I felt very badly.

Mom, I hope this makes up for it.

Logan used this blanket his entire life. It covered him in his crib, and even at 23 he had it on his computer chair and would often be seen wrapped in it. It's currently by my pillow. It's one of those items I'm not sure I ever want to wash.

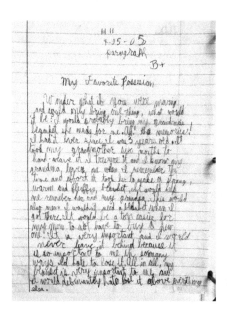

## FEBRUARY 14, 2018

Happy Valentines Day!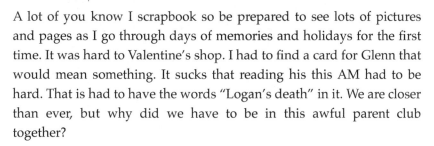

A lot of you know I scrapbook so be prepared to see lots of pictures and pages as I go through days of memories and holidays for the first time. It was hard to Valentine's shop. I had to find a card for Glenn that would mean something. It sucks that reading his this AM had to be hard. That is had to have the words "Logan's death" in it. We are closer than ever, but why did we have to be in this awful parent club together?

I always have some gifts for the kids and this was the first time I had to only think of 3 of them. My brain...as I stood there yesterday looking over the candies, I kept thinking...Logan was so good at helping hide the eggs. Ya know, I don't even want to buy jelly beans or whatever to put in them. I'll buy some candy, but the baskets will just have to be filled with their gift and candy, no plastic eggs. I'm not in the mood to stuff them and certainly don't want to hide them...Amaya is big enough, she will understand.

Bought some pink bags because I still don't like going to the basement where the baskets are (and Logan's room)...and then it wasn't until today, as I'm filling these bags, that I realize...it's not Easter. I don't need eggs.

PS. Two of these precious kids in this preschool picture are no longer with us. Next to Savannah is Keaton Allison (Jan). Today is a day about love. Let this picture remind you that no matter what is going on between you and your loved ones, love them. Love conquers all. Ask Jesus to help you love them. Life is so fragile and precious. You, or them, might not be here tomorrow. 💔

## FEBRUARY 15, 2018

Did gaming contribute to Logan's death? Such a complicated and loaded question.

For as long as I can remember Logan played. As a young child, he would compete with his brother and dad, something they really bonded over. As he got older, like his sophomore or junior year is when it became a problem. He began withdrawing from family activities and spending countless hours in his room downstairs. My discussions of gaming addiction and limiting time on the computer were met with fierce denial (and his grades were good so I couldn't argue that one those years). I remember in HS presenting his rushed attitude with us, as I could see the nervous excitement in every extra minute I was able to drag out of him to remain upstairs. And then after academic probation his fall semester at School of Mines, I thought for sure he would recognize the negative consequences of his continued obsession, but he instead attributed the behavior to the school not being a good fit. This was when we knew it had become a very serious issue, as he was a kid with serious money consciousness.

However, Logan was also a kid of facts; he saw things very black and white and he liked proof. So therefore his main proclamations were there was none against gaming. At times, he would read upstairs to prove the hours he wasn't spending glared to the screen. Books were definitely a love of his and it was part of his plea that gaming wasn't all he did at home; and I agree it was never forced. I wished I would have engaged him on those story lines.

In the end, my opinion is depression was the fatal blow, but what I'll never know is which came first. Did he use gaming to escape like many experts suggest, or did the gaming contribute significantly to the downward spiral? Genetics and mental health play a role together, and there's no doubt it runs along both sides of the family.

Unfortunately for Logan, The World Health Organization (WHO) announced it would list gaming addiction as a recognized mental health condition in early January 2018, ahead of the publication of the 11th International Classification of Diseases diagnostic tool.

One month too late for Logan. Could this statement alone have saved him? Would he have recognized the attributes he possessed that mimicked those in the reports leading up to these decisions?

A major contributing study by researchers from Nottingham Trent University and the University of Oulu, Finland, and included over 130,000 gamers, found addiction to video games can contribute to depression, anxiety and low self-esteem in players, affecting them both psychologically and physically.

Excessive game playing caused physical ailments including cardiovascular stress, wrist pain, issues with sleep and the nervous system among others. Is it ironic then that Logan complained about these symptoms, researched them vigorously on his computer (mostly the wrist pain and headaches), and then deduced in his goodbye letters that they could never get better? "I feel terrible all the time...my hands ache constantly...everything hurts...my life situation may improve but my health isn't likely to...I'm 23, none of this should be happening..."

Concluding gamers were also at risk of mental side effects, ranging from depression, anxiety, and lack of concentration (to a few others Logan didn't display), seems to lock him into a sure diagnosis. He verbalized his struggles with attentiveness in the classroom, but never having these issues in the past, I allocated it to his lack of motivation. If only I delved more into why there was a lack of drive. Putting all these pieces together at that time, I recognized there was a problem, and that he was likely suffering from depression, but what I didn't know was the difference and seriousness of 'clinical' depression.

Logan wasn't 'sad' and he wasn't 'lonely' like he and most believe go hand in hand with depression. Because of this, would he have disregarded the new published findings and continued to make excuses not believing, as he stated in the end, that there wasn't anything "was wrong with his head"?

Regardless of what came first, both seemed to contribute to the other. Was he especially susceptible and how does one predict that? Does this mean everyone who is into gaming will exhibit these results?

Of course not. You learn a lot about a person after they're gone; our eyes have been opened a lot into the competitive gaming world and the amazing friends Logan had within there. We have spent much time with them and they are close with their families, most have degrees and great jobs, and some even wonderful marriages. They have shared amazing bonding stories and it's obvious from some of their customs and FB threads how much they care about life. They appear to be healthy, happy people. And for them, this apparent hobby can be far greater than I imagined. We have been enlightened how Logan wasn't just playing, he most definitely excelled in this massive phenomenon. Tournaments are huge much like sports, and nationwide, Logan was considered one of the best in the state. At one point he was ranked 2nd in all of North America in a game 70 million people play.

...and we didn't know any of this...

Unfortunately, because of our rejection of his habits that had contributed to his separation of us, we didn't ask and he didn't tell. I knew he frequented tournaments but had no idea they were to this grand caliber. I often wonder, if we had engaged this interest more, would things have been different? Would we have seen his friends differently? Would we have been supportive of this 'practicing' that contributed to so many ailments? Because let's face it, if you're going to be good at something, you have to work at it. That, he was doing.

...but just when I feel have talked myself into supporting his passion, I found one final gust that lures me back to the other side. As I dissected details as to why he descended to ultimate darkness on that night, seeking answers, I searched his computer. I found something that stung, haunted me, and continued my head debate into the controversy of gaming (at least certain games?). In the early morning hours of the 14th, Logan played a game for the first time that I can't dismiss as anything but pure evil. Doki Doki Literature Club is a visual novel, gameplay designed to lure players into a sense of comfort before destabilizing their expectations. It's psychological horror genre containing suicide, self-harm, mentions of depression, and graphic images of death. The more I read about it, the more disturbed I became and I will forever wonder what drew him to explore it. Obviously not for the weak-hearted. For Logan, it was the perfect storm.

So, regardless of the final and actual answer to my question, there is no doubt the community of gamers is strong and close. In an ironic twist to our years of perception, one of my greatest treasures from his death is in how they have honored him and embraced us: A "Smash" charity tournament was held and those gathered made contributions given to us in a card at Logan's service. What a genuine gesture from many that had never met us and were mostly starving students. And all over YouTube and FB, the group honored Logan through videos, cover photos, and dialogue.

I truly love these kids.

I'm just not sure I love gaming.

Oh be careful little eyes what you see...oh be careful little ears what you hear...

#suicideawareness #mentalhealthawarenss #misshimsomuch

## FEBRUARY 17, 2018

Would love to share an amazing thing that has happened in the last weeks. I already talked about how absolutely grateful we were to have SO many of Logan's friends come to his service. But what is so meaningful to me is how they continue to want to be a part of our lives.

When I texted 2 of his closest friends within a couple hours of Logan taking his life, I told them we would love for them to come by. I honestly did not expect them to. I have known them and heard their names many times over the years, but they rarely came here. I wondered if it would be awkward for them, and being very young men, would they want to avoid the pain, the conversation, the questions?

They both showed up within a few hours separately. We hugged, we cried, they both talked about how they had no idea. Jared had just spent Wednesday night with Logan and couldn't recall anything unusual. Shocked is how they continue to describe their feelings.

Others showed up, even 2 from out of town. I love that they chose to be a part of our first days. They continued to communicate with us and we saw them and other friends throughout the first week.

As a mom, you can be happy about a goodbye (service) that was amazing, but it was certainly a fear of mine that everyone would quickly move on and lose touch.

I know I've already said this, but I feel even more strongly now; Logan had amazing friends. They continue to message me, check in on me, send me memories when they think of them, and this week...

...most people know I don't like to cook, so how awesome was it that Andrea Meletis came over and was our personal chef! She also brought Athanasios Meletis, Jared Severn, and Alec Filer and they filled our evening with JOY. I loved how comfortable they were at talking about Logan...

...how he was such an "old lady driver" never ever going over the speed limit. Not even by 1. Even joking they didn't know a certain street was 25 until they rode with Logan.

...they showed me a video where the leader in the state at a certain game they all play (smash), was critiquing a top player. It happened this guy was challenging Logan and the analysis turned into a constant verbiage of how amazing Logan was as a player.

...they shared how they each met him.

...they looked at his photo albums and we laughed at old pictures and even found some of Jared and Mitchee and others I had forgotten I had.

...and of course "I" got to share some of my updated thoughts and things they didn't know. I did the mom lecture on how they need to be talking and taking care of themselves. How I've read so much about them being "at risk." This has and will affect and shape their lives forever.

...we even all agreed on what Logan's facial expression would be if he walked in and saw us all sitting around our dining table!

In the past, it's been a little weird to me when people ask me, "do you feel him with you?" The answer so far has always been, no. But I can honestly say that during that evening, I felt like he was with us. And Jared has so many mannerisms and similar personality traits and even shares common wording as Logan, that I found myself so drawn to him. When I told him that, he said, "Well when someone is your best friend for as many years as he was, I suppose you become a lot like them." ...a reminder that you are usually like the 5 people you hang around the most. So thankful he had amazing people in his life. So thankful I have amazing people in my life that make me so much better than I already am. So excited (and grateful) I get to spend a long weekend with some of my most favorite people in the world. I'm sure we will laugh. I'm sure we will cry. I hope that you have some of those people in your lives.

Throughout the evening we again laughed together. We again cried together. The night ended in a group "cry hug" which will remain as one of my top Logan memories now. We made a promise to keep in touch. I hope to one day hold their babies in my arms and be able to come close to feeling like the grandma I won't get to be for Logan's kids.

#findingjoy #misshimsomuch

## FEBRUARY 26, 2018

I so vividly remember taking this picture. I was walking the dog like I did every day, and this was my view as I approached the house. On this day I knew Logan would be leaving for college in a few hours. I wanted one last pic of his car to remember what it was like when it was parked in the driveway...bittersweet I thought at the time.

...if I only knew it would become memories only marked by a horrific scene playing over and over in my mind.

#misshimsomuch

## FEBRUARY 27, 2018

Yesterday it was a Sergeant from the Marine Corps calling...I never answer the home phone but was expecting a call that might have had that number. Instead...he asked for Logan. I had to ask who was calling, thinking it might be a friend that didn't know. Poor guy, although he was very polite and gave his condolences, I could tell he had probably never received this type of answer, stumbling through his words; including ending the conversation with "I'll talk to you later." 😳

When people say it comes in waves and the littlest things will trigger free-flowing tears, they were spot on. I was having a halfway decent day (despite attending a funeral in the morning) and never expected that call to affect me the way it did.

Today it was a freaking receipt.

Logan loved Bertie Botts jelly beans (a Harry Potter thing); loving to trick people with vomit, earthworm, and even soap flavors. I can picture him laughing so hard when he was able to trick the unknowing friend or relative.

This afternoon...I was rearranging some household items and found this in a hiking book I had purchased in 2003. We had enjoyed hiking on our recent family trip to Hawaii so much we were wanting to explore more of Colorado together. Logan surely was with me, he would have been 8...I wouldn't have bought these jelly beans for anyone else. 😔

Not sure why I would have kept this as I used to file receipts and then toss them after a bit.

Not sure if I am happy to have it. Right now? No. But perhaps sometime later it will bring me a smile.

## FEBRUARY 28, 2018

How is it that something that consumes my days, my life

Is something I only allow myself to actually think about

Deep enough (or perhaps clear enough)

to where I can actually have a tinge of belief that it happened

A couple times a day?

# MARCH 2018

### MARCH 2, 2018

Ugh...so hard to see my FB "memories" these days...

#suicidesucks

#mentalhealthawareness

### MARCH 3, 2018

I feel suspended in time;

Without the past....good times and family memories darkened by an unnecessary act = death.

Without the present....I've lost entire days, weeks, and now months while my body deals with the shock. I've lost my grounding in so much ...the things I've loved, or even things I thought I understood. The immensity is this truth leaves me very stuck in time. In some ways, I don't want to move forward.

And without the future....like introducing his wife into our family, the accomplishments we could have celebrated, knowing what he would be as his adult self, the joy of holding Logan's babies and passing some of who we are into another generation (probably the one that stings the most for me right now)...

But I know who holds the future.....🙏.

And so thankful for the hope. I need that hope. And if you're not a believer you might think it's just a cushion...some made up comfort to get me by. And I would tell you, you can call it what you want, this comfort is saving my life. Molding me and making me a better version of me to come.

#suicideawareness #hope

## MARCH 6, 2018

I don't agree with the statement, "God only gives you what you can handle".

I think God wants us to draw close to Him and use Him to get through rough times. If he gave us what we can handle, we wouldn't need Him to carry us.

I know when times are good, I am still leaning and thanking, but when times are bad, He is SO much more involved in my constant thoughts and doings.

#Godisgoodallthetime #suicideawareness

## MARCH 8, 2018

Do you wonder what it means when people say their lives have been changed by Jesus?

It can mean a million things.

For example, do you have anger? Get angry a lot?

Anger is a reaction to feeling threatened. It's a normal emotion, but can you imagine not getting angry so much? For starters, Jesus protects us and when you know you have that protection consistently it give you so much more peace about every situation. What does protection mean? When you know he holds everything in His hands...when you know "we win" against Satan; this situation is so temporary and great life in heaven is eternal.... etc....

He teaches us to love and models turning every situation into good. When he is a part of your thoughts, your day, you are way more prone to look at things differently, in a "how can I help this situation become positive, how can I make it a loving situation, can I see things from another perspective?" I'm not saying your life suddenly becomes anger free, but it sure starts to lean that way and practice makes all things better!

You might say, I can do all these things without Jesus. Can you? Are you so great that you can do everything yourself? Or should you lean on something that is much more powerful than you? Something that created you and knows you better than anyone? If you're troubled by the science of God, there is plenty out there. I love learning about it and it only strengthens my faith.

Let's talk about GRIEF. Here are just a few Jesus things that have helped me:

I have a huge community of believers praying for me. Who doesn't want friends coming together and using precious time, spiritual thoughts, on their behalf? my family's behalf?

Not gonna lie, it feels good.

Then, there is the "Peace that passes understanding".

Have you ever prayed for that? Have you thought about what those words actually mean?

I have many many moments in my day and have from the beginning, where I can't explain...

...why I'm not crying...why I'm not curled up in a ball...why I can smile and say thank you to the grocer who asked me how I was doing a few seconds before and I wanted to scream at them...how when I question "why me," I don't break down just thinking about that question...how I answer it with, "what do you want me to do with these feelings"...how I am comforted that each month will get better and KNOW, really know and believe, that it will get better.

It's all peace I can't explain, other than it comes from Jesus.

I can't understand how I could be feeling this way? The worst thing that could ever happen just did. My beautiful blond baby is not here and I will never be able to hold him. How can I even sit in the same house typing this and not cry all day long that he will not come up and say, "Hey, mom?" It doesn't make sense...until I bring it back to....oh ya, I've prayed for that peace to move forward, to be thankful/grateful and not dwell on things I can't change. I've prayed for that peace.

And then there is that hope.

That hope in things WILL get better. (Yes, this was in the peace paragraph, too.)

That hope that this WILL be used for good.

That hope that each of you will see something in my testimony that when you're in a dark place, you will reach out to Jesus for a new beginning...or that you'll reach out to me and ask me questions, ask me how/what/why.

Love each and every one of you.

## MARCH 9, 2018

Completing this task totally caught me off guard. Yup, I had to fill out your taxes...

It was so freaking hard checking "that" box...that you are deceased. I still don't even know what that means.

Logan Boarman, I miss you. Last year I made you watch me fill this out so you would know what the process was like. I would give anything for you to be annoyed watching me do it again, or helping as you attempted it by yourself this year. I would have never imagined you would not be here. That you would never, ever be a tax-paying citizen again.

#misshimsomuch #suicideawareness

## MARCH 9, 2018

Triggers.

Survivors are said to have triggers that can hit at any time. I thought I had become really good at hiding my reaction to them in the past couple weeks, for the most part in public, until today.

The first one was a shared reading from a friend. The short story was all too similar to mine and I should have never been looking at my phone in the parking lot before I stepped into Starbucks, for my quick trip to get my coffee and pupa-chinos. I could only read about half of the picture clips, and even after a few moments, the tears came when I stepped inside and I was asked, "How are you?" I was so frustrated. Why couldn't I control this one?

The next one was in the cereal aisle. Can you believe, I opened this book tonight and these words were on the first page? This. Her example happened to me! What does this mean? Anything?

On my quick trip to the grocery store, I turned to the cereal aisle and saw General Mills cereal. Right there, sale priced tags glaring at me.

Logan loved their cereal, particularly Lucky Charms, and I would stock up the garage shelves when they were on sale because it was something even his picky adult self would eat. I wanted to be ok with the pool of tears, but I just didn't want people thinking, what is wrong with her, what happened? I don't want them to ask because I don't want to talk about it. I'm fine talking about it with people that care about me, but random people? But then what if that's a chance to tell his story and help someone?.... I just don't have the energy right now.

Camp.

I thought I was excited to drop Amaya off at her first winter church camp for the weekend. Guess not. I was singing along with her in the car to "The Greatest Showman soundtrack" when it hit me. I know I've said it before, but camp was something Logan really loved. Memories came flooding (omg I'm using that word just like the books talk about). My emotions overwhelmed me. My aunt, volunteering, was at check-in. Despite cleaning myself up for the entrance, she intuitively knew this was hard. She gave me a big hug and said it was ok. Ok to cry and reminded me it didn't mean I was weak. I thank God for using her to remind me of that. The tears flowed and my waves crashed even more as I drove home. But I knew it was ok. Ok for the public to see me grieving. It doesn't mean I'm weak, just that I really miss someone I loved so much.

I feel bad Amaya had to start her weekend being reminded her mom is actively hurting so much. But that is just how it is right now. I hope it helps to show her it's ok for her too. I always take pictures. I didn't today. Thankfully her cabin leader sent me some.

## MARCH 10, 2018

My husband is a 6 foot tall, healthy built, and well...by all reasonable definitions, the epitome of a 'manly man'. As expected, I've never seen him so torn up. But not as expected, is *how* torn up he is. I know, because I see it.

You say you can't imagine. I say, while I had never tried to, if I had it wouldn't have looked like this.

Even if I tried, I honestly never could imagine the depth of how the death of our son has affected him, the man I have only ever seen cry maybe 5-7 times in our entire marriage of 27 years. Usually so emotionally controlled like the stereotype, now I am witness to his breakdowns nearly every day, sometimes multiple times within that day. Unlike what most anticipated, he is not using strategies of avoidance and minimization. He tells me that Logan's birth was one of the happiest, fulfilling, days of his life. And now December 15th, 2017, is most definitely the worst day of his life. The suffering is so evident, I see it in his eyes as he attempts little by little to keep going. But unlike me, he's a man of few words. While I know he's truly a softy, he has never been filled with too many emotions and rarely has verbalized them. His dad, like so many do, told him "not to cry", and so he has lived much of his life inside. Like so many men, he was discouraged from expressing vulnerability and encouraged to accept pain without complaint.

He recently sent me this picture and no words were needed. It's of his work desk and it told of frequent stares filled with what-ifs and despair.

While it's surrounded by the many accomplishments of his time as a deputy and pictures of happiness, the rock with Logan's name written in his handwriting predominantly stands out. I don't remember now the message during that church service; if we were talking about the symbolism of rocks and building your life upon this firm foundation, but the idea was to label this rock with someone/something you wanted to passionately pray for and place it somewhere you'd be nudged frequently to implement that commitment. While it's presence has always been obvious, now it's a striking reminder of what obtrudes every inch of his life.

If pictures can speak a thousand words, this one speaks a thousand emotions as well. And while most men like to push grief back into those dark corners, based on what I've witnessed in the past months, I'm betting (and proud) that he will leave it precisely the location it is in this picture.

#suicidesucks  #mentalhealthawareness  #depression #misshimsomuch #whatifs #proudmymangrievesopenly

## MARCH 13, 2018

My aunt recently came back from a mission trip from a third world country. When I asked her how it went, she smiled like she always does after these journeys and said, "Amazing because not only did we give them dignity, we saw *hope* in their smiles." We engaged in a conversation that resulted in me comparing and analyzing grief (where nearly all of my thoughts still reside).

You know how sometimes you are aware of something, but you have an "ah-ha" moment where you actually come to a realization of it? Well, we examined what that actually meant for these people to have *hope* alone and how just a small amount can change their lives so much. You can live without food for approximately 21 days while only 7 without water, but what if you don't have *hope* for either one of those? It's likely less…  And what if you don't have *hope* that anyone cares?

I'm not going to get all sciency and look up stats on this, and I'm sure there is a plethora of information out there and it's widely known in the psychology world, but it makes so much sense to me that without *hope* all things perish. I'm sure there are so many stories where people survived a shipwreck or being lost in the desert because, well mainly because they *hoped* they would be found. And there are probably just as many people who gave up because they saw no *hope* in sight, and therefore, perished; some only to be found and if they would have just hung on a bit longer it would have been in an alive state. Anything you strive for, you have to have some sort of a belief it can be done or you wouldn't be doing it. It's got to be the earliest and most needed state of being. If life is to be sustained, you have to have *hope*. It's true that it was the ultimate killer of my son. Logan gave up on having any *hope* left as he stated boldly in his letters: "I'm sorry my *hope* has run out".

I have found myself conveying many times now, "I don't know how people do this grief thing without *hope*." For me it's a *hope* to what is to come; focusing my perspective as an eternal one. And I think the answer to my question is that they don't. They might live for a while, but they don't survive. They are the ones that end up in severe depression, addicted to whatever substance, withdrawing from life, and doing anything but living. Because once you give up on *hope*, you don't see things can be different, better, or even that the sun will shine in the morning. *Hope* is created moment by moment through our deliberate choices.

So my friend, what are you struggling with, and how can you add just a little bit more *hope* to that? Talk to others about where they find their *hope*; I'm happy to share mine with you.

Can you slide just a little bit to the *hope* side? ...whether it be for a new job, that you can make it through this grief thing, that you will escape the depression you're in, that there is a reason you are here, that your kids will come around again, that you can ever move on from your divorce, that you will ever feel good again, or even that there is someone out there- like a creator- that loves you. Have just a little more *hope* and you'll be surprised at how much things can change. It might save your life.

#suicideawareness #mentalhealthawareness #hope


## MARCH 15, 2018

What I learned from last night (hashtags compliments of Bon Jovi songs):

This shirt, this SONG...it's always been one of my favorites from my fav band, but it has a totally new meaning to me now.

#livingonaprayer #itsmylife

It makes some people look better; I miss his brown. At 57 he is certainly getting older, that doesn't mean I want to see older, feel older. I respect that he is himself, but I'm not gonna lie, I don't like comparing me and my band to all the older people in my life and The Rolling Stones. And when I see older pics of him, it brings me back. I want that back. #justolder

I still have the best friends. Lee Ann, everything you did to make last night happen, thank you. Wendy, you are a champ....living on 4 hrs of sleep the night before, not feeling well, still hanging with us most of the day into the morning...you ROCKED it (yes, pun intended 😊). You had fun, like lots of fun, despite your circumstances. Doesn't everyone want those kinds of friends? Sure makes me a better person.

#thankyouforlovingme

I can still have a good time.

Yes.

I can't tell you how many times I wanted to go to that place...in the middle of songs I wanted to feel guilty; I wanted to go down that path of feeling sorry for myself. I wanted to stop bouncing in my tracks, and just fall to the chair. I may have even thought things like, "I wonder if anyone has recently lost a child to suicide in here...I may be the only one of these thousands." If there is someone, are they thinking about me? Are they a little lost in their pain, too; and instead of focusing on the concert trying to figure out that statistic number in here—how many of us momma survivors are out there?...BUT...that's not fair...just because I've lost a son, doesn't take away there are other kinds of suicide survivors. Sometimes I want to make this about me. Totally not fair, especially because....as I look aroun...

...My two friends next to me both lost a dad and a husband to those awful circumstances. Yes, it's been some time for them, but they were having fun. I couldn't ruin that for them and just continue to be lost in my pain? And why would I want that for me?

Sometimes you "fake it till you make it."

I chose to not go beyond those initial thoughts. I kept jumping, kept singing, and pretty quickly it became real. I was having a good time. I found myself going back to the places I always think about with each particular song...and I got lost in many moments.

When my thoughts caught me off guard again, and they did multiple times, I just faked it again, and soon it became real again.

I suppose this might be a game I play for a while, but I'm choosing to work hard at this game so that I win. I do like to win!

#welcometowhereveryouare

And, I was even able to smile thinking about how I had 'brainwashed' Logan into loving this band. How at age 9 I have a video of him saying they were his favorite group! I thought about how he may have actually come with me this time...but it didn't make me cry...it made me smirk and say, ya...probably not...maybe to the concert....probably with friends, but not his mom 😉...but that's ok. I'm glad he had friends.

#whenwewereus

## MARCH 18, 2018

What prepared me for this journey?

Nothing and everything.

Nothing prepared me for the physical symptoms I would feel. Just one of them...you know that saying, "it took my breath away?" I've heard it in stories, movies and on TV, but I thought it was just a metaphor. Nope, definitely not. I can tell you it's a literal thing. Many times I have felt myself hyperventilating, or breathing heavily because I feel like I'm suffocating and need more air. I felt this for the longest period, in fact, all hours, the day of the service. Getting ready was so surreal and I felt like I was shaky and out of breath the entire day.

Everything...I turned to everything I had acquired in my short 45 years. My family, my faith, my friends, my experiences...

....An experience that would change my life was when a friend lost a child to suicide 2 years ago. Instead of being one of those that said, "I can't imagine what you're going through," I TRIED to imagine. Maybe because I had kids her kid's age. Maybe because our kids knew each other growing up. Or maybe because as a mom I just grieved for her. All I ever wanted to be was a mom, and I imagined she felt the same. I somehow felt if I could imagine, it would take some of the pain away from her?

I know many grieved with her, but somehow I feel like it was different with me? I attended the funeral; I thought about her consistently. Not just for days, but for months, and even as the second year came around. When everyone had moved forward in their lives, I still reached out. We met for coffee many times. I tried to find that perfect book to get her through this tragedy. I prayed with her. I cried with her.

.....But never, ever, did I think that I would be able to tell her, "My advice, well...now it's from a club perspective." Because we all know it means so much more when you are a member.

This experience...was I being prepared to face something so similar? To be forced to use my words directed at myself?

November was my birthday month. I was shopping when this "door-way" print caught my attention. There were many things I loved in that store, but my eyes kept rolling back to this one. "Mom, have you bought all my birthday gifts? I really love this," as I sent her a picture of it.

Since that day, it hangs at my front door. I see it daily.

Preparing me, reminding me it will get better?

Two days before Logan ended his precious life, I was at the gift shop at my work. I don't read much, but I was particularly drawn to this bookmark. I hesitated using my work card for such a small purchase, but I really loved it and I'm trying not to buy things I like anymore and only things I love.

💡 Preparing me for the many books I would begin to read on depression and suicide?

I had begun redecorating recently, which included painting my walls the grey everyone loves now. The picture that hung on the basement stairway wall, wouldn't match. Savannah and I picked out a new one and I made into a canvas...recently also purchasing this "thankful" sign...being visible for all who walked in to see. It was like being stabbed in the gut when it arrived on the exact day my family was shattered, December 15th. What was this about?

That week I kept coming back to that picture and it's the one we chose to blow up for Logan's service; my favorite of him.

💡 Preparing me to be reminded to be thankful for family?

We existed (maybe only physically) the day the police knocked on our door in our living room with a newly purchased sectional. Previously we would have not had the seating to accommodate all that visited...more preparing?...

But...at some point, hours later in the day...and I'm not even sure which family member it was....someone noticed this ornament Logan had made.

At the exact center of the Christmas tree facing all of us.

Turning it over we discovered the date: December 15. Glenn cried as he spoke about how many times he had glued that puzzle/ornament back together. Now he would have to glue his family back together.

Was this reminding us Logan would be at the center of our thoughts this entire next year, at least every Christ-

mas?
maybe forever?

💙 I think it was preparing us to be reminded that Logan is hanging onto the "tree of life," the greatest hope that exists.

#thankful #grateful #suicideawareness #suicidesucks #hope

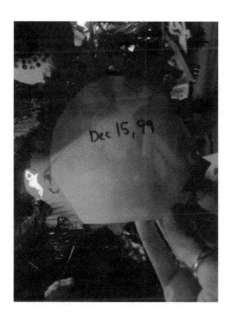

## MARCH 21, 2018

I've been waiting to dream about you Logan. I didn't want a bad dream but wondered if I could find clarity on anything? Mainly I just wanted to see and experience you again.

I vividly remember so much about this first dream. I was in the kitchen at Grandma Ruth's house. Close to the hallway, I peeked around the corner sensing someone was there. You caught my eye but took a slight step back as if you wished I hadn't seen you. Exhilarated, I immediately ran and hugged every part of you I could, as tight as was possible. With so much emotion, I told you I loved you so much. I could feel your thin body, and it was just like it had always been...I could overlap my arms despite me being fairly small myself. But I also remember having the feeling of getting lost in your arms because you're so much taller than I am. Once you realized I had clearly seen you, you became really happy and were smiling. You then, with me still hanging on and embracing you, walked me to the living room where we landed in a recliner. Atypical, we were in reverse order with me in your lap. I had an overwhelming sense of excitement and joy flooding through every part of my being. You were smiling and I could feel your happiness, too. You then spoke, "I just needed to go for a bit." With this statement, I reached for your head, placing my hands just below your ears to feel the holes you had placed through them. They appeared healed but I could feel the scars, like a thick patch that had smoothed out a bit. The same familiar touch I had experienced while you were in the casket. You then reached down and aligned your fingers in the same position searching for my bullet holes. It was at this point my thoughts drifted between consciousness and this alternative state. I began thinking, this is not real, this all can't be happening and can't be true. Like I was arguing with my 'conscious' self, emotionally I cried out as if I was pleading, "I'm going to wake up and this won't be real." I was scared, sad and angry. And then abruptly I awoke. As if I was still in the dream, I continued to feel extremely sensitive, vulnerable and the tears released soaking my pillow. Somehow I had known I was right and with a thud, the actuality of the day before me, and Logan not being in it, had presented itself all too quickly.

Shortly after this dream, I met with my counselor. Knowing we are all just sorta guessing, her interpretations of my dream made a lot of sense and gave me some peace. She analyzed Logan not wanting to see me was his sense of guilt and embarrassment but realizing how much I still was happy to see him gave him peace and he was able to recipro-cate the feelings. He took me to a place of privacy and comfort (the recliner) and then let me know he would only be gone for a bit; we would meet again. Reaching for his head, I found his wounds healed; he is pain-free. Reaching for mine was him showing concern for the healing of my head.

Even though this was incredibly emotional, I can't wait for the next one.

#suicideawareness #mentalhealthawareness #misshimsomuch

## MARCH 25, 2018

Headed to beautiful Mexico!

Well...Juarez that is. I think they have really cute Chihuahuas there at least?

So some of you may remember Logan loved going on these mission trips over spring break "helping people" by building a house in a week. We directed the memorial funds to this trip and as time went on thought it would be a great opportunity to go  this year and "honor" him. Over 80 people are going and we will be building 4 houses! So happy so many of my family could go. 🩶

Please pray for our safety, health, and that God would use us in amazing ways.

#herewego #missiontrip — with Jim Anders, Becky Korf Grant, Katie Anders, Savannah Boarman, Collin Grant, Eli Grant and Aspen Rae Wolfgang.

## MARCH 26, 2028

I received a phone call from the charge nurse at work the other night. I'm not sure if I didn't want to hear what she was saying, or the entire situation was so unbelievable that I wasn't the only one that couldn't communicate clearly. It took me a few more questions to clarify the urgency and trauma of what was going on. A co-worker's daughter had tried to hang herself. This child was 13. She (Heather) had just arrived at work only to get the call that Haley was on her way in ambulance transport.

And she wanted me to come be a comfort.

She worked nights and I didn't know her super well, but she had been reading my posts. While I'm usually very calm in stressful situations, my head was spinning so greatly I couldn't even think of who Heather was? Of course I will go, but embarrassed, I texted another coworker for help after not finding her on FB and thankfully she sent me a picture. Yes! I know Heather, we had hit it off in a few brief conversations and I really liked her. Wait...back to reality. She wants me to come witness sobbing? potential death? Rip any scabs right open to bleeding? I don't even know how to comfort myself, how will I comfort them? and 13 years old? this is inconceivable.

I left and prayed for God to calm me, use me, and help me to understand why. And God gave me everything I needed that night. Not my strength but His.

I was rerouted as they needed to transport Haley to the local children's hospital because she was requiring much more than our hospital could provide. Her heart was beating despite her efforts to make it stop, but she was not responding and they wanted to do further testing and see what time would tell, but we knew it wasn't good. I got there before everyone so just sat in the waiting area. As people (strangers to me) arrived I was somewhat hidden in the agony of their hugs and confusion. I wondered how many would notice and think I was another guest just waiting to chat with a friend. Soon I began to recognize the faces she had described and not having a clue what I would say, just began reaching out paying particular attention to the kids (siblings). What does one say to a 10 year old that had just seen the most horrific thing of his life? This experience will surely effect and haunt him all his days to come. What important words does he need to hear? I told them in one sentence how I knew them and why I was there.

Grief was my new best friend that went everywhere with me. I knew what that was like, but all words escaped me. Shouldn't I know what to say? Come on Lori, what would you have wanted someone to say to you? How do you not have these answers?

Fairly quickly Heather arrived and she spotted me right away and we had a hug I had yearned for...someone that knew my pain. I had peace in that moment that I could do this. I didn't need to say much, I just needed to be present. To be a representative of hope and that they aren't already in isolation.

I don't know if everyone has such similar experiences but my life is constantly witnessing and have encounters of "it's a small world after all," and this night was no different. The nurse that was taking care of Haley, it was her husband that was the deputy first on scene. Really? And the doctor here tonight advising on end of life decisions, well he was the same doctor that assisted in the beginning of life care of one of her babies in the NICU many many years ago. Really?

The hospital chaplain came in. After explaining I wasn't family and only there for support I listened to his words intently. My daddy did this very job for years, how did I not ever recognize the difficulties his job before now? Really. Then some guys from the county police department arrived. I texted Glenn inquiring why his co-workers would be there. Apparently when they are dispatched to situations like this, they follow up and offer support. Then it happened, the sergeant asked for my name and association to the obvious. Being my last name isn't a common one, he immediately embraced me. "I am so so sorry. I was at your son's memorial service. I pray for Glenn and your family all the time" Really? Until now I had remained stoic in emotion, but my insides were now shredding and I'm sure it displayed on the outside, if only for a moment.

All I can tell you is that my mind these days just goes in constant circles. Something like: Is this my life? What is this guy talking about—a memorial service for my son? Am I really living this? Is Logan really dead? What am I supposed to be thinking? How am I supposed to be acting? What should I be doing? Okay, Lori, back to the present, how can I help Heather right now?...her babies that witnessed this awful event? It's now midnight...I'm not tired..will they want me to go see Haley in that room? Will I want to? Do I wish Logan would have made it this far so that I could hold his hand while it was still warm? Would I want to be faced with these awful decisions Heather is now faced with? Look at that pregnant sister...she better cherish every day with her child. Now this sergeant guy is only thinking about my dead son. Is he focusing on Heather's family or the awkwardness of me being there. And I'm thinking about his alive children he just told me about.

How is this affecting the nurse inside those doors? And the volunteer…will she go home and hug her grandchildren a little tighter? Why am I still here? Should I offer to leave now? Is this really my life? Back to the call earlier…why didn't I understand the charge nurses explanation of the situation…and what posts of mine was Heather reading that she thought I could be a comfort?

It became late into the early morning and most of the family had left as little changes were being made. The oldest daughter, still living at home, needed to get some sleep, but also had a dog left behind at the house. The house where she had bravely called 911 and followed their directions in doing everything possible to resuscitate her sister. I have constant memories of looking out the window to see the police cars across the street after they rang the doorbell. What will hers be?

I remembered that there were many times, especially early on, that I literally couldn't make a decision. I needed people to just tell me what to do. So I told her she should leave, that I would go with her to the house, get the dog, and she could spend the night with me. And that's what happened.

She wanted to have her car, so I followed her and as I exited onto the highway from her house to mine, instead of praying (which I often use my car for), I turned up the radio. "Control" by Tenth Avenue North, was just starting its opening verse. A song I had held close in my thought wanderings as to God's plan on how the heck He's gonna make my tragic experience into a good one. "God You don't need me, but somehow You want me…I give You control…I've had plans shattered and broken. Things I have hope in…You have plans to redeem and restore me".

Really? This song comes on Now? Thank you God for reminding me I just need to follow your prompting.

I tucked Chloe and her beloved best friend in with a prayer and left her to attempt some sleep, and I as well. As dawn arose, the text I had dreaded came in. "Lori she's gone." I was privileged to hold Chloe during those intimate first moments. She may have still been considering me a stranger, but I didn't feel that way and certainly we were both comforted by our furry friends allowing us to engulf them with our sorrows. I was so familiar with all those feelings and emotions she was experiencing. Nothing one could prepare for, except to maybe have been through it. And now is me realizing, nothing needs to be said. 'Just be there and know.'

My calendar is on my phone these days. And instead of adding new birthdays, I now have to address death anniversaries of those that are in 'the club.' Please Lord, "Control." Allow me to witness and helps others be "redeemed and restored" as you are doing in me.

#suicidesucks #suicideawareness #mentalhealthawareness

## MARCH 28, 2018

The foundation is up and so are the walls!

**MARCH 30, 2018**

It is finished. #yourhandsyourfeet

*The dedication ceremony*

# APRIL 2018

## APRIL 1, 2018

I'm going to be blunt here and just say this day is not all happy like it should be. It sucks actually.

I know as Christians, this day is to be celebrated. I get that part and I'm happy for it. I "can" (still) be thankful. We can be thankful...especially that our grief doesn't go on forever. Thankful that one day we will live eternally in the happiest of times.

...But despite being thankful, it doesn't mask my overall sadness today. It's the second major holiday without Logan. How can that be? I still don't even believe it's real and it seems he was here just yesterday? But another holiday, already?

Another truth that life goes on.

All I can think about is how sad I am. Sad that I didn't get to make 4 baskets. That I didn't need to buy skittles. That I didn't have to ask him to dress up (he didn't like to dress up but Easter was a day I insisted). Sad that our table wasn't complete—and never will be again. Sad that I didn't have the energy at church to ask someone to take a family picture...we got one at Christmas...that seems sufficient for now.

Sad that I couldn't be more joyful with my kids today...ruining the day and spoiling it with sadness.

Sad for so many things...too many to list...

...and I can't seem to get the images of Logan coloring eggs and his sweet voice out of my thoughts. He was so cute. I want to tell him that and share this video with him so he can see...because he forgot?

I'm having a day where the feelings of wishing he had been hit by a car, instead of suicide, are so very strong. I feel like I could miss him and be joyful (if he had died for other reasons), but today I'm sad thinking about his prolonged internal suffering. That he had lost all hope tears me up. I know that's "not fair" to those that have lost children to accidents, cancer, and such. But today it seems ok to be living in the "not fair world."


My brain knows. My heart is just taking over today.

I read in a devotional that "A successful day is one in which you have stayed in touch with God, even if many things remain undone at the end of the day."

At least it was a successful day.

Happy Easter. He is risen.

#misshimsomuch #suicideawareness

Lori Logan Boarman
April 8, 2012

Great Grandma and the kids playing cards after afternoon dinner.

Memories...another in my timeline. 6 years ago. Amaya's first Easter here. We always had family over and good food and...well...created memories. So happy I got this one of my kids with their sweet smiles and their Great Grandma. When I used to see pictures like this, I always envisioned myself as the Grandma, being in the picture with my grandkids. Spending time with them and enjoying seeing parts of me, parts of my kids in them. That may happen for me, but it won't be what it could have been.

I'll never get to see how Logan would have raised his kids.

I'll never get to see what kind of woman he would have chosen.

I'll never get to be mad at the in-laws for inviting 'them' to Easter dinner first.

I'll never get to hide Easter Eggs for his kids.

I'll never get to make an Easter basket for him again.

I'll never get a complete Easter family picture again.

I'll never get to see him be annoyed that he has to dress up.

I'll never "fully" get to be that proud Grandma.

Oh, I'm sure I'll be a proud Grandma someday, but it won't be the same. Just like it will never be the same at Easter again.

#mentalhealthawareness #suicideawareness #misshimsomuch

## APRIL 2, 2018

Love this picture from 7 years ago. It was such a fun family day up at camp Elim, one of Logan's favorite places. I have wanted to spread his ashes there, particularly where all the kids run, jump and play. I feel like he could then still be a part of their "happy times;" the evening games were where I saw him smiling the most, chasing kids with squirt guns, swim noodles, or even water balloons. My family thinks that's weird. For now, his ashes sit in a makeshift memorial in the dining room.

I don't really know what we will do with them.

And I'm not really sure it's that big of a deal to me either. I don't "feel" him when I hold the urn. I don't "see" him when I look at it. He was alive and his soul is what matters, and you can't 'bottle that up' (no pun intended); that's not him. If someone stole his ashes, I would be upset because of what it represents, but I wouldn't feel like "he" was gone then. Because the truth is, he is already gone.

#misshimsomuch

## APRIL 4, 2018

~"Control." Somehow you want me~

He doesn't need me, but somehow He wants ME?

Alright...so this song has been following me around for weeks and weeks 😳 (couple months now actually) so I think it's time to talk about it.

I'm a fixer. I like to make things optimal, and rarely can I hear about something without my brain traveling down the "how can I make that better" road.

So when Logan took his life away from all of us, very quickly my mind was creeping into action mode.

"How can I help this not happen to another child?" "How can I help this not happen to other families?"

Already many people have reached out to me with their own struggles with depression, their children's struggles with depression, their spouses, and the list goes on. This started almost immediately. However, I have to admit, my early first reactions to these encounters was me thinking, "Why would anyone talk to me? I failed. My result was not good."

But thankfully now, as time has rolled on, I understand that we are all searching for answers. Searching for someone to relate to. Searching for someone to listen. Searching for similarities that maybe, just maybe, we could take pieces and figure out the puzzle.

So I keep asking myself...

What do I have to offer?

How is my story different?

Do I want to make this something I pursue with all my energies?

A non-profit?

A speaker?

A book?

What???????

I am following God's lead...just not sure yet where it's going.

Back to this song.

I was in the middle of a crisis situation (something I may share at some point with permission) following God's nudging of, "go," and literally had only a few min in the car...when this song blared at me. I already hear this song daily. I already feel it's speaking to me and it's telling me He is calling me to do something for Him. But, in that moment, wow! Reassurance there is something I'm heading towards or am I in it? I realize I was doing something in that moment. But does He want something bigger?? I feel like for sure He does.

Would you help pray with me regarding what that is? 🙏 That I might have clarity where my story, Logan's story, is molding and leading me to?

## APRIL 6, 2018

It's not his birthday. It's not our anniversary. It's not even the day we met however many years ago.

Today is just another day.

But today is another day that I am so appreciative, grateful/thankful, for Glenn, my best friend.

I know I'm never alone in this journey; people tell me that all the time. But what they don't really know, is that it's obvious to me - every.single.day. -

Because Glenn is that person that makes my loneliness seem a far away emotion, a place I can't reach because of his presence. Because of who he is.

We share something so special. Our son. Both in death and in life. It's human to search for those that can relate to your experience. I draw close to those who have lost a child. I draw closer to those who have lost a child to suicide. I find myself wanting to find those that have experienced my near-exact circumstances. Of course, this can almost never happen. Even if there is someone whose "son" took their life, but their son was on meds, or had threatened before, or was struggling socially, or other situations that weren't affecting Logan; you see, they are still not the same.

In fact, the only person that really can know is Glenn. He is the only exception to the "almost" no one. His circumstances are the exact ones as mine.

In addition:

He was there when I was angry at Logan.

He was there when I felt bad for being angry.

He was there when I begged him to get help. Many times.

He was there when I told him I loved him no matter what, unconditionally.

He was there when I cried and cried at being frustrated because I felt I wasn't getting through.

He was there when I was worried about his depression.

He was there when I gave him many of the hugs I like to give out.

He was there when I begged him to keep playing guitar...he seemed to stop doing all the things he loved.

He was there when we had many of our debates. Some ending bad but mostly ending very positive in the last couple of years.

He was there when I praised him.

He was there when I took everything personally.

He was there when I was excited that all his friends came to our house to play board games.

He was there when he told us he was done with school. He was there when we told him we didn't care what he did, we just wanted him to be happy.

He was there when I came back from counseling sessions with him, in tears.

He was there when I bought him a gym membership and then "nagged" him to go more often then he was.

He was there when I begged him to come upstairs and spend time with the family. To experience more sunlight.

He was there when we ate weekly dinners as a family. Many times multiple times in a week.

He was there when we took a family vacation and he seemed to have so much fun.

He was there to see me put up walls in fear of being hurt.

He was there to see Logan the happiest he's been in years...those last few months.

He was there in the love. He was there with the struggle with that love.

He is the only one that knows my story almost as much as me.

And he loved him as much as I did. He's the only one that knows what it's like to love Logan that much.

So thank you, Glenn. For becoming a better and better man. For acknowledging your feelings and helping me discover mine. Without my faith, without you...I can't imagine. I don't want to imagine so I'm not going to.

🩶 I love you

#suicideawareness #inthistogether #findingjoy

## APRIL 7, 2018

Logan looked so much like me.

This was always something I loved and was special about "us." People always comment on how much my daughter and I look alike, but I always used to tell them it was my son that looked more like me. At least in the majority of his years, the younger ones. After probably 5-6th grade, his masculine features were more prominent and he also developed a longer, more oval face more similar to Glenn's. I used to wonder what his kids would look like. Would my grandkids look like their daddy? Would they look like me?

Now I don't get to tell people he "looks" like me. I can only say it in the past tense. And my grandchildren....well they are no longer available to imagine.

#misshimsomuch

## APRIL 9, 2018

Depression isn't always because something terrible happened, sometimes it just shows up. It's stuffed and tucked and disguised and ignored but remains that constant companion beneath the dull-eyed smile. We frown upon it; frown because they must be doing something wrong, they're not trying hard enough, or they aren't thankful for what they have.

Wrong. Depression can show up anytime, anywhere.

#mentalhealthawareness

## APRIL 10, 2018

8 years ago things were so different...so much excitement. Can you imagine a post on December 14?

"Bout to become a family of 5"

I haven't said it out loud, but it pains me so... just doesn't make sense...to think of how hard we worked to adopt Amaya. The prayers, the emotional turmoil, the financials, the

effort and the time. All to have a child join our family so that we could share more love.

Only to have a child leave our family.

This is one thing I have really wrestled with. Screamed at God about it. I often imagine the first hug Glenn and I gave that 4-year-old scrawny child eager to be welcomed into our family. A hug that would grow to 3 more once on US land, but then ultimately be left at 2 today.

I have never taken for granted my fertility; and besides being married, having children was and always has been my number one desire in life.

And one of the hardest questions I now get asked: how many children do you have?

Many have told me, "Lori, you have 4 children. You will always have 4 children. You will always be a family of 6".

...but I have a hard time with this. Let's be honest. And I'm a realist. I don't "have" 4 children. I did have 4, but now I only have 3. Logan, of course, will always be my child, but he is not here and "have" is a present tense word.

Yes, I want to include him. I 'always want' to include him. But my response usually depends on who is asking. What will that person gain by me being honest? Or if I do the...half-truth thing...and it then depends on how the convo goes if they get the other half of the truth...

It's like a game I'm trying to predict the ending. Figuring out if there should be a "moral of the story" or just a generic "Hello, how are you" encounter.

If it's someone that is likely to go down the "How old, what are they doing, or where do they live" type questions, I'm finding, at least right now where I'm at in my grief, that it's simply less painful to just say 3. It's weird how I am eager to help and share with people that know but shy away with strangers. Maybe it's because there is a piece of me that is still exhausted. It's a story that takes effort. I'm not ashamed of it, I just haven't quite got the "elevator speech" rehearsed.

I hate the question, how many kids do you have? I hate the question, how many in your family? I doubt I'll ever change my mind "bout" that.

#suicideawareness #mentalhealthawareness #misshimsomuch

## APRIL 12, 2018

7 years ago today the courts blessed us and we were able to become parents of Amaya and for her to join our family forever. 🩶

Adoption stories don't always end up as happy as ours. We are grateful every day for her, and the smooth ride it's been. She did grieve her home country, important people to her there, and she did have a transition time where things were a little hard. But overall, she has been a ROCKSTAR at embracing her story, her journey, and what that looks like in a predominantly white neighborhood/school. I'm always amazed at her resilience and her loving, giving attitude. She is a pleaser and wants everyone to get along.

I'm especially sad writing this though. Logan is not here to celebrate. He loved her so. He was extremely patient with her and was the best at helping her with homework. They watched a movie together down-stairs only a couple of days before he left us. She was the last to see him. He gave her a big hug and said, "goodbye Amaya".

His last words he left her:

"I hope I helped you have fun and taught you some things. I hope you grow up to be an amazing person and I think you will. I'm sorry I didn't stay to see it".

Oh, how I wish he had stayed to see it.

#suicideawareness #mentalhealthawareness #misshimsomuch

## APRIL 15, 2018

Today it's been 4 months since Logan's death.

I didn't want it to weigh heavily on me, but it is.

You never know what today's "day" is for someone, so never stop smiling...even if you have to muster it...and be nice...even if they're not nice to you.

I was already in a down mood but found myself a mess after doing something as simple as entering the 4 way stop sign intersection on the way to the store. I know I'm not always thinking clearly, and in this case, I started to go before it was "my turn;" but it wasn't a situation where I was going to be hit or cause any harm. However, apparently, the other driver didn't see it that way and proceeded to honk and flip me off, as if his evil eyes were not enough to leave me shattered. I sobbed. I know his anger was likely directly at me, meant for something else in his life; but on this day, I took it ever so personally. It ruined my shopping, it ruined my drive home, it ruined the rest of my day. When I'm not so emotionally fragile, I can shake these things off like swatting a fly. But right now, I'm just a mess.

So please be nice. You never know what today's "day" is for someone.

#mentalhealthawareness #misshimsomuch

## APRIL 17, 2018

Thankful.

Another gift to receive this message about my Logan. Things I didn't know are so bittersweet, but I love being able to add memories to my ever wandering mind. These ones trickling in....well, you have no idea..... 😭☺️

Please, if you knew Logan and have stories or encounters or anything you remember about him that you're willing to share with us, please know how special and grateful we would be to hear them 🖤.

This one is shared with permission but some names have been omitted.

> I met Logan in 2013 when we started attending Mines. We both lived in Bradford hall. We both made a lot of friends there. I threw him a

surprise birthday party in his room complete with cake and balloons, turned out he didn't like cake, so 👤 and I sat on the floor and ate it without him (who doesn't like cake??) I made Logan a build-a-bear of Fluttershy as his birthday present because that was his favorite pony. He seemed to really like it. I remember he liked Avatar the Last Airbender and he is the only person I have ever met that genuinely enjoys the Animal Crossing games like I do. One time, Logan, his roommate, and I turned their dorm room into a blanket fort! I thought we had grown close by the end of the semester so that maybe I could ask him on a date when we got back from winter break. He was totally perfect in my book - handsome, funny, and sarcastic. But he didn't come back after break. He didn't tell any of us that he was leaving Mines, not even his RA, just left his room key on his bed. He didn't respond to my texts or messages for almost a week after the spring semester began. I was so worried, I even managed to find your number, Lori, in an online phone book so I had someone to call to track down Logan in case he was still MIA after 4 days (I told myself, "okay, if he still hasn't responded after 4 days I'll call his mom and find out what's going on.") Finally Logan responded to me and said he transferred to UCCS, saying that it was cheaper. I really didn't understand why he left so abruptly, we seemed to all be having fun together and he wasn't failing anything - I was under the impression that he was getting A's, actually.

I didn't know Logan suffered from depression. He hid it very well at Mines. None of us had a clue, not even his roommate. I tried to stay in touch with him after he switched schools, but he would respond infrequently, if at all, and I felt like I was just annoying him. I wish I could have done more for Logan.

Brains are just tricky things sometimes. I think you and your husband raised an amazing young man. I'm very sorry for your loss, Lori.

Sending lots of love, 👤

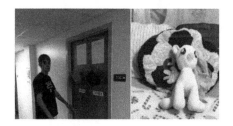

Move-in day 2013. Logan didn't want us to stay. I wanted so badly to help him unpack and organize, to be a part of this adventure. But he was cold and after putting his things in his room, basically said: "Bye now". Savannah saw my tears that day. I didn't know how to take all of it, but I was so sad. But I didn't know…. I didn't know how badly he was likely already hurting.

## APRIL 18, 2018

I've been so thankful (blessed I would really call it) to have had all my kids home way longer than most. They might disagree 😮, but they hopefully would tell you they enjoyed the family dinners on a regular basis that other families don't get, even when they're growing up.

Bryce's training with the National team and traveling so much made it silly for him to have his own place yet. Logan had been going to school at UCCS; but once he started working with dispatch, he had a plan to pay off his loans within 6 months and move in with a good friend. And Savannah stayed home to be able to have some money in the bank when she graduates from UCCS.

Because of this, I have always had someone, it seems, to be around to help with the dogs or with Amaya's activities.

4 months out and my thought process constantly goes something like this:

"Ah, my indoor game is at 8:00 tonight, Amaya's practice gets over at 7:30…Maybe someone can meet me halfway home so I don't miss so much of my game…"

Glenn- he's working late tonight

Bryce- he's out of town for work

Savannah- she's playing in the game too

Logan- he's dead"

Yup. Just like that.

I wonder how long before I don't go down that list?

Bryce is looking to buy a house this summer. Savannah is moving in with soccer teammates in July. Guess maybe then, when I don't have a "list" to go down, it will be easier.

Or maybe not.

Going from 4 kids at home to 1.....it will very much not be easier. I guess I'll stick with the list for as long as I can...

#suicideawareness #misshimsomuch

## APRIL 22, 2018

There's no good way to tell people of a Suicide.

I'm one to always worry and analyze everything. In the past few weeks, I've thought about how to tell people of Logan's death. What's the correct way?

And how different is it for those that knew him, and those that didn't?

I was in the front yard recently and met a 'new dog friend'. As we are talking about our furry family members, Logan's death is ever-present in my mind because this is just how I think these days. Because she lives by the elementary school, our conversation goes into kids. She doesn't need to know, it will change the way our conversation goes and all of her thoughts surrounding me. For now, I'm living in a world of my own.

But now we've had a few puppy play dates I keep wondering when is the right time to tell her. I fear that she will then have to go through the steps of apologizing and trying to figure out exactly what to say. But then if I don't am I lying about a huge piece of my life? Is that fair she finds out from someone else? This is such a struggle as I know there are no right answers and most of the time I can just 'take it one word at a time', but it's hard to even concentrate on any given conversation because I'm analyzing this topic. It's paralyzing.

But that's timing. What about what exactly to say, what words to use? Sometimes I seem to get it right and it goes smoothly, and other times it just blurts out like a cold washcloth waking you up...it can have a burn.

It got me thinking more about how I told people initially. What does someone in shock say, because if I had time to think about it, it would probably come out differently, right?

The thing is, I actually didn't "tell" many people. I just couldn't. I'm usually a verbal person, not afraid to tell you how I'm feeling, or ask you how you are. I ask the hard questions and like to get details and even give them. But...and this is going to sound cliche...I literally couldn't find the words to tell people. What ended up being texts, should have been phone calls. When I got phone calls, I couldn't answer them either.

The first person we told was my cousin. Because he had experienced suicide personally (his dad) and he is so close to my kids and especially to me. I wanted and needed him here. I sent him a text: "let me know when you are up, can you come over" after a few minutes I added that "Logan committed suicide" (I was conditioned to use that word, "committed," and try hard not to now, but that's another post). I neglected details that would have helped make his drive a little easier because he thought Logan had been found here at the house.

Then I contacted Randy, the kids' youth pastor for years and someone we consider a family friend. This conversation is pictured, but at least I learned from the first one to add a few more details.

And then we waited...and once they were here and we collected ourselves, we gave Collin permission to call my mom and dad (Glenn had called his mom) and Randy to call our longtime pastor and good family friend, because I knew I would be unable to hold a conversation. Collin called a few more people like my aunt and grandma and then after a bit, I started letting a few close friends know. I don't even remember how we found Jared's number (Logan's best friend), but I texted him too, not knowing how devastated this impersonal message would be.

The thing that bothers me the most is how I mostly unannounced what my message would contain. Two of my close friends were at work and I hadn't even thought about asking what they were doing or if they were at home. One, a nurse I work with, was put in an awkward position as people wanted to know why she was crying. Why didn't I think this would affect people like it did?

I guess the truth is, I didn't think. I couldn't think. I usually pride myself at processing well and reacting calmly under pressure or in stress, but not this time.

#suicidesucks #mentalhealthawareness #suicideawareness

## APRIL 25, 2018

Grief hit me hard today when I saw Logan in Glenn.

I'm always hoping for a whiff of his presence. Something to give me peace that I won't forget the many things I want to contain in the forefront of my thoughts. I thought this was an evil way to remind me, but reflecting now I'm grateful for it.

Most people, including myself, have always thought Logan looked a lot like me, especially as a child, but even as an adult he resembled me more than Glenn. He even dressed as a girl one time for Halloween and we were all intrigued at how much those pictures could have been mine. However, he did have some similar characteristics of Glenn, including his frame. Yes! Before Glenn started eating well and working out all those years ago he was quite skinny. Logan had his old frame, but definitely didn't resemble his new one in any way, except being his same height. I did, though, always think they had a similar facial structure too, mainly the longer, oval shape.

Today, Glenn was doing something and I saw Logan. I really did. Crazy. For that half-second, it was the exact expression or look that included the same eyes, the same nose, the same mouth, the same everything as my baby, my son. I suppose maybe he didn't look exactly like Logan, but the expression resembled him so much that it blinded me from anything different. I froze in that moment and could see my adult son, standing there in front of me. It caught me so off guard I burst into tears. I wept. My body just overcame me and I became angry my mind was betraying me. I felt I needed to apologize to Glenn.

That incident sorta set the precedence for the day. I'm trying to not let moments like that interfere with joy and so it's a constant battle to redirect my thoughts. But I was able to, and thinking about it now, and as hard as it was, I'm glad that happened. And...I still have some day left to see joy...to be glad Logan had some of Glenn's physical features so I could remember how much he (Logan) is a part of us both. I hope I can see Logan in Glenn many times again, and smile and have peace that he would be happy and proud that I could see him in his dad.

But as much as I want them to be alike, I'm also thankful Glenn isn't plagued with mental illness that constrained Logan's life.

#Grateful #suicideawareness

## APRIL 28, 2018

I love these friends (yes, they are from work, but they are truly great friends)! Some of the celebration was hard, knowing I'll never get to do that with my Logan. These times are ones I dread the most. Milestones. Am I going to cry the whole time, will I take away from others joy? How can I not think about the what-ifs the entire time? Or the "nots." Not gonna get to do this with Logan. Ever.

It turned out ok. Yes, I cried just a wee bit, but overall I was able to celebrate another mom's joy.

We did have an encounter that left my heart a little softer. One of Logan's friend's sister approached us. She was the event planner for the wedding and recognized us there. She easily could have stayed out of sight and we would have not ever known she was there, but she took the time to come over. We knew her family from soccer; her dad was Logan's coach for a couple of years and her brother played with him and attended the same JH and HS...

And ironically, her mom was "that" mom that I would sometimes see at the gym and wonder, did she know? I mostly found a way to avoid her so it wouldn't ruin my workout. I hadn't encountered someone that actually knew Logan but didn't "know," and was afraid of the typical "what is Logan up to" question and wasn't sure I wanted to speak the words, "he is dead." I mean, I am sometimes fine talking about the situation and am eager to educate, but then there are situations and times I just don't want to live in reality.

I figured she probably knew, but this mom wasn't on social media and I'm never sure if kids "remember" to tell their parents things like this.

Well, this girl knew.

Her maturity came through in her ability to approach us, speak of Logan, and express her condolences. It was a refreshing conversation and I'm sure she doesn't understand what it's like to hear your son's name. You hang on to every word as if you are opening up another page of his life you didn't know about, even if it's not new information. To have someone not be afraid of you, especially such a young person, is a gift. When people ask what they can do? Please, just don't be afraid.

I can't wait to see her mom now. To tell her how proud she can be of her daughter. And now, even if she didn't before, she will know. I will not be afraid to approach her.

Happy wedding celebration day to Olivia!

#hadfunseeingyouall #friendsstrong @ TILL Kitchen

## APRIL 30, 2018

Another unexpected...

Amaya had her yearly physical today. I went in frustrated with her worrying about "how much she was going to weigh." (So sad that she cares at 11 and is so focused on it despite my education regarding the scale, etc.)

But...very quickly the thoughts shifted to a place I was trying to avoid this AM. (Some days you just want to not be sad and try to avoid memories, because right now they are still pretty painful.) I had to fill out paperwork. Again this year, I suppose, just like every year. And, there was this one separate paper with a few questions and one stared me down. I suppose this question has been here before, but I have never noticed it.

"Have there been any unexpected deaths in the family?"

I suppose that is good for a doctor to know, but I was hoping to not "go there" at this appointment. After all, we have Amaya in counseling, she is thriving at school and with friends, and so I figured it didn't need addressing. These questions are so hard to read, so hard to answer, and so hard to stare at as I'm turning them in.

After a weight and height check (thank goodness for the amazing height number that distracted from the weight one), time for the assistant to ask questions. We've been going there for probably 15 years...and they have to ask, "Do you have brothers and sisters?"...and then they want to know names and ages? Generally, I am still answering I have 4 children, but I guess neither Amaya or I saw it as appropriate to name Logan as a "current" sibling. Regardless, you would think it would be in the records...😤

It's hard to know what's right or wrong as far as answering that question. Thankfully, I haven't been asked it hardly at all. But I dread it every time. I wish I could get comfortable answering it a certain way (I suppose there is no right or wrong), but I'm just not there yet.

During the appointment, I almost thought it wasn't going to get addressed (yay), but then Amaya mentioned she was in counseling and the doc then wanted to know if there was a specific reason why. And then the tears flowed. Geez. I didn't make it through this like I planned. Like I wanted. Even though I know it's ok to cry, I just hate doing it sometimes. Crying just gets old.

Starbucks for Amaya and her teacher (thank you, teachers- we love you) and it seemed to get better right away. For her at least...I so love her resiliency. It's one of her strengths.

PS she is 5'6 ¾ ! 😮

#suicideawareness #mentalhealthawareness #suicidesurvivors

# MAY 2018

**MAY 1, 2018**

Happy First Birthday to Mia! 🎉🎂🍰🎂🍰🎂

#boarmanbernards  #saintbernard  #painsucker

## MAY 4, 2018

"AWARENESS". That's my new word.

It's National Mental Health Awareness month and I have so much to say.

Even though it's called, "faceBOOK", I realize no one wants to actually read a book here, but I'm not good at conversation without including all the details. Some of you are laughing and going, "this is for sure true! the girl can talk!". Just know that I try to condense, I really do ☹.

When Logan first took his life, I had many....., many, people contact me. Some with their friend's story, some with their child's story, and many others with even their personal story. So many are struggling and I suppose they reached out for a variety of reasons, but I found myself asking over and over, "why are they contacting me? we failed! they don't want my advice....we must have done it wrong".

And then there were the times early on that I talked with educated people: like my counselor, good teacher friends that work with these issues in schools, and even Logan's best friend's mother, who knew Logan since about 9th grade and is also a high school counselor. And after rehashing and rummaging through the last few years and explaining the details that led up to that awful day, I heard the same thing over and over: "Lori, there is nothing you could have done".

Really? I mean.... really?

One perspective is... this is exactly what I wanted to hear because it confirmed my works and love as a parent. This made me feel better. That somehow I didn't have to blame myself so much.

The second perspective was... complete frustration. How could that be true? ...because if it is, then how can we prevent this? How can "I" help others not have to go through this?

So, as my journey is playing out, I analyze everything to the core (over and over again), learn from others, and pray about my purpose. The answer I'm finding, to that last question, "how can I help if I did every-thing (mostly) right", is this:

Share. Share your story. Share what you're learning. By sharing, everyone learns. It becomes "awareness".

Maybe you remember my very first post the day Logan died, when I said, "We loved him so much and as best we knew how."

Well, how about this one I discovered only recently?

> "Do the best you can until you know better. Then when you know better, do better." ~ Maya Angelou

This quote brings me much comfort. It gives me peace that we fought the battle with the tools we had, but also a mission to share the things we now "know better". We are learning and regardless of whether the knowledge we have now, could have changed Logan's mind (his denial is certainly a contributing factor and something that needs to be shared about as well), it might have changed the circumstances in which we played out our roles as his family, friends, co-workers, etc. We don't get new chances with Logan to put in place what we know now, but my prayer is that our experience and gained insight can help prevent others from suffering the way we have. The way Logan did.

So I'm going to share more of his story. I'm going to start sharing more about mental health and how it affected our lives, Logan's life. About depression. About the stigma surrounding mental health. About denial. About suicide. And I'm sure I'll be adding more as I go along.

"Awareness", that's what I'm praying for.

#mentalhealthawareness #awareness #suicideawareness

## MAY 8, 2018

Clinical depression is not just a feeling of sadness or "blue" for a few days. It's a SERIOUS medical illness.

This second part is something we did not fully understand before Logan took his life, and certainly I question if he did either.

Clinical depression is just like cancer, heart disease, or diabetes. You can't just wish it away. You can't just "get over it." It's a medical diagnosis that can have serious implications if not dealt with (obviously.... right? 💀)

Normalizing it as something everyone periodically experiences, we come to believe that those who are impaired by the illness are somehow weak and not managing their "depression" like everyone else can. I firmly believe this is one reason Logan denied the diagnosis. Sadness is a normal range of emotion, clinical depression is not.

Clinical, or major depression, is defined as: A mental health disorder characterized by persistently depressed mood or loss of interest in activities, causing significant impairment in daily life. This can lead to a range of behavioral and physical symptoms. (Mayo Clinic)

While people do often feel low or severely sad for an extended period of time, the physical symptoms that Logan displayed are many, but I don't include sadness (I'll talk about them in my next post). I believe he may have felt sad at times (don't we all) but I don't feel he had a persistent "sadness." In fact, we all agree he was "the happiest in the last 4-5 months than he had been in the last few years."

It's important to know that repeatedly I pointed out symptoms and how they were related to depression; and he would reply, "But I'm not sad," or "But I'm not depressed."

Individuals who display some or all of the symptoms can find themselves locked in a state in which they cannot even respond to painful stimuli. This is the part we particularly didn't recognize...he was incapable of making his own decisions at a certain point. I just want to scream...and why didn't I realize this and step in even more than I already was?

In the end, he didn't make a choice. A choice is when you have options. Those that complete suicide see it as the only way (thank you to the book that I read that clarified that for me).

Logan registered a very strong protest to that word, "depression." I believe he did so for more than one reason (remember this is my analogy, not what he told me):

1) The stigma is that people that are depressed are "weak." He was a self-proclaimed "incredible guy" who had a hard time "swallowing his pride." I think he assumed he would be seen as weak, and certainly didn't see himself that way. I definitely want to help change this, especially for guys/men.

The truth is, admitting depression is one of the strongest things you can do. It takes a lot of courage to say, "I need help."

His goodbye letter contained the words, 'I'm sorry I'm so weak." Ironic that one major attribute he lived to deny was the hallmark he described as taking over in the end.

2) He was a super intellectual guy (and he knew it) and I think he thought he could "outsmart" something like that, a 'mental illness'. He could not be 'tricked' into alterations in thought process. He could 'outplay' his brain and he could 'fight off' anything that was causing a 'war'.

3) And if he could outsmart depression, certainly he didn't think he could have a medical diagnosis. Since he was still smart, he thought the disease could not have affected him.

Let's be honest. You can be super smart and still have cancer. Why can't you be super smart and have depression?

He even wrote in his goodbye letter, "I don't think anything is wrong in my head,"... confirming that even at the point he had succumbed to...it couldn't be his head...it certainly couldn't be that mental illness thing people talk about...

4) He wasn't sad or lonely, which is most often associated with depression. Logan actually had a plethora of friends so I'm sure his social activities ruled it out for him.

The unfortunate truth is that we describe a feeling state the same as the name of a DISEASE. This seriously downplays the severity of the disease itself.

#mentalhealthawareness #suicideawareness

## MAY 10, 2018

My last post I talked about Depression being a serious "disease" or medical diagnosis. Please check it out if you didn't see it and, as always, please share if you'd like. Expanding today on what we saw with Logan.

Common symptoms with clinical depression and the ones Logan displayed were:

☞Difficulty sleeping: He was strict about how many hours he "needed to sleep," but would frequently tell me he didn't sleep well when asked.

☞Altered energy levels: I knew this somewhat at the time, but looking back at messages sent to friends, he frequently stayed home telling them he was "too tired, exhausted, or just not feeling up to it."

☞Lack of appetite: Even when he would try and eat, he couldn't eat much at a time before saying he was "full" or not "feeling wel.l"

☞GI issues: He frequently complained of stomachaches. I even took him to the GI doc and she informed me it was likely stress/anxiety.

☞Pain: His hands hurt, his feet hurt, his head hurt/head sensitivity and he had frequent headaches. Many of these I attributed (and told him so) to the long hours spent on the computer. I still believe this definitely contributed, and I believe he was truly in a lot of pain, but I think it was very much psychosomatic, as well.

☛Lack of interest in things he once enjoyed: This happened around age 15-16 and was the most obvious and sudden change. I include "withdrawal" as part of this. He stopped being interested in us and what was going on around him in our house.

☛Lack of motivation: He knew he was struggling with school (despite being very capable) and just didn't want to do the work.

☛Concentration: I remember, now, him complaining of this in the classroom (college) early on, and didn't have an answer other than I kept telling him I think it was maybe a part of something bigger with some of the other things. More recently, in fact as little as 2 weeks before he resigned from his job, he came home saying he didn't feel good, that he couldn't "concentrate well enough to be doing such an important job that day."

☛Other symptoms that were not displayed until the very, very end, were changes in self-esteem, and thoughts of suicide.

WOW! You may be thinking, "How on earth did you not see all of this, that's a lot!?" I may expand on some of these in another post, but for now, I'm trying to keep this at a few minutes' reading time.

The truth is, some were evident throughout and some displayed only intermittently. Some seemed to affect his daily activities and some seemed like normal things any teen/college student would exhibit. Some seemed like "Logan" (because we all knew he seemed to have amplified pain...but now we wonder, did he?) and some of it was just confusing. For example, our most frequent argument would be regarding the length of time he would spend in his room, where it was dark and isolated (the basement). But then he would go out with friends often and be involved in actives with them (board games, frisbee golf, etc). So he was living somewhat of a double life. We, or at least, I, thought it was "us" (family)...for some reason "we" just couldn't connect with him, and I couldn't figure out why? Analyzing in hind-sight, one perspective I come to is that he was spending so much energy socially and trying to have fun (I do think he genuinely was having fun when he was with his friends), that home is where he land-ed...exhausted.

The other truth is that we exhaustedly tried to help him (what did we do...another post later). I guess because he didn't wave at me saying he was sad, he repeatedly told me he was fine, and he never threatened to take his life...it somehow caused me to worry less (not that I didn't worry, believe me, I did).

We certainly knew he had all the symptoms of a depression, but didn't realize:

1) He had a "major" depression—a disease. A disease that doesn't go away (he needed to develop resiliency, skills, and awareness, or when it came back, he would struggle. And he would likely struggle with it all his life.

2) It could strike at any time and quickly, despite things seeming to be going in a great direction.

3) Depression could be dangerous. I mean, people take their lives every day and certainly if I pondered it I would tell you the root is depression...but that did not seem like Logan. He wouldn't actually do that...he didn't have "that kind" of depression. We were wrong.

⭐⭐ Don't be afraid to ask someone, "Have you thought about hurting yourself or taking your life?" We seem to think if we ask, it will cause them to think about it if they haven't. This is actually a ridiculous conclusion. Everyone knows it's out there, you are not giving them a new idea.

Many will find relief by being able to say it out loud. Others will realize someone else cares enough to wonder. For some, it might be a way to open up wounds and a conversation...a conversation that could save their life.

This biggest reason people don't ask? They don't want to know the answer. They can't imagine what that would be like to hear those words. Well, you don't want to imagine what it will be like if they complete suicide and you didn't ask...so if there is someone you've been worried about, take the time and seek them out and ask. Today.

And if you find yourself in the future worrying about someone, don't wait to ask. Do it at the moment you realize you are questioning.

(Photos are Logan with his friends. They saw him as happy and had no idea what was going on in the inside.)

#mentalhealthawareness #suicideawareness

## MAY 11, 2018

"Young Authors Night" at the school is an evening set aside each year for the parents to visit the classrooms and read all the "writings" the kids have done throughout the year.

I have wanted to share some of these great stories that Logan wrote (he had such a creative and imaginary mind), but today I can't go there. I not only can't read any of them right now, but I also don't even want to shuffle through them knowing what some of them say, based on the pictures at the top.

So...instead, I'm going to just share the introduction piece we saw at Amaya's desk.

Yup. That really sucked to see. Instead of being able to smile and tell her what a great job she did, those words penetrated our brains for the rest of the reading time. Sorry, Amaya, we have no idea what your stories were about.

Another evening of emotions in the life of survivors of suicide. Thankful once again the sun always shines in the morning. #suicidesurvivor #suicidesucks

All About The Author

Hi, my name is Amaya I was adopted from Africa when I was 4 years. I have one sister named Savannah and a brother named Bryce, I used to have another brother named Logan but he commited suicide. I love sports, my favorite sport is soccer. I play the trombone and I love hearing music with just instruments. I love pop music and watching hip hop.

## MAY 13, 2018

I thought today was a perfect day to share the NUMBER ONE thing I've learned as a mother.

Parenting is hard, we all know that. But for most of us, it gets really hard when they are old enough to really hurt your feelings. When your 6-year old says "I hate you" or "You're so mean," you are strong enough to take that, right? But what about when your teen doesn't respond when you say, "I love you," or even, "Have a good day."?

When Logan came back from School of Mines after his freshman semester, he had stopped communicating nearly altogether with us. He wouldn't say, "I love you" and was so very distant. I had already put up a few walls from the previous 2-3 years (when he began to withdraw and told us he didn't like spending time with us—which now I know is a huge part of depression), but this seemed more extreme. More hurtful. He reluctantly agreed to go to counseling, but he could be shockingly honest. I could have never been prepared for some of the conversations that took place regarding feelings, emotions, and how he perceived life. Although it was some of the worst moments of my life, it also helped me really recognize the most important thing I could ever do as a mom:

Continue to tell my son I loved him. All the time.

He was very lost. He was never rude or disrespectful to us, no foul mouth and never threw things or slammed doors. But what he did do, was hurt me in a way he didn't even realize. Not intentionally, but when he stopped saying those words back, it was hard to not take it so personally. He said he didn't know what love was or what it was all about, really. He lost his faith somewhere in there and he was obviously very empty. We had some hard conversations and although I knew he was struggling with "life questions," it's hard to hear from your son that if you got hit by a truck tomorrow, he wouldn't probably be very upset. You go back to those days of breastfeeding or rocking him to sleep. To those days of dropping him at camp and feeling like you just gave him the best weeks gift in the world! To hugging him when he brought you a homemade gift from school so proudly. How could those slip away in memory so easily for him? Didn't they mean anything?

It was so frustrating, most of his thoughts, that all I could do to protect myself, was to attempt to put up walls so that I didn't hurt so bad.

The counselor quickly analyzed and revealed to me, through our sessions with Logan, that he did not understand "unconditional love." He wasn't seeing it as an emotion or feeling, but more as an action...something I'm required to have for him, and he for me, since we are family.

She told me, as HARD as it is, you HAVE to keep telling him you love him—ALL the time—even when it hurts—even when you know you won't hear it back.

If you're not a parent, then maybe you don't know that can be something really hard to do. Seems easy? We all love our kids, and maybe for some of you, this comes easy to say all the time. However, it comes easy for me when things are going all great, but when I'm feeling hurt and not appreciated, it's really, really hard.

But, THOSE ARE THE TIMES YOU NEED TO SAY IT THE MOST.

So I pushed through that next 6 months-1 year. Every time I didn't want to say it, I prayed for strength and the words came out, "I love you, Logan." Honestly, it was sometimes a real struggle.

I'm still unsure of all the things that transpired over his course, but slowly Logan started responding again. He started giving me hugs. He started telling me he loved me back. His internal battle obviously continued, but he was able to regain the 'feeling' of love. I felt I had contributed, if even just a bit.

Monday, December 11th, just 3 days before Logan took his life, Logan turned 23. I struggled with wishing him Happy Birthday. You're probably horrified I would think this, but it had been my birthday just a couple weeks before, and although we were out of town, I didn't receive a text, a phone call, nothing from him that day. In my mind, I wondered if he would realize how much he hurt me sometimes, just by his inattentiveness. If I only knew how badly he was struggling just to live at this point.

He also had resigned from his job a couple of days before but hadn't told us yet. I was confused and even intermittently angry, unsure of what had happened. This was supposed to be his new beginning, but then again, getting a degree in Engineering and attending Mines was, too. Although a large part of me was worried, he had done things before that didn't make sense so a part of me was full of frustration. Again, if I only knew how badly he was struggling just to live at this point.

So when he walked upstairs, although I hesitated because my emotions were getting to me, I thought to myself, "Lori, this is your son and you have to wish him a happy birthday. You have to remind him how important he is." With that, I walked over and hugged him and forced my words out. Immediately as he hugged me back, my heart was already changing and softening.

Turned out, he was probably barely capable of responding, but he did. He was struggling each moment and one will never know, but maybe my hug and words helped him get through just one more day. I smashed my pride and am forever grateful this, one of the ultimate final memories, was so positive. Imagine if I had not talked to him that day. Imagine the increased pain and regret I would have.

I hope you remember this story when you are struggling with someone. It obviously didn't change Logan's decision to take his life, but I have SO MUCH peace knowing he knew we loved him no matter what. I know we had said it many times before, but I believe our persistence in telling him that, even when he didn't expect it, is what paid off for him to be able to write these last words to us, ...."I know I am loved".... "I love you all."

I plan to get a tattoo with his handwriting with these words. To remind me of that love we shared. Unconditional.

#Iloveyouall #mentalhealthawareness #unconditionallove #misshim-somuch #mothersday

## MAY 15, 2018

A lot of people have asked about work 👧 (at the hospital). Are you going back? Do you want to? Are you dreading it?

First, let me express that "we" (work and I) have a love-hate relationship.

I hate having a schedule (it's a control thing...I want total control 😷), and also not being able to be here to watch my Mowgli (he has seizures and when he has one he needs meds to stop his clustering) leads me to feel helpless on those long days. I love having time to meet with people, to be at church each Sunday, to do projects, to always be able to support my kids in their activities, and I love being home with my doggies. I don't get bored. I don't feel like I need to work in order to fulfill a purpose or even to have an identity. The biggest problem is, I just don't seem to have "time for work."

But...I LOVE what I do. Having a NICU baby once myself, I feel like it was an area I was called to be in. I can relate to my families, and I love feeling like I am ministering in a way that not a lot of people can. When I'm there, it's great. I love the people I work with, and I love helping others...And...well, then there is that money thing...I mean, we could make it happen that I could stay home, but I don't want to live tight. And Plexus has definitely been a wonderful lifesaver as I've been out, and one that I know will eventually give me that time freedom, but for now, it seems, God is calling me back to work.

As always, I do keep feeling pulled in other directions; sometimes it's missions, sometimes it's teen pregnancy (something I can relate to), sometimes it's ministry....and, of course....well, right now it's mental health, and suicide prevention. My biggest war: I like to do things 100%, I like to be good at what I do, and I can get obsessive about things, but I know that is not 'healthy' for me, for my family, and I have come to accept that I can't do everything to the fullest. Yes, I'm one of those people that wish I had 10 lives to be able to accomplish everything I want. But how do I know God is calling me back to work?

At the end of the day, I'm healthiest when I just listen. One day at a time, I listen to what God has planned for me the next day, the next week, the next month. I pray for His will to be done and that He would help me see clearly where I'm supposed to be. I pray He will close doors on opportunities I shouldn't be seeking and He would open them widely if He wants me to go in there. Is there an opportunity in front of me, maybe through a text or an email that is in line with what He teaches (love, patience, kindness, joy, etc.)? What is giving me peace? And sometimes I don't want to do what is seemingly being placed in front of me, but that "tug" that it is the right thing puts it right down in my schedule or causes me to act. And that gives me peace, as well.

Yesterday was my first day back at the hospital. Nothing in 5 months happened that made it really clear that I shouldn't be there. We didn't win the lottery, and I still want to buy a house with some acres for my dogs 🐾. It's also not clear that I should be creating a new nonprofit in Logan's name (there are so many out there...maybe I just need to find the right one to join venture with). And, my 2 workdays a week are still allowing me to do so many of the things I enjoy.

I am always looking for confirmation that I'm doing the right thing for His purpose. Sometimes it a little shady and I'm uncertain, and sometimes the answer screams loudly at me. Yesterday I was screamed at:

Dreading the drive into work and that I would show up with my makeup already ruined, I had a peace that came over me and I sang instead. As I could see the hospital in sight, the song, "I have this HOPE," played on my radio. I have even written a post about this song before and what it means to me! I know I shouldn't be videoing as I drive, but I wanted to share it with you all.

I walked in and was greeted by SO many special friends in my life. They didn't ask me anything, just over and over throughout the day I got hugs and was told: "it's so good to see you." I wasn't sure what I needed for the day to go smoothly, but the caring and genuineness of each and every hug turned out to be perfect for me.

And I ended up taking care of 2 precious babies. Babies of one of our own; a NICU nurse, a co-worker, a friend. It's been an emotionally taxing ride for her and she has other little ones at home on top of it. I feel like yesterday I was meant to be her baby's nurse, she was meant to be my baby's mom. As I continue to deal with death, and as she struggles with new life (lives!), we were able to make it through the day together with the support of love, and hope, and even smiles.

There is no doubt, yesterday, I was exactly where I was supposed to be.

#notmywillbutyoursbedone #Luke22:42 #hope

## MAY 16, 2018

You know what a super hard day looks like for me lately? Field day.

Those of you that know me well, know that I LOVE sports. I love watching my kids compete. Elementary field day for 5th and 6th grade is one of the first events where our kids' athletic ability is on display and can be compared to others in our surrounding schools; the kids they'll be competing with, or against, in HS (we have multiple elementary schools that all feed into one JH and HS). I normally LOVE field day.

I have never missed a field day for any of the kids, and so I wanted to be there to celebrate with Amaya, to cheer her on. I was genuinely excited to see her do some track events, especially since we know she is really fast...

...but the day took an unexpected turn for me. Another one of those "waves."

I usually love the atmosphere, but this day was so different. It brought so many memories; memories I guess I wasn't willing to share with a crowd of people. Thank goodness for the sun, thank goodness for sunglasses.

There was the reality of driving into that parking lot at the HS. A parking lot I had been to so many times for all my kids. Only for some reason, this place, like so many others, chose to trap my mind with Logan memories and didn't allow me to think of the Bryce and Savannah ones. At least, for now, that seems to be the way it is with many of the things all the kids shared in common. Maybe I'm grieving all my children being done with HS? Being done with living in my house? I want those days back so badly.

I think my longing to hug my Logan again, just exaggerates the tears for everything else I'm feeling.

There was the kid that ran the 400, giving it all he had, with his hair flowing and long enough to scrape the bottom of his chin—I swear I saw Logan running.

There was the goofy kid behind me telling stupid jokes. Did I just hear Logan?

There was the dancing at lunch break—I could see Logan clearly doing the moves and not caring one bit who was watching.

There was me sitting in the stands, just thinking about a track meet. Logan had run track and I remember traveling to some of the different schools to watch him. He always told me he didn't care if I went, that it was no big deal, but I so longed to be a part of anything he did. I watched him plenty on this very field, playing soccer as well. He was only on the track team his freshman year, I think his depressed body didn't have the energy the years after.

And then there was Mr. J, the PE teacher, who has been there throughout all my kids' school days. When he announced Amaya Boarman wins, I somehow only could hear him saying Logan's name.

I chose to not stay the entire time. I needed a break. It was a day where memories wouldn't stop and I just couldn't get a handle.

Glad I was there to watch Amaya win a bunch (6 total ribbons!), but even more I'm glad she knew I was there to support her. Because sometimes we don't love doing things for our kids, but we do them because we love them. I just hope next year my smiles at this event for her won't be so forced.

#suicidesurvivor #suicidesucks

## MAY 17, 2018

A great commentary on the state of mental health and men.

Men, you think it's ok to stifle your feelings? To ignore them? It's more macho to get

Help!

Suicide is the SECOND leading cause of death in all age groups of men 10-39. Wow.

#mentalhealthawareness #suicideawareness

## MAY 18, 2018

Revolutionary War Day. I have done this 4 times now. Don't have much to say about it. Hard to enjoy any of these days when all I think about are memories. But they aren't pleasant memories yet, just painful, sad ones.

#suicidesucks #suicideawareness

## MAY 22, 2018

I'll be really honest here. And while I respect everyone's different views of faith, I hope you can do so in turn and recognize that I'm just writing about *my* personal struggles and how my beliefs have influenced my thoughts. While I list some references to persuade, it's really to back up my thoughts and help people understand where I get them from.

Because of my faith in that if you believe in Jesus Christ you live eternally with Him in Heaven, I've not been afraid of death. But for those that I love, it's really scary to think about them not coming with me. I don't know what I think Heaven really looks like; are we reunited with our family? Will all our souls be a certain age, and we might have a "feeling" of certain people being closer to us, or will everyone just be brothers and sisters? While this "perfectness" (whatever it looks like) I'm certain will be all we need, right now I long for joining my family and being able to recognize each relationship. But if it is pure joy and happiness up there, it's realistic to know we won't be aware of who is left behind. So the pain of separation is an earthly feeling, but I guess at least we can have hope we will be content in the end.

But what about those that don't accept Jesus? What about my Logan, who struggled with this the last couple years? While he had become a believer at a very early age and had been baptized in his teens by his own free will, he had taken an AP biology class (I think his junior year) and had struggled with some science aspects of God after. We had some great conversations over the last couple years and even read a book together discussing a chapter at a time. We almost always ended our talks pleasantly usually mutually agreeing that there are things that just can't be answered on earth and this is where faith comes in...only *I* could go there, but *his* science brain couldn't, he wanted definite answers.

So what about my Logan?

This is the SINGLE hardest thing I have dealt with...because I believe Hell is real. (I know... so many people just don't want to say those words, or hear them because they are exclusion words. But truth is truth—there's a great podcast on this and a few good books on truth, too, that I can share if you're interested—and Jesus doesn't exclude anyone that wants to come to him). So if my sweet baby is in Heaven celebrating his everlasting existence, I can seriously have complete peace about his death; and although it's painful to not have him here, I know this isn't the end and we win. I can smile when people say, "at least he is pain-free now" (even though that's not something you should tell a grieving person really). But if he's not...well that's when my heart aches the most. It makes me not well. I can be *sad* thinking about these aspects regarding people I care about, but it's totally different when it comes to your own child.

So after Logan's death, I was honest about this with those that know the Bible best: my pastor, Logan's youth group leader, my cousin Collin, etc. I cried to them that I didn't want to hear fluffy answers, and I feared people would tell me things just to comfort me. I wanted truth.

While this is something that continues to pain me just a little bit when those thoughts cross my mind because let's face it, I can't know 100%, I have been mostly reassured by them and find comfort. I thought I would share so that if you're struggling too, maybe it will help you gain a new perspective?

Logan was baptized by his own request. This is a testament of having faith in Jesus and in doing so, he was identifying with Him. While baptism alone doesn't ensure salvation, Logan lived a life before and even after this event acknowledging his trust in Christ and baptism was just another way of showing it. Watching him mentor kids at camp, or when he would close his eyes in worship as he played the guitar in youth group affirmed his faith to me more than anything. I suppose if these circumstances were not true, there would be the struggle not knowing if he had ever accepted Jesus and believed in Him—even in his last moments; but thankfully I have this knowledge so, therefore, it's easier to be reassured with these designations:

So, the Bible says that *"nothing* will be able to separate us from the love of God" in Romans 8:38-39.

It seems the point of this whole passage is about security. God wants his people to experience deep, unshakeable confidence that we are secure in his love. Things WILL happen to make you feel separated from Christ, but this is reassurance that He will never leave you. If you are a believer, you are called according to his purpose which is this everlasting security.

Nothing means NOTHING, but let's explore briefly things that help me especially.

In verse 38 some of the entities particularly listed are *"angels nor princi-palities nor powers,"* likely referring to angelic or demonic beings (or supernatural powers). I believe Logan was suffering an attack of evil, telling him lies; thankfully all these were all defeated on the cross. There are many other verses that refer to the triumph of Satan, but this one means the most to me as I do believe he was in an altered state. Also, in verses 38 and 39 it talks about time and space.

Time: *"...nor things present, nor things to come.."*

So it didn't matter how bad it got for Logan, his circumstances don't change anything. And lastly significant is

*"...no other created thing"*

which translators say covers everything that is not God. So if that includes no thing, no person, then it certainly means not 'ourselves' either. "I'm sorry for being weak and being a failure." "It's easy for me to ignore it when others say I've failed, but I can't ignore my own thoughts on it," were depressing words Logan left. It's obvious he had become his own worst enemy, but the Bible says that even we can't separate us.

John 10:28 says regarding us sheep, *"I give them eternal life, and they shall never perish; no one can snatch them out of my hand."* As our shepherd, He protects us from eternal harm.

My cousin, Collin, reminded me early on: we ALL have struggles in our life and sometimes those bring doubts of faith. I don't believe a loving God would punish us for that.

It does makes sense to me. I always compare my relationship with Jesus to the one I have with my own kids. There is nothing that they could do to release my love for them. I may not like circumstances, but will always love them unconditionally and so I need to apply this to Logan's relationship with God.

Isaiah 53:6 *We all, like sheep, have gone astray, each of us has turned to his own way; and the Lord has laid on him the iniquity of us all.* Whew, love this one.

2 Peter 3:9 *The Lord is not slow in keeping his promise, as some understand slowness. He is patient with you, not wanting anyone to perish but everyone to come to repentance.* Some of you might think you are really, really slow. He is still waiting.

Mathew 7:7 where it says, *"seek and you shall find"*. As mentioned before, Logan was open to reading books on God and science, discussing faith, and even attended the movie, *The Case for Christ*, with us just a few months before his death. God knew he was searching with all that he had, and although I wished it would have come easier for Logan, I believe God is a JUST GOD. The Bible describes Him this way many times, and if he *is Love* = just. I may not understand, but at the end of the day, if I believe He is just and fair, I must have peace with that. And even if I don't have some of the answers, and certain passages can be argued, I do find immense comfort knowing he is *just*. Faith steps in and helps me remember to not worry.

While there are surely other verses and situations (feel free to share them with me), these are the ones I've discovered have the least controversy. I'm sure people have their doubts and arguments surrounding this, I wanted to express *my* thoughts and feelings and explain where *I* get my peace from.

If you don't know Jesus, now is the best time to meet Him. God wants us to persist; don't give up after a few halfhearted efforts to find Him. I do believe if you are asking, seeking, you will find. Sometimes it's just perspective and if you start looking for signs He loves you, I promise you will find them.

Regarding the Bible: I think many times us 'lay people' try and interpret the Bible and that's where we get into trouble. If you're struggling with its understanding and truth, get a Bible like the *Life Application Study Bible* where there are notations throughout that translate/explain history and interpretation made by over a hundred trans-denominational scholars working directly from the best available Hebrew, Aramaic, and Greek texts (more about this see the front of this Bible). If science is holding you back, I promise there are all kinds of books, Youtube videos, Ted Talks, etc.that you will be blown away if you take the time to watch them. Because of Logan's questions, I have become a much stronger believer because I was seeking to find the answers he was bringing.

And if you just don't get it, "Why Jesus?" search for those words and Erwin McManus-Mosaic on Youtube or it's a Podcast. He has a lot of really, really great messages; but if you're not convinced yet, this one is an excellent place to start ("Deep Mind" is a good one too). Another genuine, super intelligent speaker is Louie Giglio. His talk, "How Great is Our God" is a favorite dealing with some science and will help make sense of so much :)

I didn't write all of this to be preachy, that really wasn't my intention. I just wanted to be real and let you know it's been a struggle for me. Thankfully by researching and listening to those smarter than I, I am reassured more than ever that Logan is in Heaven, but that might not be how you are feeling. For those of you who have lost loved ones and you simply don't know where they stood, all I can say is I'm sorry. Painful. Hopefully, the "just God" part might help?

And although we can't change the past, we can engage and act in the future.

Seek.

Hugs

## MAY 26, 2018

Eating at Logan's favorite place and acting like Logan often did

#dorks #5guys #missyou

Who would know eating at a burger joint could stir up so many emotions?

#suicidesurvivors #suicideawareness

# JUNE 2018

### JUNE 2, 2018

Missing you isn't really the problem...

It's the part where you're never coming back that's killing me...

#misshimsomuch

### JUNE 5, 2018

"Kate Spade's suicide reminds us once again that wealth and fame do not equate to an immunity to depression. People who are shocked that successful people can possibly kill themselves do not understand the challenges of mental health."

### JUNE 13, 2018

6 months.

Wow.

Is this possible?

And at 6 months, we are at 26 weeks. Half a year exactly. The 15th falls on the same day of the week we learned Logan had endured too much pain to keep climbing. I sometimes wish we would have been notified in the daytime, because every night I cry myself to sleep laying in that same bed, thinking of the abrupt, deep, and intense banging on the door that woke up the entire family on that cold, dark, (no cliche here) Friday morning. 3 am to be exact.

6 months.

And it still isn't even real. As I awake each time, a thump overcomes me and the realization that it's still true. That Logan really isn't here anymore. I haven't been in a dream (another cliche, but the truth). Why does this have to happen Every. Single. Day? Every. Single. Time I awake?....midnight, 3 am, 7 am. Every time.

When will it become a part of my life, that I no longer question? I think the reality is that this thought might not be at the forefront when waking. Eventually. But that it will creep in regularly, forever.

Some moments I think, "I got this. I can do this." Like it's a destination I'm trying to reach and I'm feeling good in the moment so I think I can do it (maybe like a tunnel that has an opening at the end). Once there, everything will be good again. Or that Logan will be standing there saying, "Good job, mom. You trusted and persevered and so now I'm back."

But then I remember that it's forever. That it's not something to get through.

I mean, you do sorta have to get through it, but we will be battling through it for the remainder of our time here. There is no ending where it's all better.

Except in Heaven of course. But what does that even look like? I know I will be happy and have complete peace, but will I see him? Will we know who is family or will everyone just be family? I know it won't be sad then, but it's so sad from this worldly end, thinking about it. And that's all I can see right now.

Living in peace, but still laying in sadness. I just miss him and no amount of faith and hope can take away my desire to just want to hug him and tell him how much I love and miss him. My faith and hope give me a rationale to get up, look for the good (and believe me, there has been plenty of that), and make the most of the circumstances. But because of love, I still have so much pain.

Maybe we were given this mountain, to show others it can be moved. The warriors that have made it, that is how the rest of us know we can get there.

But please don't be fooled into thinking we are moving it without scars, without pain.

#mentalhealthawareness #suicideawareness #misshimsomuch

## JUNE 13, 2018

When my husband told me he wanted a tattoo, never did I think it would be a faith-based one. He is very much a believer, but not one to draw attention to it. But things have changed a lot in our lives and so I don't know why anything surprises me at this point.

I love the tattoo, and I love that he's willing to wear his faith boldly. But what means even more, is to witness last night a conversation with his longtime best friend. Nearly in tears, I hear him saying that he doesn't know where he would be without his faith right now. I love that this is reality. That his faith has continued to grow and is stronger than ever. It makes him a stronger man and makes us a stronger couple.

I don't care what journey you are on as a couple, I am convinced with God you can get through it. You NEED God right there in the middle. There are many reasons for this and I won't make this a long post, but if you're struggling as a couple, consider exploring church together. If you don't find the right church fit for both of you, keep looking. If you go to church by yourself right now, keep going. Keep praying. Keep living it. God is faithful.

As always, I am open to sharing our journey (it wasn't always as it is now). Message me if you have questions, or if you maybe just need some encouragement. 💕

#notmywillbutHisbedone  #heisgoodALLthetime

## JUNE 16, 2018

Did you know that if you text 741741 when you are feeling depressed or suicidal, a crisis worker will text you back immediately and continue to text with you? Many people, especially younger people (and introverts), do not like talking on the phone and would be more comfortable texting. It's a free service to ANYONE - teens, adults, etc. - who lives in the U.S. It's run by the Crisis Text Line.

#mentalthealthawareness  #reducethestigma #suicideprevention

## JUNE 17, 2018

Dear Glenn,

Happy Fathers Day.

I know you are struggling today and I'm so sorry for that. Of course, I wish, we all wish, we could take the pain away.

Dad, I've always looked up to you. I love you all
Logan

Never did I expect to see you, my husband, the one who has cried less than a hand full of times in our entire marriage, be torn apart over and over again since December. Sometimes, that hand full of times happens over in one day. Catching your tears in my shirt, in my embrace, is somewhat comforting, but so so painful at the same time. But I'm glad you don't feel you have to be "strong" for me always. It reminds me over and over how much you loved Logan and so I'm grateful for that. I'm thankful you can let them fall, even though I know it's not always easy to show emotion. That makes you a real man. An amazing husband. And an amazing father.

I'm sorry you were not raised by the "best dad in the world." I'm sorry he propelled you to not show emotion and to just "be a man" whenever you had feelings. I'm sorry he didn't wrestle with you on the floor, cook you breakfast, and take you to the movies. He wasn't there when you won awards, played in a football game, or even got married. He didn't encourage you in all things, give you worldly guidance, and certainly didn't show you how faith is the answer to life. I'm sorry he didn't treat your mom with respect and love her in a way his mom would be proud. I'm sorry he wasn't like you are as a dad.

But life is not fair and I hear you say that often...in fact, you habitually (yes, I'm admitting it) have such words of discernment.

But you don't just talk, you live by your words. You have given no excuses to your unrightful relationship with your father...

But...

...Last night, when you saw Amaya's card, and your battered mind left you confessing out loud that you didn't deserve those #1 dad words...well, you were so wrong.

You are the man I would choose to raise my kids with again if I was starting over. You have done everything you had no example for. You took everything that was wrong and made it right, even when it was, or is, hard for you.

You love our kids unconditionally. You are there for them through anything and everything. You lead with the highest integrity, and importantly, you have modeled what a partnership of marriage looks like.

All of these things you have done as a father is without example, and you have done them exceptionally well.

No, my gifts were not meant to draw you to me to dry your eyes. They were only meant to show you, remind you, how much your son loved you. He saw all those things in you, but he wasn't thinking about us when he surrendered to his pain.

I'm sorry he isn't here today, because I know he would agree, you ARE a #1 dad. Again, Happy Fathers Day. This day, for you, is well deserved.

I love you,

Lori

# JULY 2018

## JULY 4, 2018

If you're wondering what kind of a season I'm in, it's honestly a season of denial. I found lately that it's much easier to not look at pictures and to stay busy. If I'm consumed with things to do, I can't sit and let my reflections roam. Maybe this isn't healthy you say? For me, right now, it's a huge part of how I'm surviving.

Bedtime is the only time I can't completely ignore my thoughts. I'm not sure if it's because it's too quiet. I'm not sure if it's because when I lay in the spot I was that harrowing night, all I hear is 3 knocks roaring at the door. Or because I give into my exhaustion of dodging my feelings all day.

I don't enjoy the quiet still of the night. Not yet. But I'm hopeful.

I had to work today. Working the holidays is a huge downfall of nursing; but today, taking care of babies and talking with parents and coworkers/friends consumed me enough, I might just be thankful I was there.

Coming home to a somber atmosphere, dispiriting. I didn't like seeing the new beautiful deck and remembering Glenn recently crumbling as he was destroying the old one. Each section like a piece of mourning as he reflected on all the 4ths he carried Logan to bed. Logan always fell asleep watching fireworks from our beautiful view. I can see him now, starting to play with his ears and hugging his blanket. This just makes me want to go back to work. Or to escape where there are fireworks and laughter.

But tonight, before bed, I indulged my urge to go inside, instead of escaping by one of my many avenues. No ignoring, just feeling. I decided to look at some pictures. To try and think about the memories attached to them. It wasn't fun, but I'm hopeful it will be, one 4th, a 4th, in my future.

These pictures represent my favorite memory of a 4th of July. A memory where Logan was so happy and carefree. Where the only battles he had going on in his mind were where the bad guys were stealing our fireworks and his powers destroyed them and protected our treasures. Or the battles of reality like where he negotiated with me on whether it was a good idea to let him have a late-night soda. We had visited Glenn's dad in small-town Shelbyville, IL, but also got to see his brother, cousins, mom, old friends, and even some good ole summer race car driving. Grandpa Jo had put on a huge fundraiser for a local injured man, and the kids got to help with many more fireworks than we will ever be a part of in our lifetime again. Magical.

Logan always played with his ears when he was tired. Something I do too and it's something special about him I will always hold uniquely to us. I can be such a perfectionist some-times and so was happy to find this picture, at the race track, him playing with his ears, cut and mounted  against paper in our album. I'm grateful I didn't see it as a "flawed" one since everyone wasn't looking at the camera and kept it instead. It is now a piece of a memory I can see when they (memories) start to fade. How many other pictures do I now wish I would have not destroyed. Memories destroyed?

I'm done looking at pictures again for a while. At least for a few days, and then we'll see what comes.

Happy 4th, I hope it was good for you.

## JULY 5, 2018

Prayer eludes me most of the time.

It's coming back, but very, very slowly.

What do I mean by that? Well....the only prayer I could pray for the last many months, and still often pray, is silence. I have sat in silence so many times. I sit in silence because I don't know what to say.

But oddly, if we had a conversation I could tell you a lot of how I feel, a lot of what I want, and even a lot of what I'm thankful for. And I KNOW God will provide these, knows these, and gave me these. But for some reason, these past months it is so hard to talk to God about any of it.

Before Logan took his life, my prayer life was so abundant and frequent.

It then became silent.

My singing was full of praise and prayer. And now I often don't even attempt any song, knowing I won't be able to get through the first verse. I stand in silence usually with tears streaming down.

But at times I can sing loudly in praise at home, why is it when I'm in His house that I seem stunned with emotion? So much that I can't even cry out in rhythm. Maybe because at home I can be doing something else and the core of my being is doing the task at hand?

Obviously, a lot has to do with my focus. I have none. I was getting bad...yes, I'm 45...but it became really, really bad after December. It's getting better, but only ever so slightly. I will start talking to God...a sentence or two maybe, and then my mind drifts.

Time spins out of control and intermittently I remember I haven't spoken to him in a while, and when I last did, it was few words.

Out of frustration, I often mutter the words, "God, I don't get it. I trust you and love you and am blessed and thankful. Why can't I have a full conversation with you?" And then minutes or maybe an hour goes by before I realize, wow, well at least I got THREE sentences out that time.

So when I tell you I'm praying about this or that or something specific related to you, I do it. I often question how nonchalantly we use those words out there, "I'm praying for you." So I want to be that friend, that if I express that to you, you can be assured it will happen.

But for now, it's almost hurried. As if I need to spit it out before I can allow myself to wander. Such a challenging game almost. And sometimes it will come back to me and I can ask God for that again, but most of the time it ends up off far in the distance.

So for a while, I have felt REALLY, REALLY guilty about this. and then I listened to a podcast someone shared with me.

"Sometimes we have to lend our Faith to others, and sometimes we have to BORROW THE FAITH of others."

Many times I have been that "church" and gathered in prayer for others. Many times I have shown up in church and sang loudly with certain people flowing through my thoughts. And oftentimes I have stopped what I'm doing to add one more request to Him on your behalf.

So I think I'm discovering that *I'm* in a time where I have to borrow the faith of others. This means to "let the church pray for me." I have to let people that are surrounded by me during service "sing for me."

I know I've said this before, but I've had a lot of down moments, but I've also had a lot of peace. And I know that's because of you all—my church, my faith.

THANK YOU for letting me (us) borrow that from you. THANK YOU for being so faithful to speak on my (our) behalf. Thank you for leaving me voice message prayers. Thank you for reaching out and letting me know you are praying, you are caring, you are thinking about us.

I have hope to be able to do that again soon for you and others.

#hope #suicideawareness

## JULY 6, 2018

Missing my son Logan so much. 💔 Hanging on to these memories.

Advice: If you haven't taken time to sit down and write some things about what's going on in your kids' lives right now...the funny things they say, their favorites, their dreams, etc., I promise it will be time well spent.

#misshimsomuch #suicideawareness

## JULY 7, 2018

So yesterday I did a thing. I took a concealed gun course with Bryce.

Now, let me first preface this by saying I don't want to get into a gun debate on my FB. I've been a hunter with my dad most of my life and I'm probably more aware of dangers than the average person because of the line of work my husband does. However, I do stand strongly on the side that no citizen should need to possess a weapon that can destroy multiple people in seconds. But that's not what I want to talk about...

...Actually talking about guns is much harder than I ever thought it would be. My son died by his own hand, but with a gun. A gun I wished he wouldn't have been able to get...at least not as fast as he did.

If you read previous posts you may have an idea of his story. If not, I'm not going to go into all those details again (you can scroll back to the week of Dec 15thish), but I will update you on the gun part:

Logan Boarman applied for a gun permit at approximately 1:30 pm online. He was approved approximately an hour later. He purchased a gun online at about 3:00 and by 4:15 or so had it in his hands. He died before the clock struck midnight and if it weren't for him loving us so much that he went and bought paper and such to write notes, it could have been sooner.

I ask and do want to debate...Why, oh why, isn't there a waiting period???? At minimum 24 hours?

Why isn't there a questionnaire? A conversation? Mental health questions...are you going to hurt yourself questions? How about one reference that must be contacted. Just one?

...I understand that he could have harmed himself another way.

...I understand he could have maybe gotten a gun from somewhere else.

...I understand that he may have felt the same way 24 hours later.

...I understand he could have made up some great story to a friend that could have been a reference.

...I understand he could have lied about his thoughts.

...I even understand this might not save the average suicidal person

...and lastly, I understand you think it's a right to be able to purchase when you want.

But the truth is...we will never know \*if\* that could have made a difference in Logan's life...or with someone else?

You see....it could have made a difference for my kid...?

...Logan didn't have access to any of our guns. They are always locked and none of the kids know where the key is.

...Logan didn't really have the means to get a gun somewhere else. I recognize this is only assumption, but his ethics would have played into him until the end (and in all ways that I'm aware they very much did so) and I don't believe he would have attempted anything illegal. He wouldn't have felt comfortable approaching random people and would not have risked getting caught by any other means I can imagine (besides purchasing at a store).

...he was a sensitive kid. He might have actually answered some of those questions truthfully or showed a sign of nervousness or breakdown.

...he knew lots of people, but I do feel like anyone getting a call for a gun reference would have been caught pretty off guard and would have wanted to know why.

...isn't it worth one's impatience to potentially save someone, someone like my son?

...but most of all, TIME would have passed.

I really think we would have had a conversation the next day. I can't predict how much we would have learned about the wandering thoughts, the job situation and what happened within the last week, but I can know that we would have reassured him that we loved him no matter what. I can imagine prying a few reluctant honest thoughts from him and being able to respond. Giving him the benefit of the doubt, encouraging him it wasn't meant to be, and even helping him see the positive of what just happened and also where the next steps are to go. And most of all I know this would have ended with a hug. Maybe some tears, but a for sure "I love you," "We love you." I could have at least gotten that chance to give him one more genuine mom moment.

Would have this settled his heart for a bit...only to end up back to 3:00 a different day?

I don't know. But I do know the laws need to change. I don't have all the answers, but I have some of them.

I ask that people send the following message to your state representative: "In honor of Logan Boarman, we ask that you work for legislation that imposes a reasonable waiting period between firearm purchase and possession to provide a cooling-off period to guard against impulsive acts of violence."

Please feel free to share.

#mentalhealthawareness     #suicideawareness   #misshimsomuch #gunlawsneedtochange

## JULY 10, 2018

Have you ever said something so weird? Something that didn't make sense to say but it just came out? I'm sure we are all guilty of speaking before thinking, but...

Grief brain can affect everyone differently (every book will tell you this), but I guess certain personality traits probably are exposed more than ever under a heightened stressor such as sudden and unexpected death. And I know I've said many many borderline inappropriate things in my life; my daughter scolding me many times for having what she calls, "no boundaries," but I feel like I am a realist. I speak and ask what everyone is thinking. Perhaps I should sugar coat it a little more on occasion, but almost always I feel I'm not offensive. However, it's interesting how I choose to get through some really awkward and scary situations as they happened in the last 6 months. Here are a few examples:

The morning of Dec 15th, within a few hours of finding out Logan had taken his life, my aunt offered to drive me to Starbucks. This is a place

I frequent and love to take my dogs for an added entertainment (their presence a treat for me or them, I'm never sure). I was searching for something familiar I suppose, something to help me feel as normal as I could not knowing if I would even stomach my beloved drink, when suddenly the moment turned very abnormal (as if it could get any more). I had chosen to not go into the store, fearing the obvious, when a friend I have known since my kids were probably 8 and 9 walked out and somehow looked directly at me. She then approached my car and so I felt obliged to open the door. Then, like a shotgun firing loud and abruptly, the same question was asked that I would dreadfully hear even this day, "I came over to see your dogs, HOW ARE YOU?". She couldn't have possibly known how that question pierced my heart, but somehow I chose to thrust it back at her replying, "Terrible, my son just took his life".

Just like that, as if it were common conversation. Naturally, she gave me the deer in the headlights look as she had to process what was just said. After mustering up an I'm sorry perhaps with another short sentence added, her cracked voice turned to the rear of the car and she commented on how adorable the dogs were as they were leaning out the windows. A hug, and then some puppuccino delivered to my hands to save the day. Oh, those dogs looked so cute lapping up the whipped cream treat. Wished that could have remained the reality of that day.

Then came a friend/work get together at Panera, probably sometime in late January? I was very overwhelmed at the numbers present, knowing many for years and business their lives contained. Despite thinking I was ready emotionally for this encounter, it was a hard hard day. As a lot of people do under heightened emotion, we turn to humor. Although I'm learning what my idea of it doesn't probably resonate the same with others. Inside I'm struggling...how do I act, how do people expect me to act, how do people want me to act, how would I want someone in my situation to act...and so forth. And reminding myself there are no rules, I literally just take one minute at a time.

As we gathered around the tables after collecting our food, people started blessing me with cards and gift bags. Being in this large group and the attention focused on me, I suddenly felt really uncomfortable and blurted out, "Wow, thank you for all the gifts! It's like instead of a baby shower, it's a death shower". Because I laughed, people laughed with me. But I bet they were struggling to understand their secret responses not verbalized.

Then, in June, I went back to work. Deciding when is a whole different topic I'm not going to touch on today, but obviously there is a lot of fear and pondering of what to expect, how to act, and more no matter when or how soon the date comes. I feel like I am one that is fairly aware and protective of an environment, wanting everyone to feel comfortable. So as I approached the door and opened it at the same time thinking, here goes, there were 3-4 people at the front desk immediately in my walkway. Certainly, most everyone was aware I would be back for the first time, but it was obvious the moment caught them off guard despite any words they had rehearsed. I believe their speech was silent, but remember their faces said it all. Another burst from my fragmented brain came, "You all look like someone just died," with expression. I honestly don't remember responses, as I think I hurried away before a conversation could be started; hoping it had "lightened" the mood of the situation, but fearing it had not.

Or the time I was having beers after an indoor soccer game. One of the players had brought a guy friend to watch and hang out. We were all sitting in a small group when the questions started bouncing back and forth, "What do you do? Where do you work?", etc. Something he inquired about led me to say, "I haven't been to work in the last few months." His reply, "That's so awesome good for you," to which I replied, "No, not really." We both repeated these similar words back and forth at least 3 times as if he wanted to 'win' the opinion war until I finally had to force my verdict on him. "My son committed (and I hate that word committed, but it's habit word I'm trying to change and for whatever reason, it seemed to sound more harsh and hit home in the moment) suicide, it isn't great". He appeared embarrassed as did my daughter, who quickly got up and left the scene. I didn't regret saying it, but I did wish I hadn't had the tone that surfaced and that exact wording. All so harsh sounding...as if I was super annoyed with him. Well...actually I was at that moment...but I'm pretty forgiving and again, a realist. I knew he had no idea and that could have easily been me on that side of the conversation if it were only a few months ago.

And then sometimes people push you and through no fault of their own or yours, you end up changing the course of how they ask questions forever:

Like when I found myself in the dental chair because of severe pain only to find out I needed a root canal. And then after digging for a bit, it was discovered that the Dentist couldn't get to my nerve and I'll have to be referred (which means I have to endure getting numb again) for that part. During breaks, the assistant was trying to make conversation as I respect good customer service, but I was already teary with again heightened emotions (when you are in my state, everything even remotely bad, turns to overwhelming sadness and bartering with your mind that if your son was still here this would be ok). I remember a few vague questions I skirted with short answers, until she pressed on. "Well, at least it was a holiday weekend! Everyone loves Easter, tell me about yours." One of those open-ended questions I decided to answer truthfully. I don't recall all my responses, but the lesson I gave her was to not assume everyone enjoys all their holidays. I should have taken time to share some of my faith during resurrection season, but this girl was just too exhausted mentally. I have those moments for sure. And normally I wouldn't want personal things in my chart that would encourage foresight with their words, but I hope it's there so no one asks me how my holiday went again.

There are other examples and I could go on and on with stories, but the point really is that grief is uncomfortable. No matter how hard you try, it doesn't have boundaries, and you won't know how you feel until you've been there. So I just ask that you be gentle with me. Laugh when I laugh, and let me be real. If I want to be raw and honest and open, let me and don't be afraid to ask the hard questions because it helps me know you aren't frightened of me.

Unfortunately, though, remember that this might not be what others need/want. Just like parenting and having all kinds of friends, relationships all need to be treated differently. It's a confusing rollercoaster but just being "there" tells us you care and are trying.

#mentalhealthawareness     #suicideawareness     #misshimsomuch
#thissucks

Whoops did I say that?

## JULY 14, 2018

Dear Savannah, #Happy22!

The day you move out is the same date you moved into my world. You will never understand how I can be so happy for you and so sad at the same time until you hold your own baby on your arms. So proud that your wings have spread greater than I could have imagined.

Be patient with me always, I just want every moment with you to last...

Cheers to many more great life adventures! Keep taking them on,

Love, Mom

## JULY 15, 2018

Today is one more 15th. Sometimes a recurring date is a cause for celebration. I hate the 15th. But trying to find something to be thankful for today and well...I've been given an enormous gift, and particularly today, have thought about it a lot. I suppose that's a reason for acknowledgment. The gift.

You may not see it as a gift, but I do...at least much of the time. Sometimes I wanna give it back. Actually, I scream at receiving it occasionally, but I know it has a purpose and therefore I accept it. At least as best as I can.

The gift?

Pain.

The worst pain many of you say you don't even want to imagine.

You see, before I would share my testimony, perhaps you thinking without much credibility. Sure, I have some awesome things I've shared that demonstrate grace and love. And even a handful of hard times where my faith carried me.

But those really didn't compare to some of the heartache and stories I've heard some of you tell.

And before when I would share how Jesus has pushed me through, I could sense the eye-rolling; the "you have no idea." "Sure you can say all this Hope stuff to me, but that's because you've never had something awful happen. You've really never felt pain."

I don't think God "tests" our faith. But I do think he might allow something to happen to enable you to trust Him. To grow closer. To discover just why you need Him. If you see life eternally, this makes more sense.

I read a book long ago (*The Power of the Praying Mother*) and after reading about releasing your children to Jesus, really trusting Him with them, I thought, "I could do that." The story of a mother losing her child to cancer scared me but drew me to Hope I could have that peace; that I trusted Him that much.

But I also felt like I couldn't really know. And so I suppose you might feel the same. That we can't really know what or how we would feel until we went through something that devastating.

I can never know exactly what your pain feels like. And you can never know mine.

But the worst thing that I could ever imagine happened to me (outside of losing more or all of my children). So regardless of what your pain is, I can relate to any level. I feel like I now know. I know that I truly believe and it's not just a fake ideal in my mind. I have used God to get me through this terrible time. And without a doubt, without Him, I wouldn't be here sharing.

My gift? Pain. But more than that, I can relate to your pain and I can share my faith in a way I could never before. You can never tell me I don't know or don't get it.

Credibility? I feel like there is no other testimony I could give of myself that could be stronger.

The song *Scars* is currently playing on the radio. The first time I heard it I just bawled. It's so much of how I feel. I don't always want to embrace my story, but with His help, I'm there more than not.

I encourage you to listen to this on YouTube. It will shake your soul.

#suicideawareness        #mentalhealthawareness        #thankful
#misshimsomuch

## JULY 18, 2018

In my quest to research everything I've come to realize that what Logan thought he died from, and what he likely really died from are different.

Logan thinks he died from failure. He said it over and over in his letters. I suppose if you want to dive really deeply, he did in the sense that 'he' was failed in a lot of ways. Most importantly, he was NOT taught early on from society or us exactly what mental illness was and how to prevent or treat it. In his lack of life experiences, he 'failed' to see hope and that things can and would get better. That the sun always shines in the morning.

But after reading more about suicide, I believe it is usually multidimensional (psychological, biological, philosophical, sociological, epidemiological) with a perfect storm of events, to cause an ending so final. (*Jordan & Baugher 2016 page 161*)

As a suicide survivor (and especially as a mother), I'm always looking to blame. That's just what we do. And ultimately not one of us can take total responsibility. But if we don't take SOME, then how do we learn and prevent the next brother, son, mother, teacher, friend, co-worker, etc. from taking their life?

Here's what I see played the biggest factors:

Fear, Embarrassment, Unawareness

Fear…he was losing his mind. He was so smart and I think he thought he could outmaneuver intrusions. His mind was his strongest attribute, how scary to have it be bleeding. At some point, he started to doubt what he knew to be the truth. When he wasn't sure, he wondered if he really knew who he was? Was his intellect failing him? How could he live with a mind he could no longer understand? He panicked with the uncertainty? He didn't know what to do with his emotions, where to channel them or how to master them.

Embarrassment…that someone might know there was something wrong with him, that he could possibly have a mental illness. He came from a middle-class family. He was a man. He bought into the stigma that depression is about someone else. He never told any friends he was thinking of taking his life.

Unawareness…of clinical depression being a disease like any other that affects the body. He didn't know the warning signs and have an understanding that it needed managing. Unawareness that moods can be controlled with the right tools and with time and that support it can get better. Ignorance of how he would rob us of his future and what exactly that meant.

Did these same things contribute to our negligence in Logan's death?

Fear...I was afraid of the unknown. When my body went into alarm mode, I was scared to ask about suicide, thinking it would trigger or give him the idea (so not true). I was reluctant to hear the answers and/or terrified I wouldn't know what to do or say regarding those responses. I was even frightened of hearing denial on his part again and how that would leave me wondering why my own son couldn't talk and trust me.

Embarrassment...society and social media give way to an unrealistic version of what it means to be a man. Need I say more?

Unawareness...

...Even as a professional (nurse) with the required psychology classes and holistic teachings I didn't understand the difference between situational and clinical depression. I didn't research his symptoms enough, and I'm a researcher.

...As a society that we need to understand that depression is a disease and needs managing. Warning signs and how to talk to someone who is depressed/suicidal.

...To the JH and HS that aren't doing enough to teach, reach, and support (our district has implemented a lot in the last year, too late for Logan but so happy for others)

...From friends who never ask the hard questions.

...To the counselor we saw who didn't see him as a suicidal risk, despite acknowledging he was in a deep depression but just saying if he didn't want help there was nothing we could do.

...To the professors who couldn't help but notice his struggles reflected in his grades. To the dean he met with in his last semester...instead of exploring reasons why a previous AP, excelling, ACT high achieving student would be struggling to show up to class, focus, and maintain the minimum C requirements, instead only informed him of what necessary grades he needed to achieve this semester to stay in the program (to which Logan admittedly informed me was daunting and unattainable) These are assumptions, but I never witnessed or was informed of any interventions attempted.

...To the dispatch trainers and staff who should have noticed his physical struggles in class and especially in those last 2 weeks. And to those trainers that were considered to have bully attitudes, just stop. To the hiring process that should screen, follow, and support those at risk in this very delicate job.

...To the legislature that can implement/support a law that one must wait a minimum of 24-48 from when applying for a gun permit to allow a purchase.

...To the gun salesman that likely didn't ask the hard questions knowing his permit was only a couple hours old.

It was all the perfect storm for Logan.

But it really doesn't matter that I can posthumously diagnose him with clinical depression, or that I can attribute certain things about his life that likely contributed. I can't even know if these efforts would have saved him. He's gone. It just doesn't matter for Logan. And no one is the sole influence on another's life.

But it CAN matter for you. What you don't do or know can hurt you or those you love.    #suicideawareness  #mentalhealthawareness #depression

# AUGUST 2018

## AUGUST 1, 2018

😖 Have you ever bought a car you thought was rare and suddenly you see the same car over and over on the road?

What about hearing a word for the first time and then it comes up a million times in the next few weeks?

Well...when we named Logan...we chose the name

1) because it was fairly rare (we liked names we didn't hear everywhere) and 2) because it was my maiden name.

Logan Ray was actually named after my dad, Ray Logan. 💕

So I'm trying to figure out why when Logan was a baby I never heard his name and we wanted it that way, that now, especially since his death, it is everywhere?

A friend messaged me this note below, and it added to my already questions on why? Why am I being reminded over and over? Constantly?

I'm sharing a few of the examples. They have become so many I started to keep track but sharing just a few ...ironic...?...or not?...

This dog tag and what it says, give me chills every time I look at it...

"Ok, this is so strange—and good at the same time...remember I told you I had to go out and walk Haley...we just left and got on the sidewalk and walked about 50 feet when Haley kept pulling me to go in a certain direction, so we did. We have walked over there many many times over the last few years because now there are just so many dogs in our neighborhood. I try to avoid them and besides we really enjoy walking over there at the park. Anyway, we made it around halfway and she stopped to do her business and I picked it up. I started to throw the bag in the trashcan they have right across from where she stopped and when I looked on the ground right next to the trashcan I saw some dog tags sitting half in the dirt and half out of the dirt. I pick them up and I just held them in my hand until we got home.

Since they were dirty I grabbed a paper towel to put them on while I went to get my glasses so I could read who these belonged to. When I turned over the one with the dog picture on it, I couldn't believe my eyes: the dog's name is Logan. Lori, I can't tell you how many times over the last six months that I have come across his name just in unusual places, unexpected places and just out of the blue like that and I think that there is some reason this is happening. A couple of months ago I was in my car looking up a Colorado Springs address in my GPS that should've easily been found the first time I looked for it but my GPS displayed another city in Colorado and when I looked at the screen there was his name again...Logan Street...right there and I thought how weird is that because that other city shouldn't come up because when I tried it again I found it right away. I see and hear his name often on the phone when people are calling in for estimates...their name is Logan or they live on Logan Avenue...it just happens over and over again. A few months ago I couldn't sleep when I got up in the middle the night to watch TV and I was trying to find something to watch until I felt sleepy and I turn on the TV and hit the guide and the first thing I saw was the movie *Logan* was getting ready to start. It is just so coincidental that I see this all the time. And when this happened this morning I decided that I finally had to share this with you.

I know I've told you before that I have felt so drawn to you ever since this happened—I considered you a dear friend to me before this—but this just feels different now and I don't know why. I feel so strongly that there's a purpose for this but I don't know what that is. I do believe in signs...I believe God puts them in our path for some reason I really believe that. Maybe this is God's way to say don't forget about Logan and always be there for Lori. I hope this does not make you sad or anything but I just had to share this with you."

Coincidence? I've been personally caught many times saying, "nothing is a coincidence." So I guess this is not either...

#misshimsomuch #suicideawareness

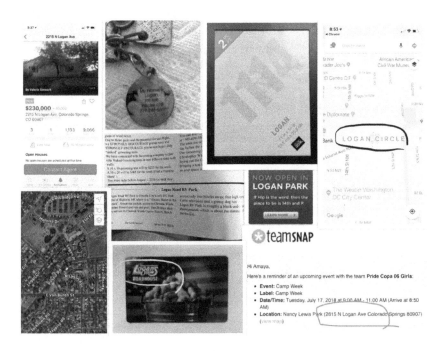

## AUGUST 2, 2018

When you have your preteen or teen talk about sex, please include depression.

Because often, once entrapped in this disease, it's hard to get out. It's a twisted and circular illness that by definition, doesn't allow one to make the obvious decisions.

Just get up? They have no energy to.

Just go to class? They lack the motivation or concentration once there.

Just get help? They don't see that anything can change.

They hurt.

But being useless or a burden is way better than dead.

If those negative thoughts and feelings are left to simmer long enough, those sensations turn to a certainty of being a burden and useless and that there is no way out—it won't or can't get better.

So we have to PREVENT before it gets to that point.

Depression should be a common talk in EVERY household.

☛Your kids should know if depression runs in your family (it's very genetic).

☛Teach them that it can affect anyone, though, and that they need to take care of their 'mind' just like any other part of their body.

☛Teach them it's a disease that is not their fault. It's like cancer...there are some things you can do to prevent it, but oftentimes you don't see it coming and don't know why. There are some things you can do once you have it to treat it, but if you do nothing for it, death can be a result.

☛Teach them that there is NO shame in getting help.

☛Teach them how to get help (tell someone how you feel—a friend, a parent, a school counselor, another family member.)

☞Teach them some treatment options (counseling/therapy, support groups, books, learning coping skills, diet/supplements, medication, etc.)

☞Teach them symptoms to watch for (in themselves AND others). These may include but are not limited to: changes in sleep, appetite, energy level, concentration, daily behavior, overall mood, or self-esteem. And you don't have to have all of them, by the way.

If this can become normal conversations everywhere, kids will see less shame and reach out earlier. The more help and coping skills they see available to them, the more likely they never get to the point of feeling completely hopeless.

Because once there, all this teaching and reaching isn't nearly as useful...and sometimes too late. 💔😢

#suicideawareness      #mentalhealthawareness      #suicidesucks #depression

## AUGUST 4, 2018

I never got a response to this text...

Can you believe I had never watched a Harry Potter movie before Logan's death? I'm just not generally a fan of what I had considered a 'sci-fi', fiction, or make-believe movie. Wasn't against it in any way, just wasn't interested. I knew if I watched it I probably wouldn't mind it even; but mainly, "I had so many better things to do."

Let me tell you, I had NOTHING to do that could have been better than spending time with my son doing what HE loved. 💔

And, man, do I struggle with this reality, even today.

How much closer could have we been if I would have shown interest in his favorite book and movie 😢😢. Would he have confided in me after a nice chat about Harry's struggles?

In our grief and loss for what to do with our thoughts and moments just 2 days after Logan's death, our family watched the first Harry Potter movie together. Only I was the only one that had never seen it before.

One of my biggest regrets; don't let it be yours.

Is there something your kids or spouse or friend is interested in that you kinda blow off? Spend an hour or two engaging that activity or interest and then smile and say, "this one's for you, Logan". #keephismemoryalive

#misshimsomuch #suicideawareness

## AUGUST 7, 2018

Just another day of picking Amaya up at camp?

Nope...because this camp is at the UCCS soccer fields. That parking lot that means so much more than a place to store cars of hopeful visitors and future graduates. Not just some concrete area that is the pathway after people leave games with either joy because of a win, or frustration/anger from a loss. Or those same feelings related to class that day as it's also a commuter lot for the buses. While I've experienced all those emotions from Savannah's time there, and certainly Logan experienced these leaving school for the day...it's also...

a parking lot that changed our plans, our family, our future—forever. And I have recent new emotions surrounding seeing it, being there...

...Because recently I was able to abridge the area and my thoughts where Logan parked his car before taking his final breath. We knew 'approximately' being told "Four Diamonds parking lot" from the officers that knocked on the door. But now I have the lot number, the area of that lot, and which direction his car was facing...

because about 2 months ago I read the police report.

I admit it's something I had always wanted to read, but then also at times felt creepy about it. I wondered why I desired that piece, but one thing I have read is that survivors of suicide often want every last detail they can get, which comforted me that my thoughts were not psychotic. We are searching for any answers, knowing we won't ever have them all. But each detail gives me one more answer to hang on to, even if that leads to more questions, or is something we wished we didn't know. But it's like I'm gathering Logan's game cards to hold tightly in a box they were purchased in, for safekeeping?

This was a known piece that still existed untouched, so it sorta left a stone unturned in my mind.

But. I had been somewhat okay with letting it go wondering if it might cause me more pain?

Then the Aflac claim letter came....."we need more information, can you please send a copy of the autopsy and police report". Mind you, I had filled out the claim form in complete truthfulness. Death listed as "suicide." Hmmm, were they considering this claim and I really just need to send them the remainder of what they were requesting? I called customer service and explained to the lady the situation. I told her I thought that this claim was invalid because the death was a suicide. If they were seriously considering its review, I would go through the painful process of getting those documents but made it clear this was not easy for me. The lady replied only to say she could give me no information and that I needed to send in the documentation. I pleaded, "If you know these types of claims are automatically denied because of suicide, can you please just tell me that! You are not giving an opinion, it's not interpretation, is it a listed disqualification in the policy?". Her response was that I just needed to send in the information requested. I assumed that meant there was hope.

So we did just that. Sent for the info and then one day I opened up my email box and there it was: "Logan Boarman autopsy." I still can't imagine (myself) what it was like opening it up. I must have sorta visited another dimension in my brain so that I could avoid much of the pain?

But when I got the police report, there was something about anticipating reading it that made me hopeful. Hopeful I would be able to find out the exact parking spot. So that I wasn't left to wonder which of the 200 spots as the most precious to me?

Spending more time filling out supportive paperwork, I sent in the forms, only to receive a letter via mail "....your claim has been denied....suicide...". Thanks, Aflac. I appreciate the added pain and lack of sensitivity for something you could have been clear about from the beginning.

Anyway, back to the report...

It was not completely but fairly informative, redirecting me to a different parking lot. While it was still within the location of that "sacred area," it wasn't the parking lot adjacent to the fields. It was the other direction from where I had often thought about, stared at, wondered about. Clarification within a much smaller area and eliminated down to a couple of spots. But oh, I had more answers.

Since gathering this more descriptive area, I've wanted to go there. I think about it when I'm home. I think about it when I'm driving on the highway along the route. Or even when I'm stopped at the stores along that front. Maybe today is the day to go there? To stand there and leave flowers perhaps? To just sit and cry and think? To look for the bullet that was never found? Maybe I could find it? Would that be special, or horrible? I just am not sure. That spot...something just lures me there, but then I somehow can never bring myself to actually make the turn and direct my car that way...

Until today. Unintentionally.

I was forced to go through that roundabout to pick Amaya up, passing by within 15-20 feet of the area I have visualized as it..."the end place." I anticipated it all week. All morning. And my heart got really heavy as I made the turn towards the east where I could see the stadium. But as I approached, all I could see was some temporary fences, big machinery, men in hard hats, working and tearing apart that area. What? Are they making a new parking lot? Paving it? Expanding a building or creating one? I couldn't tell...but my thoughts were of another ending. I would probably never find that bullet now. I will never get to visit the dirt as it was. My provisional grieving area that I had only visited in my mind thus far...was gone.

Never to be what it was before. Just like everything else.

Yup...just another day picking up a kid somewhere...

#misshimsomuch #suicideawareness #mentalhealthawareness

## AUGUST 11, 2018

Sometimes I don't have the energy to cry.

And sometimes I don't have the energy to stop from crying.

P.S. Recently found this sweet picture on my mom's phone. Taken a year ago this week. Thankful for pictures I didn't know existed.

#misshimsomuch #suicideawareness #mentalhealthawareness

## AUGUST 12, 2018

I posted the following letter in my work group a few weeks ago. Because so many people told me it was very helpful and because this (suicide) is happening all around us and people don't know how to respond, I decided to share. Every circumstance is different and this, of

178 · HOPE REMAINS

course, is directed to a work situation, but hopefully, it will give you a little insight.

"Hey, all...

Heather has to come back to work next week (some feel so ready and some of us come back because we have to) and is feeling very unready. I can relate so much to this. It's such a high anxiety time, for many many reasons that no one can really understand completely or that time will even allow to explain. But even I, can't relate exactly, or know how she will respond to things. We are all just so different.

With her permission though, I thought I would give you a little insight on how you can help make it as smooth as possible for her.

For those of you that are new, Heather's 13-year-old daughter took her life a few months ago, a couple months after Logan.

What I can tell you is that I was super worried about crying all the time and that I wouldn't be able to complete a task at times. I wasn't sure how I wanted people to respond when they saw me for the first time, and it's always a hard thing to predict how you might respond, or even what people might say. And sometimes you think you got it down, but your emotions on certain days or even moments can be very unpredictable.

A few thoughts...

Try not to ask "how are you?". That's one that is always hard to answer. People will ask because it's just such a common greeting that comes out without thought, but try and avoid it if possible. You can say, "I've been thinking about you instead".

Although I didn't (and don't) want to pretend nothing happened, I also didn't want to be addressing it over and over at work. But...my opinion is that if you don't say anything at all, it's hurtful. You just went through the worst thing that could ever happen, and so when it's completely ignored, it makes you feel like people think it's no big deal. Or that the event is over and you have now moved on and back to work (I know people aren't thinking that necessarily, but that's how it feels).

I realize some people just don't know what to say though so here is my advice: just let her know how much you missed her, or that you are happy to see her. Let the hugging come naturally and not forced. If you are a hugger and it's genuine, it's okay. But if you aren't, don't force it and feel like you should. It's better to not then! We aren't all huggers so that's okay!

So many of you reacted these ways to me, and it was very comforting. I didn't feel like I had to say anything back except maybe, "thank you". Then, if I wanted to elaborate or say more, I could, but didn't feel obligated to.

Lately, give her the chance to verbalize if she needs help/time out/break. I think when people check-in "too" much, it causes you to feel like you're incompetent or that people are worried about if you can do your job. I know that's not anyone's intentions necessarily, but that's how it can feel. Or, just makes you feel like people are thinking about it all the time. You want people to love you and care, but you don't like to feel or be reminded that's it's so on the forefront of everyone's mind..... because you already know it is.

Hugs! and thanks for taking the time to read this. You guys are seriously "friends", not co-workers. 💜 "

## AUGUST 15, 2018

Today is 8 months.

I bought this little wall hanging about a year ago. I thought it was different, was a good reminder, and so I stuck it in the main bathroom where I would see it...a lot. I was looking at it intently this week and thought, "that's exactly how I feel."

Injured

I have nails everywhere prodding me, sometimes being hammered so deeply, more than necessary.

But...my faith is still very intact.

If you're wondering how it feels to lose a child, I would describe it right now as being injured. I've seen it written that it's like a hole in your heart that can never be filled and so you are never whole again. I guess that is pretty accurate and one way to describe it.

But lately, I would describe it more like this:

I walk around "injured." I don't always think about my injury or feel it as intently, but it's always there. There is a pain lying within my being that doesn't go away, even if I'm not actually focusing on it or how bad it's hurting. Sometimes it's just in my head, and sometimes it's in other places, and sometimes it's everywhere.

I don't (and I've read that I won't) feel the same as before, and I suppose that means I'll have a 'pain' that will never totally heal. I used to be the "old Lori." Old Lori that had some bad days and some good days just like everyone else. Old Lori that had some really good high emotions, and old Lori that would sometimes feel super sad about things. Old Lori that was pretty much like anyone else.

Now I feel like a different Lori. And different too, than almost anyone else. And all my emotions have a piece of me that is not like before. Have you had an injury that you have never recovered from? Sometimes it hurts really, really bad, and sometimes you can keep yourself busy enough to cover it up for a bit. But it's still there.

I'm not saying I don't have Peace, but...I think I will always feel like there is something hurting. Not a monkey on my back, but a chronic pain.

I'm thankful that I have that hope that God will continue to buffer that pain, and even show me why it can be good to feel it.

I'm thankful that my faith is wrapped up in those nails, just like my wall hanging.

#suicideawareness #mentalhealthawareness

## AUGUST 17, 2018

Have you heard that phrase, "your worth is found in God, and not in the opinions of others?"

What about the opinions of yourself? Because man, this is really hard.

This is something suicide survivors (those left behind) immediately race to. Why didn't I do this, why didn't I do that, how could I have not known this, how could I have ignored, or missed, or misinterpreted or forgotten or...and the list seriously goes on and on.

And it doesn't matter if you were his friend, his teacher, his sister, his neighbor, his Boy Scout leader, his gaming partner, and especially his mother, we all feel like we were "bad" at our affiliation.

I certainly have felt the bad mom role and it has taken me to deep dark places many times. Particularly when I reflect on the last couple of days leading up to the knock on the door from the police. So many things I thought to do at the time. But I didn't. I prayed and prayed, but I didn't act.

Even though most of the time I try and focus on the 'good' things I did as a mother when I 'go there,' it's a constant battle with myself, and I have sobbed for hours wishing I was a different mom for Logan. When you do this, you will feel broken and depressed. At the end of my tunnels the only thing that has been able to get me to the other side where there is light, is when I remember that it doesn't matter what I think of me. I often pray, "I don't want to feel like this. No want wants to see me like this. There are people that love me so please help me help myself."

As a believer, it's about Jesus. It's about Him and my purpose on earth and how I'm supposed to be fulfilling that. He knows all my imperfections and still loves me exactly the same. If He can forgive me knowing everything He knows, I should be able to as well.

Now I'm not saying I have totally forgiven all the things I regret and wish, but I'm able to take a deep breath and keep on living just remembering these things. Sometimes I can't even remember them and have to literally read them. I have to see it in writing:

**Romans 5:8** *But God demonstrates his own love for us in this: While we were still sinners, Christ died for us.*

**Song of Solomon 4:7** *You are altogether beautiful, my love; there is no flaw in you.*

**2 Corinthians 12:9-10** *But he said to me, "My grace is sufficient for you, for my power is made perfect in weakness." Therefore I will boast all the more gladly about my weaknesses, so that Christ's power may rest on me. That is why, for Christ's sake, I delight in weaknesses, in insults, in hardships, in persecutions, in difficulties. For when I am weak, then I am strong. -*

#suicideawareness #mentalhealthawareness

## AUGUST 19, 2018

Last night was one of those really lonely moments. I was on my way to see my parents. Both my girls on each side of me in the airplane. All day had been sad/bad, but once my headphones went in and the lights went out, I just couldn't stop the tears. A bunch of 19-20 years olds behind us just laughing and talking the entire time. I was so jealous of the fact they get to be on a trip together (going to Vegas) but also wondering which ones were faking it. I always think that. There have to be many in each crowd struggling. The stats say so. I should have been thankful I have my 2 girls and we get to spend time together, but honestly, it just wasn't enough at the time.

Anyway, sometimes I just go deep and sometimes music makes it worse. I sat there thinking about only me. Being selfish and knowing surely there are many on the flight hurting too, I couldn't imagine they were hurting any worse than I. I hate it when I feel that way. And so lonely. I know my God is with me and usually, it's a comfort, but occasionally nothing is. 😥

I just want you all to know, this happens occasionally. So if it's happening to you, you are not alone in your lonely thoughts.

## AUGUST 21, 2018

Memories...

You may see this picture as a pair of shorts with a paint stain. But....you see, yesterday this simple paint stain tore my husband to pieces. He said, "Do you know what this is? It's paint from when I was helping Logan paint his ice cream truck costume." Seeing the pain in his face was just unbearable. It's unbearable as I'm writing this now. Logan always loved Halloween and would have such creative ideas for his costumes...I'm pretty sure this was his last costume. I guess maybe the last time he had the energy to be creative and excited about this day on the calendar. Halloween is coming sooner than I think. I'd be happy to skip that day this year.

...These sheets...these twin sheets...they've been under Amaya's bed.

 She recently moved to Savannah's old room so I've been cleaning and going through things. Stumbled upon these sheets and my day suddenly turned into a tunnel again. These sheets were on Logan's bed since he was probably 3. He used them for years until we made his room into an army room and changed everything to camo (because, as a little boy, he wanted to be in the military). We don't need these sheets. I don't need to keep them. But then...my heart struggles with the memory. I held them so closely and just like they write about, felt suspended in time.

My brain and heart argue all the time something like this:

"Don't need."

to

"Not sure I'm ready to part with."

to

"Lori, you're being silly....they are just sheets."

to

"I seriously can't believe this is my life."

to

"I just want to give you a hug again. You...laying in these sheets on your top bunk. Your skinny little body with your shirt off and a board game at the end of your bed."

Getting rid of these sheets means I'm standing true to my "not going to become a hoarder, keep it clean and simple, lifestyle." But getting rid of these sheets is one more step to forgetting. Healing maybe? which is what I want? but if that comes with more distant memories than it's not what I want?

...And then I was cleaning off books

from her shelf. I really wasn't prepared for this one....inside my mom had written a special note to 3-year-old Logan. Geez, really? How did I not know what was inside this book before opening it? Why did I think it was just another book on that shelf...

And then I began to read it. This book was created just for Logan. With his name throughout the story. That name is so hard to read. I wanted to be able to smile but I couldn't.

..."Adventures."

..."Make believe."

Ah...that was definitely him. Seemingly a perfect description of who he would become. An Omen of his life?

For a little while at least. Then he stopped believing. He lost his adventurous spirit. Why couldn't he had just found some fairy dust? He could be flying...

I'll just hang onto the last words in this book...where he says, "follow me" as they flew into the sky.

Heaven is in the sky, isn't it?

Can't wait to follow you there Logan. I know it's the greatest adventure to Neverland that could ever be. 💕

#misshimsomuch    #isntHeavenN-everland?

Logan felt very happy. Carefully putting the necklace around Tink's neck he said, 'Could you please return this and thank the mermaid for *her* special help?' Logan turned to Peter. 'I think it's time you showed me the way back to 1679 Ensenada Way, Aurora.' I can't wait to get home and tell Bryce and Savannah.
'Follow me, Logan,' he called, and they flew high into the sky. Soon they were in Aurora at Logan's window.
'Thank you, Logan,' whispered Peter Pan. Logan waved goodbye and slipped back into his bed. He was soon fast asleep, dreaming of a wonderful place called Neverland.

## AUGUST 26, 2018

I have all kinds of notes in my phone for different things. This one is on sizes...so I would be able to look quickly if I saw a deal or wanted to buy something for my kids or Glenn.

I just can't bring myself to delete Logan's info.

I know I don't have to. But I wonder when I will feel like it shouldn't be there anymore...

#suicideawareness #thissucks

# SEPTEMBER 2018

## SEPTEMBER 2, 2018

When Logan took his life, two of the hardest people for me to see were Angela (one of my best friends) and her mom, Connie (my second mom). They had shared so much of life with my Logan. I knew they were hurting for me. I knew they were hurting for themselves.

Angela and I became close even before Logan was born, but she also quickly became one of his main babysitters. He loved her and she was super special to him for many of his early years. She would have been at Savannah's birth, but she was watching him!

Living in Grand Junction the first 3 years of our marriage, we were not too close to family. Connie became my second mom and I have always felt so comfortable and loved around her. Really, Angela's entire family became mine, as they are all such great people.

I'll never forget the Christmas EVERYONE wanted a Tickle Me Elmo (remember that, ya...!), and Grandma Connie and Angela found one for Logan. I was like, you could sell that for so much money...but they didn't care, they wanted to give it to my Logan. We stayed at their house for a few days and I think the batteries surely died at some point. He loved that creature so much, and I can still hear him laughing with it. I have it in a special tub and will probably display it somewhere because it's such a special memory for me.

Connie is truly one of the most giving, loving and wonderful people I know. When she told me she wanted to make me a picture quilt, I knew it would be special.

Wow...special I'll say. Do you see how beautiful this quilt is?! She gifted Glenn and me with it today and I just can't tell you how much it surpassed what I expected.

It's so perfect.

The colors are perfect.

The picture layout is perfect.

The stitching is perfect.

The fabric choice is perfect.

And what is even more perfect, is it was made with some serious 🤍🤍 🤍. 3 special people worked on this quilt to gift it to us. Even "Great Grandma" Wilma (91)!

I know, because they loved Logan too, that this was a hard thing to spend so much time on. I'm sure each time it was touched, an old memory, a thought of sadness for us, or even a thought of sadness in how Logan felt, was surfaced for them once again. How could such a happy, constantly smiley kid, end up in such a dark place?

I am also very sure, that it was hard for them as they thought about the suicide part. Because, just like so many, they have been touched by it as well. Angela's dad took his life and it was back in a time when no one talked about it, but Connie is not afraid to talk about it now. Connie has come through blazing strong from her experience and has gifted me with many, many words of wisdom. I love her for sharing her feelings and thoughts and hugs. I love her for sharing her hands...

Our quilt is beautiful, thank you, my family. 🖤

## SEPTEMBER 5, 2018

I was invited to a BBQ going away party for 2 of Logan's friends.

Theo and Andrea are a young married couple that Logan met through his online gaming community. Their house was the "place to be" for board games and fun. I had never met them before his death; however, shortly after Theo told us a story of "how Logan helped him break into ours." There was supposed to be a board game night up the hill and Logan had locked his keys in his car and couldn't get to the board games. He called Theo since he lived close and said he needed help. "Here's my garage code. Go in there, grab the keys. I'm not sure who is home but knock first. If no one answers just open the door and you don't even have to go inside, the keys are hanging just inside." Already cautious, Theo comes over and no one answers but there is a car outside so he calls Logan, "Hey, are you sure no one is here, because there is a car outside." Logan replies, "Oh, that's okay it's just my dad's cop car," as to which Theo is now questioning if he should really be going into a cop's house in case he should arrive home and stumble upon a stranger! So Logan stays on the phone, Theo's heart already beating louder and faster now, Logan then tells him, "By the way, when you open the garage make sure you don't let the big dog run out." Now, Theo says he is used to big dogs in his life...150 lbs or so but then he opens the door and he sees "a mammoth of a big dog staring him down. It was the most terrifying moment but then turned to adorable." (Mowgli is 210 lbs or so and is the biggest teddy bear.) It was quite the adventure for him and I could see the emotion as he told me for the first time the details.

I have come to really appreciate these 'kids' so I was saddened to hear of them moving but then came the BBQ invite. Theo is in the military and would be stationed in Alaska and all the "community" would be coming over for board games, food, and fun. Glenn didn't want to go.

Savannah didn't want to go. Bryce didn't want to go. They are all similar in personalities and certainly more private and introverted, but I had hoped at least someone would come with me for support and because I had asked them to. I didn't understand their denials and it made me kinda bitter at the time. I really appreciated everything Logan's friends did for him, and us, and wanted to not only show appreciation but longed to be around them. They were my only 'living' connection to him at this point; they help me feel close to him. I hoped for more stories, and details that I could grab onto as if I had discovered the lost pieces of the puzzle, knowing it would still never be complete. I needed to somehow mold this time into my own memories with Logan as if he was still there amongst them.

So I went alone.

And it was amazing.

As people arrived and congregated in the kitchen, I at first felt awkward as I wasn't sure of some of the faces and wondered how many were trying to figure out who I was, as well. Soon the games appeared and I was asked to join. Instead, I observed (after all, I didn't want to be an inconvenience as they spent time teaching me the rules). This began one of the most surreal afternoons of my life.

Logan's friends gathered around the table: gaming, laughing, telling stories, just very much enjoying their time together. I have pictures of these times when he was present. I imagined him sitting amongst them and couldn't help but keep thinking, this is a movie, right? I'm that person that is present but no one else knows I'm there...I'm observing and weeping inside and trying to understand the moment I'm presented with:

How could a mother not agonize her thoughts?! Why wasn't he here? He *should* be here. And what would he think if he knew I was here? Would it make him smile? Or would he be annoyed? Was this a part of his life he would be proud of it he knew how much I enjoyed being here and would he invite me next time? What food would he have brought? I'm sure he would have a coke in his hand. These are good people. Man, Josh and Jared mimic his personality...I found myself staring at each of them...Jared talks and laughs and smiles just like him. When he talks with his hands, it's like I'm seeing Logan's same body expressions. Josh has the same hair, the same beard, and I'm pretty sure Logan would have been dressed in the exact same way. His lips and teeth are even the same. Man, I bet he would be creeped out if he knew how much I was studying him. Is what I'm seeing reality or am I reaching for similarities and making things up in my mind?? Lori, pull it together ...MAN THIS SUCKS.

Food came and went and I spent a little time trying to mingle outside by the grill with those that introduced themselves. I wondered how his relationships played out with each of them. I've heard stories of his hospitality and could visualize him going about the room making funny sarcastic remarks and being a clown. I remember how his energy heightened when he was around board games and friends, doing something he loved. He always became louder and vivacious. Then we congregated in the living room for a video I don't even remember the substance of. After feeling satisfied in my presence, I signaled I was leaving. My announcement prompted a renewed and focused conversation. What a great new round of stories containing Logan that were told! Amongst the chatter was the upcoming date for the annual suicide walk and many said they were planning on coming. I had thought about it but now eagerly put it on my calendar.

To hear the anguish so many were still feeling and the raw, unapologetic emotions tore my heart to shreds but greatly comforted it at the same time. How can I pride myself on being such a compassionate person, but then find so much pleasure in seeing and knowing their tears continue?

A group hug not initiated by me, and a 'selfie' pic to capture the moment, brought me to euphoria. I wish it were a movie I could play back on a screen and experience again and again. I wish I had recordings of all the exchanges because as much as I try and hold on to each and every memory shared, I know I won't remember...I'll remember he wasn't there, but I won't remember all they said about him.

#suicideawareness       #mentalhealthawareness       #misshimsomuch
#hehadfriends

## SEPTEMBER 9, 2018

Dawn of a new era.

My mom and dad sold us their "rig."

This is both exciting and sad. Just like nearly all my emotions have been in the last year and a half. Constant clashing from within.

We are excited for the road trips to come. Hopefully, a lot of them to dog shows 🐾, but we are excited about doing some camping too ⛺.

We are sad to know how much it broke my parents' heart 💔 to come to a realization that they won't be using these two babies anymore. As they closed the door to release them to my sister (who graciously drove them to us 😊), my dad said they both cried and said, "it sucks to get old" 😔.

There are so many memories within these walls. Hunting trips, excursions across many miles, and more. My favorite is a trip that they took Aspen (my niece) and Logan on to Yellowstone National Park 🏔. I treasure those pictures taken there; here are just a few.

Thanks, daddy, for the amazing deal, and don't worry, we will take good care of your babies and create new memories you can be so happy for.

#memories #findingjoy

## SEPTEMBER 10, 2018

It's National Suicide Awareness Day.

I worked today so haven't had time to write a thoughtful post, so I decided to share some tips instead:

👉 What you can do to help a depressed or suicidal friend:

Take suicide threats seriously.

Ask questions.

Ask your friend if he or she has ever felt this bad before, how did he or she handle the situation.

Be non-judgmental and validate your friend's feelings.

Be especially concerned if your friend takes alcohol or drugs because their judgment will be impaired.

ASK THEM THE QUESTION ARE YOU HAVING THOUGHTS OF SUICIDE?

Be specific and direct.

Give your friend a hotline number (Local: 719-596-LIFE, National: 1-800-SUICIDE) and make sure your friend calls.

Stay with the depressed person.

If your friend is a teen and is suicidal and refuses to get help, tell a responsible adult as soon as possible.

Make a specific plan.

Offer hope that alternatives are available.

Also, do they have a family history of mental illness/suicide? Do they have social stressors (problems with work/school/home/social life)? Do they have access to firearms?

Take action: remove means such as guns or pills.

What to say:

I'm here for you.

I want to hear about what's bothering you.

I really care about you. Let's talk and figure out how to make things better.

Things are tough now, but you've got to hang in there and I'm here to help.

I would feel horrible if you hurt yourself and I don't want you to die.

No one and nothing is worth taking your life for.

I hate to see you suffering like this—let's think about where we could go to get some help.

What not to do:

Don't keep suicide threats a secret.

Don't ignore your friend.

Don't put your friend down.

Don't change the subject.

Don't try to handle it alone if your friend doesn't respond to your effort to help.

Don't minimize the problem.

Don't suggest alcohol or drugs as a solution. Most teens complete suicide while taking a chemical (alcohol or drugs).

Don't act shocked or condemn.

Don't make promises that you can not keep.

Don't point out how much better off they are than others.

Don't interject your own problems and feelings.

Don't minimize the person's feelings and don't offer simple solutions.

Don't leave the person alone.

Don't try to be a therapist, get professional help.

Save these to a note on your phone. You never know when you will need this!

## SEPTEMBER 13, 2018

Another moment I would have never dreamed of.

Glenn and I had dinner, at Logan's favorite place with his best friends.

Mitchee was in town and set it up and I'm so glad these guys were all available. I cannot tell you how healing these friendships are to me.

We talked about what we are up to in life. We talked about past funny memories. We cried about the ones that won't be. We wished we could have hung out like this when Logan was here.

These guys thanked us over and over for taking the time with them.

Are you kidding???? This is a connection I cherish. I am the one that is so thankful. I never expected or imagined we would be spending time like this.

I have so much respect for a younger generation not being afraid to invite us to hang out. To not be afraid to ask the questions they did. To overcome any awkwardness that might always be anticipated.

To just want to show themselves.

The love and maturity they have presented throughout this journey would make any mom smile. It makes me proud to think if it were one of them and not Logan, he would have been sitting alongside that friend's parents.

They don't realize how much this shows me what my son was and still is worth. 🤍 These relationships make me feel the closest to Logan I can get right now. I love that...so much.

Thank you Mitchee, Jared, Galen, Corbin, and Leslie. Thank you.

#mentalhealthawareness #suicideawareness

## SEPTEMBER 15, 2018

Well.... we made it through 9 months.

Saturday had a lot of sadness, and it was hard not to just completely feel sorry for myself the entire day...my mom's 15-year-old dog passed away, the 9-month anniversary date, and driving away from Bryce's new house leaving him and all his belongings there, left me bawling like a baby.

...But I still believe that focusing on the blessings of any incident is always the best way to get out of the dark.

Today I wanted to share one of the very best things that has come out of Logan's death.

The reconnection with my sister. A renewed and wonderful relationship.

We have had many rocky times over the years and actually hadn't spoke in like a year and a half.

Shortly after Logan took his life, my sister wrote me an email apologizing for many things. Like all of us, she had/has many regrets (she continued to speak to Logan during our silence) and couldn't bear having the regret of not having a relationship with me any longer. Death sometimes brings out the worst in people. For her, it brought out the best. We quickly jumped back into being sisters and have a stronger relationship than ever, in my opinion.

During these last few months, our family has taken on more stress than you can imagine. Between both of my parents' health issues (including multiple surgeries), their move from Hawaii to Las Vegas, and cleaning out their house of 20+ years in Colorado, we have stuck by each other and supported each other in a way only God could configure.

I am so thankful for the help she has offered my parents and keeping things afloat with them.

What I love the most is how we can laugh like I can't with anyone else. The pee your pants kind of laugh, and only we understand. There is history there and we have so many family inside jokes, and, well, maybe even secrets...we share.

When I went to visit some weeks ago, my task (I learned upon arriving) was to assist my sister in putting up a gazebo my dad had managed to purchase, not realizing it says 4 people and __ hours (not telling). If you ask my husband if I typically put anything together...well don't ask him. In 113 degree weather, though, my sister and I spent no less than 12 hours, using idk, 542 screws? to put this gazebo together. There were tears and there was laughter, even a moment where some PTSD of death overcame us both. But we didn't fight. Not even for one second. And what a wonderful accomplishment we could be so proud of together to present to my dad's backyard.

I hope as she sits there, many times in the quiet of the morning or night, that she thinks...not about her regrets...

but about the beauty that came out of ashes...

I love you, Heidi.

#beautyinashes #findingjoy

## SEPTEMBER 16, 2018

This is what grief looks like. In the middle of the day. On a random day.

#suicideawareness #griefsucks

## SEPTEMBER 18, 2018

This was a "live" I did on Facebook. The sentences are broken up, as that's how I talk and I tried to transcribe this word for word (except for the ums, way too many!)

I don't remember now what prompted this, but maybe reading back on Logan's letters:

*Hey everyone, I am not going to do what a lot of people do and wait for people* to jump on, I'm just going to start talking because I want to make this short and sweet.

I've been wanting to go live for a really long time. Ummm, I just, of course, I'm really drawn to wanting to educate people about mental health awareness, suicide prevention, and um obviously we have a story to tell. And, I...I guess I always chicken out because I don't have the time to create a script...time is the biggest thing...as much as I love to educate and teach, I've just not been sure I can do it, but I kinda feel like people just want a genuine me.

And so...I wasn't going to get emotional (voice cracking),  but I just want to begin.

I guess the biggest thing I wanted to do today because I do want to do these more often, and so really I just wanted to talk about what my number one advice is, right now, for you moms out there and you dads and this is probably more pertaining to the younger kids, the parents with younger children, but I will tell you that...I really think that it's important to let your kids fail. Obviously, if you've done any searching on how to be a better parent they're going to tell you that. But I think one of the biggest things with Logan was that he didn't feel like he had failed before.

I'm going to read you just an excerpt of his letter:

He said, "I've had trouble being motivated all my life. But the feeling of trying my hardest, and failing, is new to me, and it hurts. The feeling of not living up to expectations kills me. It's easy to say that other people's opinions don't matter, but I can't shut out my own opinion. I can't respect myself anymore."

So I think for Logan...it didn't matter what we thought because I feel like he certainly knew that we didn't think he was a failure at anything, but it's obvious that he says he had never really experienced failure before. And we all know that he had experienced little failures here and there, but obviously nothing that bothered him. And so yes, he was good at so many things. He wasn't always the best on his soccer team, but that was okay for him. And so I know that it's gonna look different for every kid because anyone that knows me, knows that I'm not that kind of mom where I'm always scooping my kids up and saving them. If there's an issue with the soccer coach, I try to make them talk to the coach. And certainly, I get involved sometimes but I really try *hard not to. Are you that parent? Are you that parent that is scooping your kid up on the playground because there is a bully there? Sometimes I just think that we have gotten so bad in our society at protecting our kids and wanting to save them from every little thing. It might not be a total failure of a project, but maybe something in that project doesn't come through, and are you the one that is saving them at midnight? It's just something that...I don't want to judge people's parenting, but even as a parent who doesn't do that, I ended up having a child that struggled with that, and so I just feel like it's something for you to think about. Are you being that parent? I think you should welcome their struggles and any kind of adversity they have. It's not always fun, and believe me, we are struggling with Amaya all the time with her race. And you know she's so much bigger than a lot of the girls and kids her age. It's not easy but we talk through it and we teach her things to say, and...well now I'm rambling and I didn't want to ramble.*

*Really, that's kinda just all I wanted to say today is think about if you're that parent. And the other thing I know is all our kids are different and the best advice is to parent your kids all individually. You know with Bryce he is so self-motivated I haven't had to pick up the pieces for him and maybe with Logan I did that too much.*

*I guess the last thing I just want to leave you with, is don't be afraid to text...if you don't want to call the suicide hotline if you're thinking that you're struggling right now watching this? You don't have to be suicidal either, you can just be really frustrated with some things and just having a lot of down thoughts; and hopefully, I wrote this right (showing card with "741741"), you can see it right, you can also text and talk to anyone. You don't have to be on the edge of taking your life, you can just be really down. Just know that I love you and that there is someone that cares and please reach out and find that person. I will hopefully be trying to do these a little more often and keeping them really short. Thank you guys for all your support, we genuinely really appreciate it.*

## SEPTEMBER 20, 2018

Someone was talking about their family today and telling a story amongst a few of us. At one point she "slipped" and mentioned a name. The name Logan. I said right away in an upbeat manner, "Logan? Your ___ is named Logan?"

She turned the mood to a somber one, hesitated and with a sigh said, "Yes. I'm so sorry."

What?? Please don't be sorry.

Please. Don't feel like you have to tiptoe around me. I feel much more at peace when you can tell me a story and not work hard at saying the "right thing" or avoid names, connotations, etc.

I love to hear Logan's name. It's not a "trigger" to me. And here's the deal, I think about what happened 14 of the 16 hours I'm awake. Still.

So if you think you will cause me to somehow "remember what has happened," you are sadly mistaken. You aren't triggering or reminding or causing. It simply is already.

So don't work too hard at trying to not.

#suicideawareness #pleasesayhisname

## SEPTEMBER 22, 2108

The Boy Scouts got me tonight...

Emotionally.

The cutest little blue-eyed boy, approximately 8-9 years old stopped Bryce and me in the driveway. He was very serious about telling us about his troop, his goals, and how we could help (by purchasing popcorn). Like with almost all things, I went straight to thinking about Logan. Only while sometimes I am probably 'reaching' for a comparison, tonight it was so real. Logan was a Boy Scout and for

many years he asked many to
purchase popcorn.

The boy spoke just as my Logan did. In an old soul and intellectual
way. And I was extra aware of his beautiful blue eyes...and he said
it....his troop number, 101...the exact troop my boys were in. We excitedly told him he was talking to an Eagle Scout (Bryce) from that very
troop. Which did divert my thoughts for about 4 seconds.

I instructed, in a mom sort of way, as I was rushing away to pick up
Amaya's soccer carpool, to stick with Boy Scouts because it was so
good for my boys.

...But as I got in the car, I doubted my words. I had one son that those
words were true for, and one son...well...I could only pray for that boy
I had just met. Comparing him to Logan, what would be in store for
his life? I prayed that he would live a full and purposeful one. That he
wouldn't live to the fullest for 17 years and then let darkness overcome
him.

I thought about his mom and how I hoped she knew. Knew what? I
didn't even know. I guess I hoped that if she saw the signs she would
act on them and that by that day, a day in the future, we would have
better resources, more awareness, that she would be able to get
through to him.

...But mostly, I hoped she knew how precious that time was that she
was spending with her son tonight.

#suicideawareness #mentalhealthawareness #suicidesucks

## SEPTEMBER 23, 2018

Today was our first suicide prevention event. A walk, a run, a balloon
launch remembrance.

Hard.

There were many people there. But for some reason, I felt like all eyes
were on us. Like I felt like I was some anomaly when I should have felt

very comforted. I felt like I wasn't sure what to do, wander around and talk to people at the booths? Learn more?

Yes, thank those that came for Logan, but it felt so weird. I kept wondering why I was there and had to be reminded over and over what it was all about.

Glenn and I talked about it after. I think we are not immune to feeling like "that can't happen to us," but yet we didn't think we belonged there. That didn't really happen to us, did it?

And yet each one of those people there, and I'm sure there were many parents and survivor families left behind, didn't think they would be there either?

No one really plans to be a victim, a survivor. What a strange word. I guess we are survivors. That word can mean so many things. We were left behind. But also we are still making it through?

I was jealous of those who were there to support a great cause and haven't actually become a survivor.

It was so great to see many of Logan's friends, and particularly his best friend's mom. She is working on her Ph.D. in suicide prevention. Go figure. But how cool. Recently coming from being a HS counselor where many teens have taken their lives, she has been touched by suicide way too many times.

Thank you to all who came out and to those who donated. We truly love you and embrace your support for us. 🩶 You truly, truly make a difference in our lives.

#suicideprevention #mentalhealthawareness #misshimsomuch

## SEPTEMBER 27, 2018

My husband is not a writer. He's not a touchy-feely kinda guy either. But he is a new, changed man after the death of Logan. He typed this up...I think...because he couldn't get the words out. He handed me this cross...and this message...and I could see so much emotion. He hurts. We all do. But there is HOPE. Not sure where the cross will finally land, but for now it's in on our memory shelf.

*(sharing with permission)*

*The Cross*

*After several days of being in the woods alone hunting, crying and praying, I saw a cross of sticks and a cross of pine needles on an aspen leaf on Thursday.*

*After walking and hunting Friday morning, I took a break about noon. I napped, cried and prayed. I was tired of crying. I picked up two old sticks peeled the bark and started rubbing them together to take my mind off my sadness, to no avail. I continued to cry and notice the old sticks were becoming* bright and polished. I did not want to just toss them and decided to make a cross out of the sticks. I used my hunting knife and a piece of parachute cord to make the cross. I tied the cross to my hunting back-pack, hunted that afternoon and went to camp. I don't know if I made the cross for Jesus, Logan, Lori, me or all of us. I felt the old stick being turned into a shining rugged cross is much like what Jesus' death did to give me salvation and why I believe Logan is in heaven.

I decided to take the cross hunting with me Saturday morning. It was my way of taking Logan hunting. What if I would have taken him hunting when he was alive, would he still be here? One of several what-ifs I deal with. I hunted Friday morning, went to the Jeep, took off my backpack and put it on the front seat. I immediately realized I broke the cross and was devastated. I cried and was mad at myself. How could I be so stupid? Then something (Jesus) told me we were are all broken and can be repaired through Jesus. I decided I was going to save the cross like Jesus saved me. I took the cross home, glued it together, retied it and now it is stronger than before, much like I am stronger with Jesus.

#hope #suicideawareness

## SEPTEMBER 29, 2018

Sometimes angels appear to me. This week it was in a FB message.

"Hi there Miss Lori. We have never met, but I have many friends who are friends with your son. When his funeral happened, I noticed the urn for him was one that I created. I was the one who made this urn, from editing the photo to lasering it onto the maple body. When my friends posted about his passing, I immediately saw who it was, and while we weren't friends, I did know him since I play competitive video games.

I hope this isn't in bad taste, but this photo has struck me for so long now.

*Reading all of what you and everyone has said about him made me feel really connected to him, everything is so beautiful.*

*I completely understand if you prefer me not to and I will respect it since this isn't my photo, but I was wondering if it would be possible to use this particular image for my portfolio? I can remove the name as well, anything you ask.*

*It's a lot to ask, so I hope this doesn't come off badly. Unfortunately I did have to leave the company and I really don't have any examples to show of the work I did.*

*My deepest condolences, and I hope this urn was able to bring you, your family and friends some peace.* ❤"

These messages mean SO much. SO, SO much. Crazy coincidence in this story or another beautiful sign from above?Thank you, Lizbeth. 🩶 😌

#suicideawareness #mentalhealthawareness

# OCTOBER 2018

## OCTOBER 3, 2018

I don't think I've cried at work more than maybe 3 times in my 21 years. But I get teary frequently now and last night broke out in full sobs. It's so much work being "ok."

Grief brings all your emotions to the surface, and they stay there...or at least it has for me. I find myself getting emotional so easily; but of course, I try hard to do this behind closed doors. Whether it just seems like a day going wrong, something I was supposed to do and forgot, or even when my coffee is made wrong. And I'm rarely 'mad,' just 'sad.' It's the "feel sorry for myself" emotion.

But the weird thing is that I rarely feel emotional about death. At least in the past year. It's a weird thing; but when I've heard that someone's grandpa died, a child dying because of cancer, or even that my mom or dad are really sick (and that has happened multiple times in the past year) it doesn't hit me the same. Even if these people are close to me and I know they're hurting.

I'm numb. Most of the time actually. I cry at the little stupid things, but the big things I just can't 'feel.' I don't really know if this is a common thing or not.

But maybe that's changing.

The baby I took care of the last 2 days is in heaven now. It hit me hard to let her go. To give her to Jesus, even though I believe that's best.

I LOVE that I work with others that are so faithful that don't see their skills, their hands, as their own. I love that we prayed together (MD, nurse practitioner, respiratory therapist and all) before an important procedure. No matter what the outcome, we knew God's hands were all over our day. We knew His will would be done.

I see it as a gift from God how we (medical people) can stay composed when we are in 'work mode.' I realized the second I released this baby into someone else's hands how tiring it was for me.

...Maybe because of all the efforts we put in...maybe because I bonded quickly to the parents...maybe because I found myself saying, out loud, "I know what's it's like to lose a child."

The mom and dad do not know this about me, but that's okay. I know their story. One that they will carry much alone, only because as they raise their other children, most won't be aware. Aware that they are missing such a huge piece of their hearts.

But I didn't share this for anyone to feel sorry for me (no need to post any comments regarding encouraging me. If anything, pray for the family). It's hard days, that test my skills and compassion, that I truly find my purpose and identity and remember why God continues to leave me here. Ministering to others, it's what I love to do. And this time it was a good reminder to me that I do have feelings. That I care about death.

#misshimsomuch

## OCTOBER 6, 2018

Do you ever pay attention to FB when they ask, "What's on your mind?"

Tonight I noticed it and paused...

...all those sayings like "live today like there's no tomorrow"

...the songs like "live like you were dying"

*Our first St. Bernard, Bosco*

....ya those... all on my mind...

have been for a while now...

...not sure why I think about them when I see that question...

## OCTOBER 8, 2018

I hope you all are having a great night. Whether you're watching football, preparing for tomorrows work or school day, or getting ready to cuddle in with that good book, take a moment and think about who you know that might qualify as one of these myths....and ACT on the fact that they might be needing you tonight.

Myth: People who talk about suicide do not act.

- Fact: 8 out of 10 people who take their life have given definite clues and warnings about their intentions (unfortunately Logan was one of the 2....he never talked about it.)

Myth: You cannot stop a suicidal person.

- Fact: Most are very ambivalent about heir feelings regarding living or dying. Most are "gambling with death" and see it as a cry for someone to save them

Myth: Once suicidal, he or she is forever.

- Fact: Those feelings can fluctuate over time and be time-limited. If provided adequate tools and support, they can lead a normal life. Multiple attempts, however, may reflect greater risk. Con't to reassess to identify current risks.

Myth: Improvement after severe depression means the suicidal risk is over

- Fact: Most suicides occur within about 3 months after the beginning of "improvement," when the individual has the energy to carry out those intentions. (We definitely saw this with Logan. The last few months he was the happiest he had been in a really long time.)

Myth: Suicide is inherited.

- Fact: It's not. It's an individual matter and can be prevented. However, it does increase the risk to close family members.

Myth: If you're suicidal, you are mentally ill, and it's an act of a psychotic person.

- Fact: Although the majority who attempt are extremely unhappy or clinically depressed, they are not necessarily psychotic. They simply were unable at that point in time to see an alternative solution to what they considered an unbearable problem.

Myth: Suicidal thoughts and attempts are manipulative or attention-seeking.

- Fact: All must be approached as if the potential act is in mind. It's always possible that the individual is crying for help.

Myth: If they attempted once, they will not do it again.

- Fact: Between 50-80% of all people who ultimately take their life have at least one previous attempt.

Myth: It always happens in an impulsive moment.

- Fact: People often contemplate, imagine, plan, write notes, post things. The importance of in-depth exploration and assessment cannot be overstated

Myth: Most people overdose on drugs

- Fact: Gunshot wounds are the leading cause of death among suicide victims

Myth: Young children (5-12yrs) can't be suicidal

- Fact: Annually 3-35 children under the age of 12 take their own lives...and not all are clinically depressed

#suicideprevention #mentalhealthawareness

## OCTOBER 9, 2018

Senior night.

Made me think about how Logan won't be anything senior.

Not a senior in college.

Not a senior in his work field.

And certainly not a senior in age.

#suicidesucks

## OCTOBER 15, 2018

10 months.

Really?

What I'm waiting on...

When will my new normal become my new normal? I know things won't ever be normal, but I don't like feeling so unnormal.

My biggest feeling, thought, emotion? It's simple, what is going on?

Have you ever had an out of body experience? Then you have a piece of what it's like. The feelings were certainly more intense in the first few days, few weeks, few months, but I still find myself, multiple times a day and even sometimes multiple times a minute or hour...thinking..."Hey, Lori, did this really happen because I'm pretty sure it was someone else?" or "I seriously can't believe Logan is never coming back. How can that be?"

## OCTOBER 15, 2018

Small world, right? Small city, right? Do you have those thoughts? Experiences? Do you wonder what they are all about?

10 months today since Logan took his life. In case you didn't know, his final resting place, where he called and told dispatch they could find him, is Four Diamonds parking lot.

Wanna know why that's is significant? Because we have to park in that parking lot each time Savannah has a home game.

There are these things called tailgate "parties" that take place many times before a game. Parties. Do you know how hard it is to have a party in a parking lot where you know your son was removed from without a beating heart?

It's a place I often think about visiting and leaving flowers. But I don't. Oh, I have visited. I have walked the spaces to see if there is leftover broken glass. Maybe hoping to find the exact spot, so that I have somewhere I can say, that is the spot.

I think we have handled this season quite well, but I have wondered if there is a reason? Because I analyze everything.

This parking lot was a familiar spot for Logan. He had parked there for school and he often met friends there to carpool to gaming tournaments in Denver. I think he also knew on a late Thursday night, no one would be around during his preparation.

I don't think he thought about how we would have to come back here. Often. That Savannah would be here sometimes 6 days straight in a week.

In his weak and narrow mind, he didn't realize these details. I'm positive of it. Because he worked as hard as he had the energy for to cause the least amount of pain for us.

So while the actual reason will never be revealed, someone early on trying to comfort me said, "Lori, think of it as a place where maybe Logan knew you would gather as a family, all together, in celebration."

Instead of dreading going there, I have tried to remember that and think of those words often. Because it's all in how you choose to create your world inside. I can dwell on the negative, or I can choose the joy version.

Friday night, senior night...a celebration.

Tonight. At 10 months. A celebration? Well, Savannah got an assist only a couple of games back from injury and she looks healthy. Yes. A celebration.

Tonight....another night standing in the bleachers in the quiet of the moment, facing the American flag waving, with my hand on my heart, I see the north side of the parking lot in the background. "The" area. You can't miss it. ...And I say the same prayer I have said each time, "Lord, thank you for loving my son. Please give him a big hug for me. I pray his life can bring others to you. Thank you for my family and that we can be here celebrating. Celebrating so much. America, Health, Hope, Love, and especially family."

#mentalhealthawareness #misshimsomuch #hope #findingjoy

## OCTOBER 17, 2018

Recent random cries and triggers...and I have learned you can definitely cry without tears and sound. You can scream without making even a whisper.

Seeing friends get together—your friends all took a trip to CA together. You should have been there. And you would have been warm there, too.

Shopping for homeowners insurance, a picture of our house popped up. Your car is in the driveway.

Every time I log into USAA, I see your name listed under the bank accounts. Not sure why they haven't removed it when they know…

I still receive mail in your name. The First Responder magazine could save a lot of money if they just take those that don't work as one (First Responders) anymore off the list.

You know when you buy a car you think no one has and then see them every other block? I encounter gray Honda Accord Coupes multiple times a week. They still always catch me off guard.

The dogs come up the stairs from the basement. The abruptness of their movement and stride sometimes still makes me think it's you.

Seeing young fathers holding their babies for the first time. I always pictured you doing that. I never saw in the future that you wouldn't have kids.

Moving things out of the entertainment center for our new TV I found your HS diploma. It froze me and I exploded inside…and then a few minutes later I was going through your scrapbook notebook and found your AP Scholar certificate. All I could think of was, "what a waste." Dad told me to quit looking at that stuff for now…

Amaya's 6th-grade band concert. I first told Amaya I wasn't going to be there, but then I felt guilty. I had my excuses but in the end, she could see in my eyes the real reason. I was thankful for the darkness that enabled me to sneak in amongst so many of the familiar faces that surely would have recognized me and casually said, "How are you?"

Seeing your favorite teacher's first death anniversary. I had you bring her a meal in her last weeks, wanting you to be close to "death," hoping you would lean into family a little more. I never, ever imagined your death would follow only 2 months later.

Our neighbor's son rang the doorbell. I wasn't home but opened up my Ring to see who it was. My heart stopped, I thought it was you. But I knew it wasn't you. But it was a moment I thought the spirits were playing a trick on me. But he looked so much like you, even his long front locks waved in the wind like yours. I had to convince myself it wasn't you. The same self that knew it wasn't. I later confided in Glenn what had happened. With a tearful expression, he acknowledged he had looked at his Ring at that time, too, and had experienced the exact phenomena.

Helping Savannah get an auto insurance quote. Your name comes up: "Drivers found, would you like to add them to your quote?" They think they found you, but you're not here.

Your blanket remains by my pillow. As time has gone on, I find myself taking deeper and deeper breaths to find your smell. It's disappearing and that pains me so much.

I still have Christmas list suggestions on my phone and scrolled through them the other day. You were hard to buy for and moving out soon and so I put down, "safe," so you could keep some belongings secure. That word seems like an omen. I should have been focusing on keeping your thoughts "safe."

Looking at your computer. Lasts ...last email sent ...your last search ... last message sent ...last message received ...last log on to your gaming account. I wish I could get into your phone.

Your dad finished new floors in your old room that Amaya recently moved out of. I was redecorating and cleaning the closets when I found your joker hat, a *Chronicles of Narnia* book on the bookshelf inside, and your half football/half cheerleader Halloween outfit. I don't know how these things were still here, they should have been in your room, not hers. So unexpected.

It's the season of gifts. I opened up my "notes" where I keep a list of ideas and previous purchases. There it was...your name. The game and desk listed that I purchased for your birthday last year. Hadn't listed anything for Christmas yet. You were so hard to buy for, so most of your gifts were now gift cards. This meant, thankfully, I didn't have to return or try and figure out what to do with a lot of YOUR presents in 2017. So grateful for a friend that returned your desk still in the box...that would have been impossible for me to do. Wishing now I would have just donated it.

#mentalhealthawareness #suicideawareness #misshimsomuch


## OCTOBER 18, 2018

Suicide Warning Signs

- Negative view of self
- A sense of hopelessness or no hope for the future
- Isolation or feeling alone
- Aggressiveness and irritability
- Possessing lethal means
- Feeling like a burden to others

- Drastic changes in mood and behavior
- Frequently talking about death
- Self-harm like cutting behaviors
- Engaging in risky behaviors
- Making funeral arrangements
- Giving things away
- Substance abuse
- Making suicide threats

These signs are good to know, BUT my son who took his life, Logan, only had like 2 of them.

At times he could be irritable...But I attributed that to his need to get downstairs and play his video games ASAP. And/but, he was never aggressive.

He did have a pretty big mood change around age 17 when he started to withdraw from family events and was not as excited about things like he used to be. Looking back it seemed to be a more sudden change, BUT at the time, it felt gradual.

There is not a certain amount of boxes to check.

#themoreyouknow #suicideawareness

## OCTOBER 19, 2018

The short story:

We became property owners today 🏔 🏠! Our eventual future home will be in Monument, Colorado...at the base of Mt. Herman. This pic is taken from the northeast corner. Behind us (along the north side of the property) is Federal land so we will never have neighbors there! The dirt is where our planned main house will be located.

First, I need to make it extra clear that we have MANY WONDERFUL and close realtor friends and it was a HARD decision, on so many levels, who we would use to finalize the details. I never want to hurt anyone and again, it was a HARD decision. But...we had peace and knew we had made a great choice and one that was right for us currently. Was this why?? Wow, he blew us away when he asked us to choose a police (protective vests) or suicide organization to donate ¼ of his fees today.

Our choice: Responder Strong (this actually meets both of his preferences!)

It's an organization recently started in Colorado for first responders; particularly police, fire, and dispatchers on the issue of suicide, PTSD, and mental health.

👉 Did you know more first responders die by their OWN HANDS then any other way, including on the job accidents?? The stresses of the job can be overwhelming and we do think that Logan's dispatch job definitely contributed towards the end to him taking his life.

This organization is doing GREAT things with awareness and the offering services. Their education is starting to reach all cities and counties in Colorado.

We are humbled by your generosity, Ray Brown. I know you wouldn't want to be named, but too late. 😉

You will never know what this means to our family. Many things about this property will follow us through our grieving journey, and this one is a special piece we will not forget. 🍃

#hope #findingjoy


## OCTOBER 28, 2018

Here it comes. The firsts of the season of parties and holidays.

Yes, we've had a few holidays and celebrations come and go already, but the ones yet to come are the ones we really dread because they are full of so many more memories. Halloween was such a special time with Logan. His creativity with costumes and wanting to "not just purchase one" was always exciting.

Tonight we went to our annual Trunk of Treats at the church. I don't think we've missed one since the church first began doing them, 1999? I didn't want to go, actually. And I was already feeling sensitive to everything today.

You see...this happens all the time...I don't want to ruin other people's parties. I know I will be emotional, and it's supposed to be a fun time, so I'd rather not have people have to think about me...to feel like they have to ask...or give a hug...And I definitely don't want to have others engage in sadness when there is supposed to be joy all around. And today, when I'm already feeling down, I didn't want to go deeper.

But I had to go. Amaya wanted to. She insisted and even begged despite me telling her exactly why I didn't want to go.

I went. I did actually enjoy seeing the trunks decorated. I enjoyed trying some chili from the cook-off, I enjoyed seeing the kids dressed up and even stealing a piece of candy here and there.

But it hurt so much too. Seeing a party atmosphere when I'm hurting inside so badly is a constant battle. Seeing the church sanctuary and thinking about the party going on when only 10 months ago we had a party there celebrating Logan's life.

There were the youth boys helping with carnival-type games. Logan was SO good at that. He loved kids and was so darn good with them. There were the unusual costumes that weren't like any others. There were the familiar faces...Logan's youth pastor, Logan's Sunday school teacher since he was like 6, friends I haven't seen for a while since they attend a different timed service, and even a teacher Logan had in school. Ugh. I could go on...

I can't actually say I'm glad I went. At least for the most part.

Regrets that I didn't dress up or use my car as a trunk (I have always before). Regrets that I didn't wear one of Logan's costumes. Regrets that I wasn't more understanding of Amaya and wasn't in a more joyous mood. I try not to have regrets but sometimes they just come.

But...I'm also trying to be more forgiving of myself. I did actually go, right? I did the parent thing, right? I did something knowing it would be difficult, right? And I don't pretend everything is perfect and great.

...If grieving has unwritten rules but "proper grieving" is about taking one more step, getting up every day, not pretending he's coming back...then today was one more success.

#grievingsucks #misshimsomuch

PS: stay tuned on Halloween for some pics of his costumes!

#suicideawareness

## OCTOBER 30, 2018

To move forward means:

(1) you have to acknowledge that things will never be the same again.

(2) you have to desire God's plan for your life now.

"To really admit to yourself, 'This person is gone, and life's got to go on, and I've got to buck up and turn the corner and get going,' is probably one of the toughest transitions in the grief process," says Dr. Joseph Stowell.

Your plan for life was suddenly changed. But God has a purpose for you, and you were created to fulfill that purpose. That is why you are here on earth right now. Find God's plan for your life and seek fulfillment from Him.

"But I have raised you up for this very purpose, that I might show you my power and that my name might be proclaimed in all the earth" (Exodus 9:16).

Things will never be the same again, and I will never be able to go back to the way things were. I will move forward with a purpose, seeking to fulfill His plan for my life.

#hope

## OCTOBER 31, 2018

When we think back on quality time with Logan, helping him make his annual Halloween costumes sits at the top. He always wanted to be something fun and not store-bought. He won many "best" contests. I look back now and laugh at how many of his outfits had to do with females...he did make a pretty girl.

The Ice Cream Truck was the last costume that he seemed motivated to work on. Glenn helped with it. Logan had been in science olympiad and was a gifted engineer, and had constructed many complicated things. So not sure he really needed help, but maybe that was his way of making us feel involved?

It was sad to see him grow up and I suppose not all adults continue the Halloween dress-up tradition...but should we have noticed he didn't want to participate anymore?

And then I found a "where's Waldo" costume at a garage sale about 2 years ago. He asked if he could have it when he saw it on the counter. He said he needed it for something with his friends.

Maybe he didn't have the energy to create or make a costume...should I have noticed? That wasn't like him...

I found this picture after his death. He's wearing his Waldo costume... He knew I didn't love video games so I guess he didn't want to tell me why he wanted the costume. It was taken at a tournament in Denver.

Today I am especially missing him. Walking into the elementary school to support Amaya brought back so many memories. I remember going every year and helping with his costume. Taking pics with him and his friends.

.....and then I saw a pink power ranger blond little girl....that's what he always said Savannah was...his pink power ranger.

#misshimsomuch #suicideawareness

# NOVEMBER 2018

## NOVEMBER 1, 2018

This year we dressed up the dogs in Logan's "Where's Waldo" costume. Of course, this wasn't a creative one he made up. I had bought these at a garage sale mainly for a back up if Glenn and I needed something someday. When Logan saw them, he asked if he could use them. I think he quickly explained what for, but those words didn't enter my brain; zooming by like any other car going down the street. I feel like I reached for positive thoughts...frisbee tag?...costumes for that?....oh maybe special night the kids all dress up while playing... something? I couldn't focus on what he was telling me (all this in like 3 seconds of my mind), so I left it at a simple interpretation: "something for Logan and his friends." I didn't really think about what he might use them for. I didn't go into that world beyond the frisbees? I'm not sure why? Because I didn't think I understood it? He probably mentioned some gaming code and I just assumed I wouldn't know what that meant. Because I was angry at his "gaming" world? Because I had put up a wall surrounding the activities I thought were contributing to his pulling away from the family? I still don't know why my mind was so flighty when my main passion was to take so much interest in my kids and their lives.

Later, when searching his computer and such, I came across pictures of him and his best friend wearing these in a tournament. He looked silly, playful; he looked like the Logan I knew that could laugh and have fun. These activities took him to a world he didn't have to 'work at.' I bet his 'tired mind' loved going back and being childlike. He had no worries except the battle of the game, which was entertaining and since he usually won, rewarding and accomplished.

I wish I would have asked more questions like I usually do. I wished I would have pictured the tournament and then it would have led to wanting even more details and I could have traveled into his world, sat in that chair with him, and imagined the brief joy he was receiving. Take advantage of any opportunity to have a conversation with your kids and their world. This was a missed one for me.

#mentalhealthawareness #misshimsomuch #suicideawareness

## NOVEMBER 3, 2018

Savannah's team (University of CO at Colorado Springs) won last night. They play in the finals tomorrow at 12:00.

As if it's not enough that we had to be in the same parking lot Logan's last breaths were all season for home games, the semi and finals of the conference championships are played at School of Mines.

The significance of this?

Logan attended here his freshman first semester. It was the beginning of an end I didn't see coming.

It's a prestigious engineering school and he had gotten in purely on his ACT score. He went in with over 30 AP college credits and wanted to learn how to make prosthesis because he liked to help people. As I sat in orientation with him, I was so excited he would be with so many kids that were similar to his intellect and figured he would find some too, that shared other things in common, like being slightly nerdy but also athletic, etc.

Savannah and I dropped him off and I remember that day so clearly. He didn't want help unpacking. He didn't want us to hang around and he didn't show us the campus. He didn't even care if I met his new roommate. As we landed his stuff in his room, he basically said, "Ok, thanks, bye." When we got in the car to leave, I just cried. I felt punched in the stomach. I so badly wanted to be more a part of his life, but he had just pushed us out in so many ways. I know kids are finding their way at this age but I wished I would have recognized more of the depression signs and not just blamed video games. He had certainly withdrawn from the family, a classic sign.

Logan didn't thrive there. He was capable, but not in the state he was in. I do believe he was "addicted" to the games and having a room- mate with the biggest and best TV and all the consoles certainly didn't help. I recognize there were many things playing here, but it's so hard to know what came first.

He ultimately moved back home by choice and transferred to UCCS and their engineering program. He didn't have the energy to work that hard and didn't have the motivation to catch up there. At least he recognized "wasting money" (it's far cheaper to live at home and attend a less expensive school) on loans wasn't a good plan.

We had just thought he was choosing the games over going to class. But I have learned differently now. He went to class. He couldn't concentrate. He was tired. He was hurting. I think his body was screaming for help while his ego told him he was fine.

Shortly thereafter I took him to a doc because he complained of stomachaches and such. I told him it was anxiety. I was happy when the doc concurred. But it still wasn't enough to convince him he was suffering from a mental illness. Even I knew he had "anxiety" and "depression" but didn't realize how deadly an illness it could be. It's a disease, just like diabetes.

Last night, the road to the fields took us by Logan's old dorm. I was getting emotional already when Amaya said, "isn't this where Logan was?"

I really don't know how she remembered that. I don't recall when she was there and we had made no mention of the relation with the school/fields, and Logan.

I hope our team wins tomorrow. I hope I can remember this school, these grounds, on a positive note. And if we win, we also don't have to come back again for Regionals (which if we lose we will because they will host and we will get a bid and still be invited).

I don't want to have to continue to be reminded of that time period. A period of such pain. Pain he was going through, and us from afar. I really don't want to go back there. I really thought that semester was the beginning of him finding himself...the beginning of the rest of his life.

Why is this such a small world?

Go UCCS.

## NOVEMBER 5, 2018

I don't like to run.

But...my daddy taught me from an early age that health was important, and running was an important part of how he maintained that.

So...I began running young and even ran cross country in HS. It's become a part of my routine.

But...I really don't love it. A couple of years ago marked a new period where I finally didn't mind running various routes around the neighborhood, as I really adjusted my thinking to the surroundings...it's beautiful and lots to see and appreciate as I pass through.

But...when it's cold, I just can't run outside. My hands hurt to the point of tears. So I run on my treadmill when I need to put in a cardio workout and there aren't other convenient options.

But...I really don't enjoy it. At all. Music, videos, podcasts help, but mostly I end up focusing on boring.

But...the weird thing about me and running? I always have this urge to close my eyes, especially on the treadmill. Maybe because my eyes get a little dry? maybe because I focus better (if I'm thinking or praying)? maybe I know the next time I open them the number on the timer will be higher, or maybe because somehow I think I can fool myself into being in a place I'm really not...visualizing beautifulness and anything but the bed and curtains that surround me.

But...of course one can't run on the treadmill, eyes shut, without having a hilarious and surely painful encounter with the floor.

But!...I recently discovered that with just one finger, my "pointer finger", I can escape my bedroom drab and enter into a world of darkness, but still stay steady and on course. One little finger placed in the middle of the treadmill makes all the difference. Wow, just one finger! And although I can't see the light, I know it's there and just knowing my finger is placed correctly, I keep my balance and feel safe. And when I peek and get just a pinch of rays through my eyelashes, I am secure in knowing exactly where I'm at on that belt.

I started thinking about how freeing this was and began to compare it to my life right now.

Lately, I feel like I'm in a lot of darkness, like my eyes are closed on that run of life. I'm not enjoying much of it. I maneuver through the day with brief eruptions of joy, but I often and quickly come back to my drab thoughts of, "Lori, just keep putting one foot in front of the other." Sometimes my breath overcomes me and I feel so tired, just like my workouts. One of the stages of grief is depression, maybe I'm treading there. It's mostly a feeling and has little truth, but it's pushing me day to day to work hard at being my best self. Grief is such hard work, just like running on my treadmill. And grief even seems to make my run more physically exhausting then it used to be.

But...the good news? I'm surviving, and it's freeing to know I can lean on where my finger is pointing. I'm choosing to point at the one who holds my direction, Jesus. Even when I cannot "see" Him, I know he's there, I just have to open my eyes and look for Him. And it may seem insignificant, like a finger on a treadmill, but it's ALL I need some-times. Where that finger points helps keep me in balance and to feel safe. When it's pointed, it's going forward; towards something better—Hope. If I move it any other direction, I fall. Not saying it's always easy to keep it that way, but that's what works. Even in my darkness, I can use my "pointer finger" to make all the difference in failing, and well, my falling.

But...I have to keep using it in this run of life.

#suicideawareness #mentalhealthawareness #misshimsomuch

## NOVEMBER 7, 2018

Five Signs of emotional suffering

😢 Nearly one in every five people, or 43.8 million American adults, has a diagnosable mental health condition. Half of all lifetime cases of mental disorders begin by age 14. In addition, 1.7M Americans sustain a traumatic brain injury each year—which may affect their cognitive and emotional functioning. Drug use is on the rise in this country, and 23.5 million Americans are addicted to alcohol and drugs. That's approximately one in every 10 Americans over the age of 12.

Often our friends, neighbors, co-workers, and even family members are suffering emotionally and don't recognize the symptoms or won't ask for help.

Here are FIVE signs that may mean someone is in emotional pain and might need help:

☞ Personality changes.

You may notice sudden or gradual changes in the way that someone typically behaves. People in this situation may behave in ways that don't seem to fit their values, or the person may just seem different.

☞ Uncharacteristically angry, anxious, agitated, or moody.

You may notice the person has more frequent problems controlling his or her temper and seems irritable or unable to calm down. People in more extreme situations of this kind may be unable to sleep or may explode in anger at a minor problem.

☞ Withdrawal or isolation from other people.

Someone who used to be socially engaged may pull away from family and friends and stop taking part in activities that used to be enjoyable. In more severe cases the person may start failing to make it to work or school. Not to be confused with the behavior of someone who is more introverted, this sign is marked by a change in a person's typical sociability, as when someone pulls away from the social support typically available.

☞ May neglect self-care and engage in risky behavior.

You may notice a change in the person's level of personal care or an act of poor judgment. For instance, someone may let personal hygiene deteriorate, or the person may start abusing alcohol or illicit substances or engaging in other self-destructive behavior that may alienate loved ones.

☞ Overcome with hopelessness and overwhelmed by circumstances.

Have you noticed someone who used to be optimistic and now can't find anything to be hopeful about? That person may be suffering from extreme or prolonged grief, or feelings of worthlessness or guilt. People in this situation may say that the world would be better off without them, suggesting suicidal thinking.

IF YOU RECOGNIZE THAT SOMEONE IN YOUR LIFE IS SUFFERING, NOW WHAT?

You connect, you reach out, you inspire hope, and you offer help. Show compassion and caring and a willingness to find a solution when the person may not have the will or drive to do it alone. There are many resources in our communities.

It may take more than one offer, and you may need to reach out to others who share your concern about the person who is suffering.

If everyone is more open and honest about our emotional health and well-being, we can prevent pain and suffering, and those in need will get the help they deserve.

You can learn more at changedirection.org.

#changedirection.org #mentalhealthawareness #suicideawareness

## NOVEMBER 12, 2018

So we did a thing as many of you know. We bought some property that we hope to build our forever home on and have been working on that just a bit lately. Scary for a lot of reasons...mostly forever is a hard word for me to understand.

When we moved here, soon after some time in 1999, I was so excited to personalize our house; I wanted to make every room count. My mom had made each grandchild a beautiful cross stitch with their birth stats that was similar to their nursery theme, and they no longer 'matched' their current room decor. So I decided to put them in the laundry room and then decorate the walls with their handprints. Savannah was yellow, Logan red, and Bryce blue.

The kids had a blast and we even put them on the washer and dryer, which made me sad when we sold them, but I took pictures and thought that would be a satisfying way to hold onto the memory.

But now...those adorable handprints mean so much more...do you think I can talk Glenn into taking a piece of this wall with us?

#misshimsomuch  #suicideawareness #suicidesucks

## NOVEMBER 13, 2018

Every day things go the way I hope they would, and then some things just don't.

Savannah's season is over. They lost yesterday in double OT PK shootout. If you don't know soccer, it's not a great way to win; it's a terrible way to lose. They were the better team but it just seemed it wasn't meant to be because the many, many shots did not float in. I hate ending a soccer game that way.

I hate that this season is over. Yes, they still went so much farther than most and have SO much to be proud of, but they should have gone all the way. They have a better team than last year (when they went to the final four!) and the experience to get there. But we were plagued with injuries...more than any team could ever imagine. Injuries are to be expected...but not us...?!

What makes it even worse is that this season just didn't go the way I imagined, hoped, or even prayed for as far as Savannah goes. She (and her team) had an amazing season last year and she earned many accolades so again, we thought it was a preface to what was to come. But this game yesterday, it was really Savannah's first complete game back. You see, Savannah has had basically an injury-free competitive life in soccer. Playing competitive soccer all these pre-college years, she missed maybe 1 or 2 games ever. Ever. Am I thankful, of course...But...yes there is a but...This year she started off with a stress fracture and every time we thought she would be back, another injury or incident would happen. She played some minutes here and there but was never 100% when the next "thing" would remove her from a game. Why?!

Why do we have to keep going to these fields, a parking lot I don't want to be at anyway, empty-handed? This thing...watching my daughter play soccer...is one of my favorite things to do in this entire world. Why Lord why?

Finally, Savannah gets cleared (from a concussion this time) once again and we have a game before us that should have been won. There should have been an opportunity to see her play again and again now that she seems to be back?! When her dad couldn't make the trip because his flight was delayed due to weather, surely we would be spared the sadness of a loss and get to play at home next!?

Nope.

She played an amazing game...surely we weren't going to lose in PK's....and then we did. Just like that. Over.

....and then the snow came and driving 20-45 miles an hour for almost the entire way gave me way too much time to dwell on it.

Let me be honest here...when life brings you the worst thing you could ever imagine...losing a child, a son...one tends to think, "Ok, now everything else should go the way I want for a while, at least this year??? Haven't I endured enough for a long time?" Right? You feel sorta entitled to some kind of greatness to follow.

Nope. This is just not how life goes and just because you're a believer, God does not promise all your days to be perfect and your dreams to come true. He does promise to be there through it all and make it all worthwhile and good, but we just don't get to see it all on a list displayed before us...there might be clues we collect and sometimes it's super clear, but usually there are seeds scattered that remain left to be bloomed in our presence.

What He did make clear, was that I could be proud of the last game. She ended "playing" and not on the side. And playing well. A last memory of the greatness of my girl.

This is such a hard concept to accept though. That it's over.

And it's a hard concept to understand God can turn all things to good. So to remind me, back in June I decided to get this tattoo on my foot. "Not my will but YOURS be done" Luke 22:42

Because God is not a cook, he's a chef. His ingredients matter where they come from. Only the finest and the creation is special and not meant to be the same for us all. Or even to be what is expected.

Oh how I have needed that reminder these past 10 month.

For me, being able to see this tattoo is a good daily reminder. What can you do to be reminded you aren't smarter than the creator of the universe?

#findingjoy #hope

## NOVEMBER 15, 2018

11 months. We have made it this far.

I thought today would be a good day to share with you an email I sent to an organization I have mentioned before, ResponderStrong. They are fairly new, created to help with awareness and treatment of mental health amongst first responders. When Logan took his life, I was looking for ways to help. I felt like his job was a piece of the puzzle and so when I found this organization and what they stand for, I couldn't help but send an email. I didn't take time to carefully think out every word. It was raw and just what came to mind at the moment. If you'd like to gain some more insight into our, and well, Logan's world and what goes on in our minds, you can read what I sent to them (written late April):

*Hi, my name is Lori Boarman and my son, Logan Boarman 23 years old, took his life on December 15, 2017. He was a city dispatcher in training.*

*I have been in some counseling with the local agency psychologist, as my husband is a law enforcement officer. She is the one that told me about this program.*

*I have been searching my mind, and resources, to figure out where I can maybe be of assistance or even and advocate for what my son went through.*

*Perhaps to try and prevent? bring awareness?*

*Logan was a brilliant kid, but since about age 15/16 began suffering from depression, maybe some anxiety. The biggest problem was that he wouldn't admit it. We tried to get him help, but we fear he just couldn't find or reason that someone so smart could have something "wrong" with his or her brain. When we were able to get him some counseling back when he was 19, he couldn't/wouldn't admit depression. The counselor figured it out easily (as did the GI doc) with all his signs/symptoms, but without him accepting this "diagnosis" he wouldn't seek help beyond the couple sessions I coaxed him, telling him it was to help with our communication.*

*He did 3 years of school for Engineering and struggled all along with many of the signs, including physical pain (difficulty sleeping/eating/headaches, etc.). He dropped out and decided to pursue a career in law enforcement, originally wanting to be a deputy like my husband, but then saw the dispatch job and eagerly applied for it stating, "it's still all about helping people and that's what I like to do." He was accepted and began his training in July. It sounds like the classroom part went very well, but once on the floor, the last couple weeks he began to struggle. We're told different things from a couple of his colleagues that he trained with, and I'm only assuming these things to be true because no one from his work in a supervisory position or above contacted us at any point, but it sounds like some of the trainers have a very hardcore and/or military like training personality. He potentially was even bullied as we found another trainee had resigned just before him for those reasons. We were given details on some of the things stated to her during training, and it made us very discouraged. It's so sad, especially because he was the sweetest kid and took too much responsibility for his mistakes. We have heard the unit referred to as a "viper pit" since by multiple sources.*

*We do know he began to "lose all confidence in himself" in the last couple weeks. He even called in sick 3 days, and another time left work for "focus" and "nausea." About a week or so before he resigned, he told me about a day where he had 3 death calls and I could tell it was very upsetting to him. Despite that he struggled with showing feelings, he was teary as he told me briefly about it. As a critical care RN myself, I assured him he would 'harden' over time. He also told me on the Sunday before resigning, he was very upset about two mistakes (I felt they were minor but I don't know dispatch) he had made. I could tell it was really bothering him so I didn't even ask about details on the second one, but he also wasn't one to share his feelings much and so it was a fairly brief conversation. He was still in training at this point and I did reassure him that he was "new, and surely they can't expect you to get everything right quite yet".*

*He resigned 3 days later on that Wednesday, and 8 days after he took his life.*

*Logan did not call 911, likely because he knew the procedure and feared he could be tracked quickly. But he did call the non-emergent line to give them the description of his clothes, his car, and where his location was. Stating he did not want to live and did not want to talk about it, he hung up and by the time the officers reached him it was too late. I have become aware that his colleagues* in training with him, those that had gotten to know him, feel very guilty. This is extremely normal after a suicide, but statements made by more than one like, "I wished I would have taken the call. I would have recognized his voice and could have tried to talk to him," bring this crisis situation to a whole new level. These people deal with suicide calls all the time, but one of their own? I'm sure these people need some longer term counseling.

My frustrations with these events are:

Why is there no depression/anxiety, etc. testing for qualifying to enter into the training program? I'm not saying he should have been disqualified from being hired, but certainly it could have brought more awareness to even himself. Maybe just testing after they are hired if it's not possible to do it before?

He could have been "flagged" as a risk, to be watched, and maybe even without him acknowledging a diagnosis, info given to him could have helped shape how he saw himself? Even if it had to be confidential, certainly it could help some.

Why didn't he get any info on suicide and these stats I'm reading about on your website, in his training?? I'm told at the time there was none given.

I wished we knew he was at such a high risk. My husband, as a police officer, and myself as an RN, didn't even realize what an impact this job could have potentially had on him. We both see sad and horrible things, but everyone processes differently and certainly when you start out with an illness (depression is just like having cancer- it's a disease), you are at even higher risk then someone who has a situational depression. In hindsight it makes sense he was at a higher risk, but we are all for more awareness (which I know is partially what you're here to accomplish) to bring it to the forefront of people's minds. Perhaps even a handout to give to family members on "signs/symptoms of when I might be in trouble and need you to assist me to seek help."

After the event, there was "crisis" intervention among his co-workers (which I see is common from your study), but nothing after or long term. And certainly nothing before.

We have learned he demonstrated many of the symptoms of depression at work from the beginning. In the classroom he had a few days where he was obviously not feeling well per colleagues (keeping his eyes shut and complaining of *dizziness). Despite this and not taking notes, he did well on the classroom tests. The abrupt changes of "he lost all confidence in himself in the last week or so" could have been addressed. And when he called in sick around these times, it goes hand in hand. Were they just annoyed that he was sick and it played into more hostility and perhaps contributed to even more anxiety, etc., or were they trying to see a bigger picture and figure out why the changes in performance? Of course, this is all in hindsight, but more education certainly can help decipher what is going on?*

*It's still unclear to us whether he was forced to resign, or he willingly did (he never told us he had resigned), but an exit interview from a neutral party could hopefully have brought some issues to light? I recognize these agencies lose people all time and probably don't "care", but it could have made a difference for my son and I would love to change that attitude.*

*Why do dispatch agencies have a rep for being a "viper pit"? Why did we hear the comment, "those __ (rhymes with witches) must have been riding him hard"?*

*We have a kid here that had a nearly perfect ACT, attended School of Mines with 30 HS credits already in place, and so was certainly capable of doing this job—if he was in a mental stable position.*

*Please understand we are not out to "blame" anyone at this point. We certainly approached him at times regarding seeking help, without success, and I'm not saying implementing more services (as you are thankfully attempting to do) would have saved his life. But, we can never know. Hearing from a party he respected and even a reduction in stigma could have made a difference for him. And I also know you are not these agencies.....you are not about going in and changing policies. I just wanted to give you a perspective, a personal story. A story of dispatcher and suicide.*

*Maybe you can use it?*

*And I'm not sure how this story can help, but I'm willing to tell it.*

*If I can be of any help in your efforts, please let me know. I know this letter might seem jumbled, but hopefully you get the idea.*

*Thank you for listening,*

*Lori Boarman*

## NOVEMBER 16, 2018

Got a sweet, sweet message from a friend (🖤) today.

Kim, Logan's best friend's mom, sent me this and like so many ironic moments in my life in the last 1.5 years, I happen to be across the street shopping at Costco while Amaya had some soccer training when I received it. I had just enough time to drive over and find this exact piece of steel still exposed and get a picture (although I wished I had a zoom-in camera for a crisp view of my son's name) before I had to wipe the tears and show up once again with a half-fake smile in front of other parents.

For those of you that don't know, Logan went to UCCS for a few years. He was within 2 semesters of graduating with an engineering degree. It's also the place he chose to be his final spot before ending his pain. In fact, this building sits in the same parking lot he chose to park in last. His dirt spot is now covered with cement.

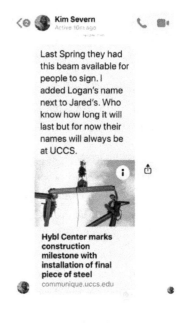

Kim Severn
Active 10m ago

Last Spring they had this beam available for people to sign. I added Logan's name next to Jared's. Who know how long it will last but for now their names will always be at UCCS.

**Hybl Center marks construction milestone with installation of final piece of steel**
communique.uccs.edu

I have to admit, driving toward pickup, the same thought consumed me (as it continues to daily), would anyone notice I had been crying? Has it been so long they would wonder what's wrong with me, why am I still having such a hard time? Time moves on...do some of these people even know our story? Do they know my son is gone? My heart beats irregularly now.

#thankyoufriend #misshimsomuch #suicideawareness

## NOVEMBER 18, 2018

At church today and greeting a couple we have seen many times but perhaps have never formally introduced each other:

Nice lady: Hi, I know we see each other all the time, but what are your names again?

Me: Yes, I'm terrible with names, but I am Lori.

Glenn: I am Glenn, you are?

Nice lady: I'm ___ and my husband is ___...I know you have 2 grown children, isn't that right?

Lori: Yes, and we have a 13-year old that helps downstairs during first hour.

Nice lady: oh, so 3?

Me: Ya...(a pause), 3

Me looking at Glenn and muttering quietly and somberly: umm...3...

Glenn looking to comfort me: it's just easier that way

Me: Yup

#misshimsomuch  #suicideawareness

## NOVEMBER 19, 2018

My post this week on suicide and the language used to talk about it opened up another issue...is suicide a sin?

This, of course, is a complicated topic and one I can only give my opinion on, because only God knows the final answer. Lots of thoughts both ways, but my question to you is, does it really matter?

I mean, when talking about someone who took their life, they are no longer with us so whether we hash it out and come up with an answer really only makes us be able to categorize a word into a box.

One could argue that if we label it a sin, we can have a more armor to prevent attempts. But the truth is, no one argues the results are devastating. Do we continue to try and prevent and show that there are other options and solutions? I sure am, but the more you learn about those that have had a serious attempt or did actually die by suicide, the more you learn about their thought process. They are so debilitated with pain, they don't actually see that they have any other options. And labeling it sin isn't going to stop anyone. If anything, it probably deters people from getting help. Another stigma that can add to someone in serious need to reach out.

There are certainly arguments that sin robs people of the fullest life God has given them. But people do things every day to rob their lives short; for instance, soda, cigarettes, and even lunch meat have been proven to be cancerous and toxic. The line is so hard to draw here on what we can consider a sin?

Suicide is mentioned only six times in the whole Bible, but when it is mentioned there is no moral evaluation given as to whether it is right or wrong.

To add to the convo....if suicide is a sin, is it unforgivable?

I think most people are aware now that the Bible doesn't say anywhere that it's the ultimate unforgivable sin. Since it doesn't even talk about it being a sin, there certainly isn't any solid evidence it's considered a straight path to Hell. That is old school thinking and if you want to know the history, a simple google will give you answers. Many people have (and still do) try and reassure me regarding this BUT because of the basis of my faith foundation, I never believed that even long before Logan took his life.

So...here is the ultimate reason why NONE of this matters. Whether you believe it's a sin or not!

The clear and consistent message of the Bible is the complete and full forgiveness of sins (past, present, and future—known sin and unknown sin) through faith. Jesus Christ came and lived on this earth, but paid the ultimate price, his blood- death—in exchange for all our sins. They (sins) are all created equal. When you believe and accept that He gave you this free gift, there is no sin that separates you from Him and therefore also never anything you could do to EARN his love. I often compare it to my relationship with my kids. I give them grace all the time AND they can't do anything to take away my love.

So although Logan did probably the worst "thing" (sin or not) he could ever do to us, we still love him more than ever...as does our God.

John 3:16

(And thank you my friend—you know who you are—for challenging me on this topic)

#misshimsomuch #suicideawareness #suicideprevention #mentalhealthawareness #changethestigma

## NOVEMBER 20, 2018

Here's how grief brain works—flighty thoughts that jump quickly and often end up with a sad thought:

I'm at work down at the lab today with a specimen I'm handing over. While the lab tech is filling out her end of the paperwork, she sorta mumbles but asks me, "What's this baby's birth date?" I tell her and stare at the medical record label...November 20th. November, what a great month to be born in. Does every person feel like their birth month is special? Whenever I hear November I think, "special," it's the month I was born. And 20th?? Wow...my birthday is almost here. Wait...I don't want my birthday to come. It's not going to be special. And then Glenn's is right around the corner. Not as special as November but December is a good month. And then Logan's birthday will come...but I don't want to think about that right now...then I think, what will I get Glenn? He deserves something special. And then I remember Glenn showing me something from his drawer a few months ago. It was like an old Coke emblem. I don't really remember exactly what it was, or Logan giving him this, but he did. Glenn stood there crying showing it to me saying it was a birthday present recently. I'm trying to remember if it was last year or the year before...but...maybe it's Glenn's favorite birthday present ever now? Logan knew he like old Coke stuff and had found it just for him. Logan didn't usually buy presents but he had this time for his dad.

I feel my eyes swelling and about this same time I come to as the lab tech says,

"You ok?"

"Ya...." Of course, I am. It's just another thought in my day...

#mentalhealthawareness #suicideawareness

## NOVEMBER 23, 2018

It's not always "what you say," but "how you say it," right?

Before Logan died, I had never thought that much about the word suicide, but particularly the phrase "committed suicide."

I have grown to really hate that phrase.

I'll be honest...even the days after his death, I didn't like using the word "suicide" at all. Instead, I subconsciously and immediately took to telling and texting people that he "took his life." Sometime very soon after that first week, my aunt and I were talking. (I talked to her a fair amount because my uncle had also taken his life and I had a sudden interest in more details, as you can imagine), and she had mentioned that etiquette was changing from "committed suicide." It didn't immediately strike me in the heart too much, but then I guess because I wasn't using it?

But shortly thereafter I could hear those words zapping my ear, even if it wasn't in "my" conversations, as if I was programmed to visibly shake my head. I hear it everywhere since and it's come up lately more as everyone is talking about "BIRD BOX". So here is my rant:

"Committed" is a word we use associating things with a crime. People commit murder, rape, burglary, etc. We use those words for actions that are considered immoral or sinful. Now, you may think suicide is one of those, but I can assure you, after lots of counseling and reading, it's not. I'll share more on that in a future post. At least, for now, I will say that it is not against the law anywhere and don't laugh....because there are a lot of stupid laws out there. I know you're thinking, well why would they ever pass a law to punish someone not here anymore...If this helps to understand, you cannot be charged for an "attempt" either.

So the term ended up mostly changing to "completed suicide." Honestly, I don't like this either. Completed is usually something that gives you fulfillment. You completed a project. You completed a class. You completed your chores. If you don't "complete" something, essentially you failed. Often times if you don't complete something, you have a sense of discouragement. It brings still a stigma that we are trying to avoid so that people are more willing to get help! And...when you think about it, suicide is suicide. The word itself is explanatory and so by saying completed you are sorta using it as an adjective and that makes it redundant.

So my advice is to not use any "C" word. Remember, C starts the word "cuss".

So what do you say?

I like, "he took his life." It's the phrase I use the most. Helping defray stigma, I feel it's the most gentle.

But other ways you can say it and sound more respectful are:

"Died by his own hand"

"Died by suicide"

"Intentionally ended his/her life"

"Killed himself" (although this sounds harsh to me too. BUT...it is what it is and that's what happened.)

I realize it probably won't be exactly natural at first. But if you practice and become aware, the wrong words will taser your ears, too. It's amazing what a different world I live in now and how it's made me not only aware of things related to suicide but also to grief, to death, to depression, to youth, to family, to...just about anything that most people mistake in everyday life...

#suicideawareness #mentalhealthawareness #stopthestigma

## NOVEMBER 24, 2018

I have to confess, I didn't think Logan's friends were all that great of an influence. Even though I honestly didn't even know them that well.

When Logan entered JH he had a group of kids he had grown up with all through elementary school and he was planning on being in this group for the remainder of the years. But JH brings out new and emerging personalities and Logan suddenly found himself at ethical odds. It was a trying and frustrating time for him, as I could see a little more anger that I had never seen before. He even punched a kid in the stomach after being frustrated that he wouldn't release the football as the rules implied (during lunch free time). Rules were black and white for him, but he had never, ever hurt anyone. And this certainly went against his integrity he was so fighting for. This was really not like him and I wished I would have seen more into this act.

Logan's giftedness came in multiple areas which made it really hard to figure out exactly where he fits in. I remember talking with the gifted counselor about how he had scored high in multiple areas of the cogAT, which made him super unique. He was athletic, but not a total jock. He was smart, but not a total nerd. He was sensitive but didn't show it.

He eventually began to develop new relationships, and with the distance of the new boundaries of the JH and having multiple siblings with various activities, I didn't get to know his 'new friends' all that well. By late HS I knew names, and had encountered some on various occasions, such as Science Olympiad; he even had them over for pizza birthday one year, but I didn't really 'know' them, as I feel a lot of moms of boys might attest to as they get in the older HS years. But what I did 'know' was that over time with new friends, came withdrawal and extended periods spent in front of his computer screen battling those buddies online.

By the time he graduated and began his college years, I had completely associated his friends with video gaming. It had taken over his life in the last few years to where he wasn't "present" in our family. He was addicted in my assessment; and I tried many times to tame this, to show him, to accept counseling, etc., but he was so good at using big words and elaborate statements to stump me into not knowing what to say next. After all, he had graduated one point away from having a perfect ACT score and over 2 semesters worth of AP credits.

But times were different after his freshman semester as he struggled to focus and stay motivated to keep on track. He continued to spend endless hours downstairs in the dark, in his room, playing video/computer games. Sure, he would occasionally ask to have over several people for a board game night and sometimes told me he was going elsewhere for the same, but I didn't really 'hear' that part. I only heard 'games', which I way too closely associated with 'video games.' It was a huge source of contention in our house and something I cried about on many occasions because at some points caused fighting nearly every day. We even made him bring his computer to the dining room and limited play at times, but ultimately we knew he was an 'adult' and we couldn't continue to push him away by controlling this behavior he saw nothing wrong with.

Back to his friends...I remember SO vividly the day Logan got his job as a city dispatcher. He came eagerly into the garage where I was sorting and cleaning. "Mom! I got the job!" his expression and voice containing the relief and excitement he was experiencing at that moment. Immediately following my "congratulations, I'm so proud of you," he stated, "Jared and I have been talking about moving in together, I'll be able to do that quickly now." My excitement suddenly halted and my mind went to "Oh great, now you can be consumed with gaming even more...terrible, awful, I can't even imagine idea. Jared will certainly contribute to pushing your gaming habits even higher; no way do I want you to move in with him," although I never said these words. Instead, I mustered up a "Why don't you stay here just a few more months and get your student loans paid off and then you can explore moving out".

Those thoughts haunt me; I was so wrong.

Today the truth is, I think moving in with Jared could have saved his life. Jared is a respectful, intelligent, motivated, spiritual, nice, honest, trustworthy, successful, happy, funny, caring guy; a best friend any guy could ask for. Jared loves gaming, but it doesn't consume his life. Logan was (in my opinion) using it to escape the reality of his pain; but in turn, it was contributing to much of his physical symptoms. It's very likely Jared could have picked up on many of Logan's behaviors that only we saw behind closed doors. Logan was living a double life and although there might have been times he would have had to work harder to mask this from his best friend, Jared certainly would have new insight and become aware of his overall mood. Living together all hours likely would have brought up needed conversations. Jared wasn't seeing what we saw.

I've written about Logan's friends before and how truly great they are; men and women of great integrity and compassion (amongst so many other positive attributes). But today I just want to apologize to Jared.

I'm sorry for associating Logan's negative gaming behaviors with your character. I'm sorry for not getting to know you better over the years. I'm sorry for not realizing what a bright light you were in his life, and just how much you meant to him. I'm so thankful he voiced that in his letter to you, despite how hard it is to read. It's overwhelmingly obvious to me now that you were key to his quality traits. Your words describing your search for him because it was so unbelievable are the most powerful that stir my emotions today. I'm thankful you've become a part of our 'after Logan died' lives and hope it continues. I want you to stick around as the memories you make give me a glimpse of what it would look like if Logan were still here. As I've told you, you mimic him on all levels, including all the way down to his mannerisms.

Except, depression.

#thankyouforbeinghisfriend  #suicideawareness #mentalhealthawareness #Iamsorry

## NOVEMBER 26, 2018

"I know the night won't last"...

Thank goodness I have an understanding of this. That the way I feel in that dark moment won't be the way I feel the entire week, the entire day, and sometimes not even the same hour.

If you struggle with having HOPE that your moments can be better, different, or even joyful, then maybe you need to meet my best friend. Jesus. He allows (and knows) me to feel these sad thoughts, but then also tells me to lay them at His feet and promises to make good out of them. Because I know He holds the future, I can have peace that these hard times are temporary.

#hope #findingjoy

## NOVEMBER 29, 2018

Twelve year old thoughts... 💔 🐾

#suicideawareness

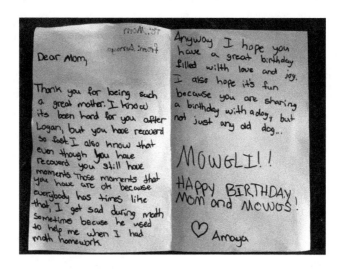

## NOVEMBER 30, 2018

Mental Health experts say it's time to normalize conversations about suicide. I couldn't agree more. What you say (and don't say) could save a person's life.

Tip 1. If someone seems different, don't ignore it..

-Talking about wanting to die or to kill themselves

-Looking for a way to kill themselves, like searching online or buying a gun

-Talking about feeling hopeless or having no reason to live

-Talking about feeling trapped or in unbearable pain

-Talking about being a burden to others

-Increasing the use of alcohol or drugs

-Acting anxious or agitated, behaving recklessly

-Sleeping too little or too much

-Withdrawing or isolating themselves

-Showing rage or talking about seeking revenge

-Extreme mood swings

Tip 2. Don't be afraid to ask. Then act.

-Ask, keep them safe, be there, help them connect, follow up

Tip 3. Pay special attention when someone is going through a difficult time.

Tip 4. If someone makes an attempt and survives, continue to be there.

Tip 5. You don't need to have all the answers.

If you'd like more details, read the article attached or visit SPRC.org or AFSP.org #suicideawareness #mentalhealthawareness

# DECEMBER 2018

## DECEMBER 2, 2018

Tonight, exactly one year ago, we sat down for dinner as a family (all of us) after being gone for a few days in Kansas City with Savannah and her soccer team's Final Four run.

My birthday happened while we were gone. And something that weighed heavily on my mind was that Logan had never acknowledged it. I remember trying to have fun at dinner in KC with a group of people, but thinking and wondering if I would actually hear from him. It had consumed me. He didn't text. He didn't call. And there was no card when I returned home. I always tried to shake it off and blame his chemistry makeup, but I longed to feel important again to him in the last couple years.

He had been so much happier and engaged in the last couple months, but very recently something had started to seem off again. He had been hanging downstairs (in his room) a lot more and I was preparing to bring it up in conversation. I always hated that part but felt as his mom I needed to. But still, I thought we were in a new place. He had once struggled with acknowledging special events, but certainly, he wouldn't actually forget it was my birthday would he? He was so much better at asking me about my day in the last year...

Back to Sunday dinner...I was angry. Or maybe I was hurt. Either way, the mood changed when I blurted out, "You know it was my birthday?" We were sitting side by side but my body language was shifted away. He slowly, quietly answered, "Ya I know. I'm sorry. I forgot, and then when I remembered I was embarrassed so I didn't say anything".

My response..."Well, next time better late than never."

I don't remember saying much else that night. My feelings were hurt. I'm not sure he did either.

I only had 2 more weeks with him at that point. If I had known that, how differently would I have responded? If I knew he was struggling so wouldn't I have just hugged him and told him how much I loved him?? That it was ok!?

Shouldn't I have known something more was wrong? Couldn't I have been more forgiving?

Logan was obviously struggling with focus, memory, and even feelings. He was already feeling numb and I'm guessing every minute was weighing on him. I am hanging on to the fact that as he worked so hard to live, he did have just enough energy to apologize.

We later found out he had called in sick a couple of days in the last weeks. It was probably during this time we were gone because I hadn't known of any time he had missed an entire day of work. While I was selfishly thinking about my birthday, my son was struggling with living. Maybe he didn't even get out of bed that day?

Who are you sitting with at the dinner table? Are they letting you down? Maybe there is a reason for that...

#suicideawareness #depressionisadisease #misshimsomuch

## DECEMBER 3, 2018

Memories on FB...Logan is becoming less and less in them. Now that a year has come and gone, the memories of him seem to be of grieving posts 😭.

I didn't even really use to look at my memories, but in the past year, I search them for any remnants of my Logan. Of a time when he walked the earth...(sounds like I'm searching for dinosaurs, sometimes it feels like that already).

I was so excited, angry, happy, weepy, proud, in pain, and more when I saw this. He was so smart, and so proud of his school and team this day. Why couldn't he hang on to these days?

#misshimsomuch

## DECEMBER 4, 2018

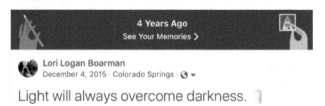

So crazy I posted this 3 years ago.

Let me tell you...it STILL holds true. Don't get me wrong, there is a fair amount of darkness in my life, but thank goodness the light is brighter.

Where I find the hardest time to be, is in my bed. At night. Where it's dark. The dark leaves my mind free to wander. When there is nothing to actually see, it's when I create things to see. A dangerous place to be. It's where I cry the most.

So I have to be extra careful in the dark.

I have to search, for physical light sometimes. It's there, but sometimes that means opening my eyes to see it. Even if it's the tiniest amount of light; the street light outside my window, or turning my phone to see the time. But even a tiny bit gives me hope. Hope that it's not completely dark. That I won't be left in the Black for very long. That light is out there and the sun will shine again in the morning.

But that's just physical "light". God is my mental light. When I'm in the dark and in those dark places, I remember that with the light of the morning, a new day will be here. That He has a purpose and meaning to my thoughts and He is excited to turn them into good. As I remember these things, my thoughts usually turn to better ones and then wander pleasantly from there. Sometimes I let the dark last longer before turning to Him...not sure why we torture ourselves like this?

But....when I do remember Him, It doesn't matter what I'm thinking or what has happened to me that day, there is an eternal picture. Get a grip on eternity, on the world to come. It's the best thing that has happened in my life...to my over-analytical mind...

If you can learn to live your life in "light" of eternity, I promise your perspective will change.

Isn't it crazy how ANY amount, ANY....amount of light, causes it to not be completely dark? And then it appears so much bigger than it is. All the dark in the world can't stop even a speck of light. You can always find the smallest amount of light...hang on to that. That's God. He is bigger than any amount of the world's darkness.

Hold a match up to the wall. Light has NO shadow.

"God is light. In Him, there is no darkness at all. 1 John 1:5"

#mentalhealthawareness #hope

## DECEMBER 5, 2018

Today my Grandma turned 92 🎂!

Because Logan's birthday is also early December, we often celebrated them together. In 2016 we had an extended family bash. So glad we got this picture of my Grandma turning 90 with so many of her grandkids and great-grandkids! Oh, did Logan seem to love that evening because we played board games after the celebration into the night. On the drive home, he was in a particularly good mood and we had more than just a brief conversation. Logan had just decided to quit going to college after 3 years, and I was throwing out my last-ditch effort words to persuade him to take even just one class. While it didn't convince him, it was a pleasant talk in that I tried to listen more than talk and understand more than argue. He did a lot of talking that night and I'm so thankful I was able to convince him into going.

I look at these memories and wonder...how fake are these smiles? Was he really having fun? Had the thought remotely crossed his mind to end his life at this time?

2016

#suicideawareness

#mentalhealthawareness

## DECEMBER 7, 2018

I'm having a moment...and felt like writing...

Suicide.

This is such a huge part of my life now and I'm reminded of it constantly:

A text from a friend thinking about me; she knows this time is so hard.

A text invite for a "board" game night for our family; this friend is always thinking of ways to honor my son.

A card in the mail; another friend is thinking about my birthday and all the "events" in the next couple weeks.

An email from a relative; I haven't opened it yet but it has the heading...Preventing Teen Suicide.

I open up FB and a new friend is posting how she can't do Christmas Cards; her daughter took her life this year. I haven't met her but we connected because of suicide.

Another text from a friend whose son is struggling and she's looking for some insight.

A prayer group on FB started for a dear family whose son is struggling with depression.

I open a sack given to me by a relative and there are suicide cards to pass out as I see needed.

Another friend messages me in FB and shares song that she hopes I can share with others.

Responder Strong creates an event on prevention and I receive the notification.

Another friend (whom I knew previously) mourns another year of her son being gone by suicide.

A co-worker stops and talks with me about how I'm doing and I find out about 2 missing people in our community that likely took their lives instead of some other accidental death.

This is what I can come up with at the moment; I'm sure there is more.

This was only the last 24 hours.

But please, don't take this as I don't want to hear from you or that it's a burden. It's just a new way of life. Trying to embrace it as best I can.

#suicidesucks #suicidesurvivor

## DECEMBER 11, 2018

Logan, today you would be 24. But instead, you will be 23 forever. My heart hurts so much thinking about this and all the things I couldn't wait to see you do.

I took some time gathering all your birthday pictures. Number 23. Nothing.

One year ago, I gave you a hug and wished you a happy birthday. When I asked you what your plans were for the day, you said you were going out with friends. I figured you meant at least later in the evening. After dinner? When you walked out the door before your dad was home, you just yelled, "Bye, I'm leaving now." I scared you because I was painting up high in the hallway. I stopped you and said, "When are we going to celebrate? I didn't realize you were leaving so early." You just shrugged your shoulders and said, "I don't know."

I never got that birthday picture. My album is not complete. I guess there are many albums that won't be complete now.

I'm struggling, but I still want to wish you a Happy Birthday. And please always know, Your mommy loves you so very much. 🤍

#missyousomuch #suicideawareness #happybirthday

## DECEMBER 11, 2018

Say I love you even in some of the hardest moments.

My best advice as a parent, friend, spouse, and child.

Please share with anyone you think needs these words.

#suicideawareness #mentalhealthawareness #misshimsomuch

I posted a video today, below is a manuscript of it.

*Hey everyone, I'm not doing this live because I'm not sure I'm actually gonna post it, but we'll see.*

*Today's Logan's birthday and I just came into his room for the first time ever. Well, not ever, but the first time since his death a year ago. And because it's his birthday and because of the importance of this week, it's on Saturday it will be a year since he took his life. There's just a lot of events and memories and thoughts that are replaying in my mind over and over again. And... probably the one that's heaviest is just something that I felt like I needed to share because it's given me some comfort.*

*Being a parent is so hard and I know you guys know that. Um, I mean this isn't just for parents it's for everyone that has a relationship with anyone which is everyone. Um; but sometime when Logan was around a junior in high school, um, he sort of lost who he was and (while it was a little bit later than this, it's actually probably more like 20, but I mean he did start to develop his depression and withdraw from the family when he was about 18...17 or 18). Um, but after his first semester of college when he came home and we entered some counseling, he just could not say that he loved me and he could not really...I mean I guess that's the main thing. You know we would talk and all but when I was leaving or going to work or going to bed and whatever and I would say "I love you Logan," he wouldn't respond. And we did some counseling that spring semester as a part of a deal when he moved back home...and...I think he, you know, he was convinced he was doing it for me, which was partly true. I just needed to know how to communicate with him and all but, you know, through that counseling one of the biggest things that came from that was that his counselor (I mean, and she said to him as well but mostly in a session privately with me) was that Logan doesn't under-*

stand unconditional love right now. Um, he just doesn't understand love— what it means. And, no matter how hard it is and how frustrated you are with him, her advice to me was that you've got to just keep telling him that you love him, even when you're mad at him, even when you know you're not going to get it back. And, it was the best advice that I've gotten because he didn't give it back to me for a long time, and it was so hard.

I'm sorry I had a visitor show up, um, and obviously I've calmed down a little bit, but I wanted to just finish. And...

So that advice from that counselor was really the best parenting advice that I've ever gotten because as we all know our 3 year olds can be very trying at times and our 18 year olds, um or 16 years olds or even 13 year olds that are talking back or doing whatever. And do we always love them, of course we always love them. Um, but to say those words, especially when you are frustrated or you are angry, mean so much more. And so for me, I continued to tell Logan that I loved him. And you know we wouldn't fight, and he wouldn't say awful things to me. Um, he would just be going about his day and be leaving and I would say, "I love you, Logan" and he would just look at me and I wouldn't hear it back and I can't even tell you how hard that was. Hurtful. Um, it would have been easier to just not say it because then I wouldn't have to not hear it back. But as I continued to say it, (I don't remember how many months that was and it might have even been like a year later) at some point he had a new understanding of what love was and I believe he met a girl (that sounds like movie and cliche-ish) but i think she kind of, you know, showed him that and he was able to open up and figure it all out again. But one day when I said, "Have a good day; I love you," he actually said it back to me. And I just knew at that time, like, wow, you know, she was right. I needed to show him what unconditional love was. It didn't matter, um, if he was doing everything great or if we had a great relationship or whatever was going on. He knew that I loved him. And so I will tell you that on his birthday one year ago I struggled with wanting to say happy birthday to him. And telling him that I loved him. Because if you read my post the other day, I was really angry at him for not wishing me a happy birthday. And the other thing is that we had found out that he had quit his job and he hadn't told any of us. And I was confused and frustrated and was scared too; but mostly he was just acting like nothing was wrong. And so I was just like, *you know I wonder, in my mind, I kept thinking, you know maybe I just won't say happy birthday and almost like pretend like we forgot. I wonder what he would think but part of me knew, because I had asked him questions before like, Logan what if we did this to you or whatever and he would say it's no big deal and you know I don't know how much that was true because now that I know how much he was hurting and numb to emotions and feelings like maybe it really wouldn't have mattered to him, um, I don't know… But…so I struggled I just keep thinking, you know, I'll at least let him maybe bring it up you know and when he walked up stairs that morning my motherly instincts took over and I remembered what the counselor said and I'm like I have to do this, no matter how hard it is. And I walked over to him and I gave him a hug and said happy birthday Logan, I love you. And… sitting here today thinking back it gives me so much peace that I did that because it was only a few days later that he took his life. And I'm not saying because of that day that he wrote this in the letter but because of all the times he knew how much we loved him, he wrote in our letter, especially to me, he said, I know that you cared. And he wrote that I love you all. And you know obviously that was huge for us, after what we had kinda been through with him. But, can you imagine if I had not wished him a Happy Birthday or had avoided it or had somehow made it a different moment. How guilty I would feel now? And I mean of course I feel guilty for other things but I have so much peace that I did that anyway. And so this is just my plea to you guys, to remember that in a moment when your son or when you're in a big fight with someone that you really love, to not be afraid to you say it. It doesn't even mean that you make up, it doesn't even mean you agree with what they're doing, but..just let them know how much you love them.*

*I hope you guys have a good rest of your day. Thank you for all your support, reaching out to me and giving me hugs. And, Love you all.*

## DECEMBER 12, 2018

Found this in Logan's album yesterday. This summed him up when he was living life to the fullest. Unfortunately, video games and an occasional book was all that was left the last 2 years…

#mentalhealthawareness #misshimsomuch

## DECEMBER 12, 2018

A month ago I planned on talking about the events of the last 2 weeks or so of Logan's life—each day—as those dates on the calendar rolled by. And then they did just that...rolled by. Each day the emotions and scenarios leading up to the tragic moment, played out, repetitively, in my mind. But mostly I didn't find the time or energy to talk/write about them. So here goes probably a long post...attempting to back track and express any glimpse. I thought I had journaled this already shortly after. If true, I can't find it. So these are my memories of that time, currently.

Logan had begun working as a dispatcher for the Co Springs police department in August 2017. He had stopped going to school after 3 years and was searching for something in law enforcement. Said he liked helping people and was so excited about getting this job. I'll never forget the day he rushed to inform me of the news. Such a huge smile as he exclaimed, "I got the job." I was ecstatic and thought, this could be the beginning of the rest of his life. A new start with a quality job that paid well and was a "career."

....He seemed to love his job and initially was eager to share stories at the family dinner table. Bryce particularity had mentioned many times, "Logan is the happiest I've seen him in a long time."

So much more to tell regarding that opening preface, but I'm reserving these writings to his final movements.

The first time I realized something was off was around Thanksgiving. I asked him how his day was, and he answered somberly "I had 3 death calls today." I asked him about each one, and I especially was interested in the "a mom called, she was hysterical, she had found her 19 yr old dead, probably from an OD." We stayed on that one for a bit as I was eager to bring out any emotion, always wanting to bring him close to death so that he could "feel my love more," mentioning that I could not imagine what that would be like and how horrific. He agreed as he stepped through the details of that call. We even talked about the process they taught to determine if the body was truly deceased or if he needed to act otherwise.

I had no thought in my mind, at that point, that Logan might be considering taking his life. If it was a thought by him by now, I don't believe he was "planning" it. I reassured him that he would become numb. That he would get used to death calls.

Sometime around these dates, I began noticing Logan wasn't around as much again. That he was spending a lot more time in his room. And I began to internally dread the inevitable "nag" by his mom to recognize it and "appear" more. Things seemed to be good with work, so it was a little confusing and I suppose because we had been dealing with withdrawal for a couple years now on and off, it wasn't particularly 'frightening' to me. I don't believe I ever had that dreaded conversation with him, meanwhile thinking about it every.single.day. Savannah's team was going deep into the playoffs and planning trips and being gone pleasantly preoccupied my mind.

**December 3rd** - the family dinner conversation I wrote about last week (missing acknowledging my birthday)

**December 4th** - I remember him coming home and I was painting in the hallway. I asked how his day was and he reluctantly stopped to answer. He stated that it wasn't very good as he had made some mistakes he wasn't happy about. I probed for details as I most always do, and he gave me minute ones, almost certainly trying to avoid discussion. Since we believed he was still on orientation, I reassured him they were minor and that he wasn't expected to be perfect.

Many times I've played this conversation in my mind. What else could I have said to help him discern "failure" in his mind?

**December 6** - Glenn and I both worked and were up and in the kitchen about 6:10 when Logan, dressed for work, arose from the basement (his room) and proceeded to the garage (where many of snacks and misc food is located). He then proceeded to the front door and was stopped by my semi-sarcastic "good-bye....hope you have a nice day" since he hadn't even acknowledged our presence. He quickly turned and replied something like, "Oh...have a nice day," as if he was surprised to see us. Reflecting within days of the event, he seemed preoccupied in his mind. I'm not sure he had actually been aware we were standing there. This was the day he quit his job. Did he already know the plan for the day, or did certain events push him suddenly? Certainly he was struggling with thoughts.

No one remembers contact with him the remainder of the day, assuming he was out with friends in the evening when we were all home.

**December 7** - Glenn's birthday.

It's hard to think about this day. I suppose it's when my "motherly instincts" really kicked it and just hits my core.

Glenn texted me at 9:57am telling me Logan quit his job yesterday. He found out from a co-worker, whose wife worked with Logan. It went something like this:

"I'm sorry about your son"

"I don't know what you're talking about"

"He quit his job yesterday"

"Oh, we didn't know"

I was heightened emotionally with these words. Angry, sad, scared, confused, frustrated, felt sorry for him, worried about what was next...every emotion.

Why would he quit? He loved that job

Did he do something wrong to get fired? No way

Could he not handle it emotionally? Maybe...but why wouldn't he get another job first

He wouldn't walk away from this job for just any reason...what happened?!

This was the first time (besides a very brief-thoughts that were very light-time after his freshman semester 2 years before) I really worried about him enough to consider he might take his life. He had never threatened or even talked about it, but my mind just went there. I had been through begging him to get out of bed in the past....encouraging him to finish his last 2 weeks of school and when I thought he was at a serious low. It was painful for many reasons, but I wasn't at the point of "worrying" about him to that degree. This time was different. He had been through so much and after all the previous events, I thought I felt what he must have been feeling.

Now what.

Was Glenn going to be so frustrated he would kick him out? Would he end up on the street?

This job was so promising, how will he get another "career" one without school?

What is he gonna do? He must be so depressed. I was so sad.

Back to anger...why would he do this and he's not telling us!

My stomach ached. My brain ached. My heart ached. I texted a group of friends that are prayer warriors and my aunt to pray.

A couple hours later my aunt called me asking if I had talked to him. He is usually up around noon at the latest to get something to eat and I hadn't seen him. She said, Lori - haven't you gone down to check on him? I immediately began crying and told her I was afraid of what I might find. Yup...those words came out of my mouth. I don't know exactly what I meant by that, but I was scared. And, if he was ok, I didn't want to be the one to confront him because Glenn was much more calm, rational, and not emotional in these situations.

My aunt prayed with me over the phone. That Logan would see his path, that he would be safe. I so regret that I didn't go down. Why didn't I give him a hug, tell him I loved him no matter what, and ask him to tell me about it? I should have asked him straight up if he was considering taking his life. He might have lied, but he might have told me. We know now from his computer that that was the first day he did research on buying a gun.

...Kids straggled in and eventually Glenn came home from work. We got the dinner birthday celebration ready when someone texted Logan dinner was ready. I hadn't confided in anyone else how I was feeling. When Logan walked up the stairs, my heart skipped a beat—relief - he was ok. And...he was in a good mood. We enjoyed our time celebrating and I suppose in his display of seemingly happiness, I was fooled and somewhat comforted. At least for the evening. He never brought up his job, and we decided not to since it was a day of 🎂. It would turn out to be our last...full...family meal together.

### December 8 & 9 (Friday & Saturday)

I don't remember much about these days, other than Logan still didn't tell us he had quit his job. He was "around" but of course that mostly meant his car was in the driveway, he is isolating himself in his room. He probably left at some point as he often did in the evenings, frequenting other friends houses for board or video game nights. Occasionally they came to our house, but it had been at least a few months.

I guess he likely assumed we thought it was just another unscheduled group of days. His routine had rotated and changed a lot so he could have easily told us it was official days off. But he didn't mention anything, and we were waiting for him to talk first. The one thing I do remember him asking was, "Could I take Amaya to a movie tomorrow"? While this wasn't an unusual question, it was more of an implication that he wouldn't be working tomorrow. I think I responded that she had something going on (I just don't quite remember what) and that it would depend on the timing. I remember her not being home at the time so I left it as we would have to talk with her tomorrow.

Then Saturday came around and after discussing it with Amaya, they decided Sunday would be better since she had plans with a friend in the middle of the day.

We may have eaten dinner together, but Bryce was now out of town and Savannah likely not around on a typical evening either.

### December 10 (Sunday)

Amaya and Logan decided there weren't any good movies they wanted to see. Instead they watched a movie downstairs: *Divergent*.

This was the last day Glenn would see Logan. Glenn had been working on finishing up a coke machine he was restoring, and upon finalizing the tweaks, asked Logan to help him move it from the garage to the dining room. I was hanging around painting my Grandmother's buffet, so I remember this occasion vividly. Logan was pleasant and fairly cheerful. No mention of his work. Glenn and I had a conversation about it later in the day...

Me: Aren't we going to talk to him?

Glenn: I'm sorta wondering just how long he's going to play this out?

### December 11 (Monday)

Logan's 23rd Birthday. His last. I wrote about this day on the anniversary, Tuesday. You can go back and check it out if you missed it.

Some of his good friends saw him briefly that night, but where else he spent the long evening is unknown to me.

### December 12 (Tuesday)

I worked my usual 12-hour shift, arriving home around 8:15pm. When I asked if anyone had seen or talked to Logan, only Amaya had. He had left a short time after she had arrived home from school, and told her he was going to work. We figured maybe he wasn't lying. Maybe he had decided to go back to Pizza Hut and work while he figured out his next step?

*Excerpt:* We are not typically worriers. We mostly live on faith and agree you can't change anything by doing so...(except maybe worsen your health). So if you're wondering how we could go to bed each night not wondering where he was, it was not uncommon for us. He often worked late hours and with 3 adult children living with us at the time, we didn't feel it was our place to question them constantly.

I did often ask him to tell me "approximately" where he was going or who he would be with. I urged him to understand that I wasn't trying to control where he was, just that "if you don't come home some night, at least I would have an idea of where to start looking." I have to think this might have played into his thoughts when he called to tell dispatch where his final resting place was...

Sometime this week, I'm not sure which, I found myself downstairs getting wrapping paper. I was just around the corner from his room and felt an urge to snoop on his computer. I was still constantly thinking about him and what was going on. He wasn't home and I was thinking I could maybe gather some insight. As the urge lingered, something drew me back upstairs. What would he think if he came home and found me in there? My mind also argued that there would be nothing there. Turns out it had a password on it and I would have never gotten in anyway. This gave me some comfort in the after days.

### December 13 (Wednesday)

My last day to see my baby alive.

I was on the computer when Logan meandered upstairs around noon. He came and sat in the same room as I, on one of the ottomans, looking at the floor and gently petting the dogs. I did say, "Hey," with a return of the same 3 letters, but overall it was an awkward silence at first. I had to wonder...does he not know we know about his job? Surely he is wondering why we haven't asked? But then I was also nervously wondering if he would bring it up for the first time with me? I was calm on the outside, but my mind was racing internally. I just kept wondering what was on his mind? What game are we playing here? I wasn't even paying attention to what I was doing, just consumed in thought.

I don't usually have a problem expressing my feelings or talking through things, but with him, I was so cautious. Never wanting to upset the situation and had tried to really respect his opinion of my communication skills with him.

I, finally, after I'm sure only 5-10 min but seemed like an hour, broke the silence, "You know, we did get you some birthday presents. There's a big box in the dining room I didn't wrap."

(I had been so proud to have spent a couple hours researching and conferring with his siblings on finding the best computer desk. It was something he needed and I thought kinda a truce gift to show him I wasn't totally against computer games, something that seemed so much of his identity).

He immediately got up and went to check it out. Coming back he came over to my chair. He leaned down and gave me a hug and in a genuine voice said, "Thanks mom, I really appreciate it."

"I will put it together when I have time (catching himself and maybe knowing I was thinking he had all the time in the world); well, I mean it looks like it might be hard to put together so when I have an extended period of time."

I calmly replied, "You know your dad will help you," and he nodded his head and said confidently, "I know."

I think that was it. I don't know if we said anything else after. Final words. Wow...if I could have only known.

I'm embarrassed to say I gave him a half-ass hug back. I didn't stand up from my chair. I did reach back, but it wasn't a full embrace. I was confused and somewhat angry/annoyed so I held back as I often do (putting up walls) when in the midst of these feelings. Oh, how I regret that. Can I just please have that hug back? I would embrace him ever so tightly and make him ask to let go...

I believe he got something to eat and then descended down to the dark once again. I left by 1:30 to go to Sams. I wanted to purchase a phone for Bryce for Christmas and be home for when Amaya walked in. I remember texting the usual family group message: "At Sams, does anyone want anything?" I got a few answers, but his number never replied. The phone purchase took a lot longer than anticipated; and when I arrived home, Logan's car was gone. The first thing I asked Amaya was if she knew where he went? He had once again told her he was going to work. Ugh. And then as expected, he didn't come home before we went to bed that night.

**December 14** (Well, that's tomorrow so I'll write more then.)

#suicideawareness #mentalhealthawareness #misshimsomuch

You ♡'d for me to rock you to sleep.

## DECEMBER 14, 2018

The clock is ticking. You have tried fiercely all day to think about something else; to do other things, to attend parties and pretend it didn't happen. Your dogs even help a little. But...it's getting closer and closer to the time you know your son would call the non-emergent line and tell them where they could find his body.

This sucks.

Suicide sucks.

#misshimsomuch

### December 14

Today, one year ago did not start out as a normal day. Because...I woke up with Logan heavy on my heart. I was increasingly worried about this "game" we were playing; him not telling us about quitting his job, and us not asking. I had worried particularly the day we found out, Glenn's birthday, but had been deceivingly somewhat calmed by his upbeat behavior. But as I drove to work, I spent all my prayer time asking for him to have direction and peace.

Much of my free time in my 12.5 hour day was spent talking about Logan. A co-worker I had often confided in asked me first thing for an update: had Logan told us yet?

I had a very small baby that day that needed more monitor watching and potential prevention then actual care, so I had a fair amount of time to reflect openly in communication.

I remember specifically talking/comparing my situation with a friend of mine, whose son had repeatedly threatened, and even attempted suicide. Talking about having peace that she knew she had done everything she could to prevent it, and if he chose to do it, it wasn't her. That it's such a hard and tiring road to be in... However, I was not thinking along the lines of suicide regarding Logan, but that I had tried, directed, encouraged, etc. regarding his school, job, career situation. As smart as he was, I couldn't control if he ended up working at Pizza Hut, although I was convinced in my heart that wasn't good enough for him. But I hated that he was seemingly taking the long and painful route. And that I was tiring.

Oh, how I wished that's what he was doing...figuring his way through life, instead of just ending it. Even now I regret that we hadn't been way more encouraging of him taking a year off of school when we saw him declining.

It's strange to me I was taking about suicide. Did my mother's intuition know that he was checked into a hotel that very moment writing good-bye letters? Was I already subconsciously trying to comfort my heart from blame—pointing out I had tried my best?

By the time my shift was over, I was emotionally ready to end the curiosity.

I texted Glenn- is Logan home?

Him- no

Me- are you working tomorrow?

Him- yes

Me- should we text him to come home so we can talk?

Him- Savannah told him we know

I left work uneasy. I usually spend my time praying on the way to work and listening to music on the way home. I drove down I-25 reaching out to God this night all the way home...please be with Logan. Please guide and direct him. Help him know we love him. Give me the words of understanding...etc. I had never prayed more intensely for him.

I arrived home and eagerly inquired on the details of the conversation between Logan and Savannah. There wasn't much more than what he had already told me: Logan came up about lunchtime and they exchanged a few sentences. Savannah told him we knew about his job, and we were not mad but just waiting for an explanation.

That was it. Oh, how I am thankful she told him we weren't mad. That has given me some peace.

I may have been comforted just enough to fall asleep at a usual time. The home phone rang at midnight, an anonymous caller so I did not answer; but I didn't remember it until reminded of it later on that next day.

...loud, very loud, abrupt knocks on the door changed all the peace of the night as we knew it. As Glenn immediately got up and I believe went to obtain his gun, I looked out the window, my heart racing. I saw multiple police cars parked across the street, closer to the neighbor's house. I started arguing with myself...one of those cars looks like it could be a humane society car...maybe the neighbors dog got out and there is something wrong and they are asking us for details/help deciphering the situation. (This was not even rational as their dog is not mean and cops wouldn't bang loudly for that...)

Those were my thoughts, but I remember 'feeling'...like I had seen this coming...that this was the moment I knew was coming and it was finally happening...

In the next seconds my mind began racing harder so much so that I don't even think I could gather thoughts.

I grabbed my robe and was coming down the stairs and Glenn opened the door to see multiple officers. He immediately responded, "Oh, this is not good." My mind immediately began begging to know the reality I hoped for...please, just be here to tell me Logan had done something bad and was arrested and in jail...but my brain argued back...they don't come tell parents of adult children these things...and what on earth would Logan have done to be arrested...not him.

Are you Glenn?...yes...are you Lori?...yes....

Before I could consciously think anymore thoughts, the lead officer began talking. Bryce was descending upstairs and Savannah down, but hadn't made it to the the living room. Amaya was halfway down the stairs I think trying to figure out if she was allowed to be present.

He began...there's been a terrible accident at UCCS...(my mind racing...but not considering it could be only an accident/my mind had already determined it was death...began trying to sort through the confusion...oh my goodness, did Logan kill other people before taking his life? The word accident didn't make sense to me)...Logan shot himself, he called dispatch to let them know where he was, but by the time we arrived he was no longer with us. Maybe they used the word deceased...I just don't remember.

Bryce arrived in the room and I said, "Did you hear what they said?" He replied, "Yes...I heard them..."

I really can't put into words what happened to my heart, in my brain after that. When people say, "indescribable," I guess they mean they just don't know how to describe something. I can't really describe those next minutes. I know I put my head in the pillow next to me and screamed and cried.

I know Glenn asked what kind of gun. (He was comforted in knowing it wasn't a gun he possessed or owned). I know that they told us someone had tried to call at midnight, to confirm the registration of the car...(I am happy knowing we didn't answer that call...we couldn't change anything at that point and were able to get 3 more hours of sleep.)

I know they told us he left letters and that we could see them once the body was released. I begged, surely you have them, can you just take a picture of them for me? No was the answer. I wondered, were they hate letters, were they good, bad, do I want to read them? Would they make things worse?

I know that as they began their "informative speech" Glenn stopped them and told them he was a deputy, that he knew the procedure, and that they could leave now. I know they left fairly quickly after that.

I know that once the door was shut, my husband, a man of little emotion and calm in all situations previously, gathered us together and cried, cried out loud as he looked to heaven and spoke these words, "Jesus, please help my family get through this." I know that we cried together for a couple more hours before notifying anyone else. The guilt immediately kicking in, we had to comfort one another when we began to explain what we should have done differently, done at all, or thought would have made a difference. Bryce seemed the most comforting, "Logan was Logan and there was nothing we could have done."

What I don't know is how we made it through those moments, hours. How the body doesn't just give out is a miracle.

What we learned later is that Logan spent the night of the 13th with his good friends (including best friend, Jared) at a video game tournament in Denver. I have heard accounts from a few different people of this night, but all were of Logan in a pleasant, happy mood. Jared saw no signs and never detected the emptiness that he was wrestling with. Was he having a great time doing what he loved? Or was he in a euphoria because he knew the pain was ending soon? Or was it all so much effort that it became clearer than ever that he didn't want to fight the battle anymore?

We learned he had researched how to buy a gun 2 days after resigning. Was he only thinking at that time and not necessarily planning? Could a conversation with him accelerated his acting, or potentially only slowed it down a short time?

We learned that he had applied for the gun permit online around 1:00. He was approved within an hour and then used it to purchase a gun online. He could have left right away but seemingly waited for Amaya to get home. He arose from upstairs around 3:45, grabbed some snacks from the garage, and came in and gave Amaya a nice hug. She thought it a little odd but had no reason to be alarmed.

"Bye, Amaya" he said as he walked out the door for the last time.

#suicideawareness #mentalhealthawareness #misshimsomuch

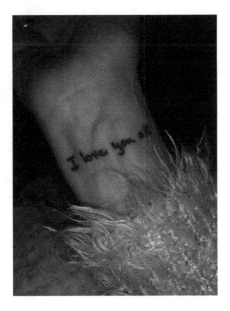

## DECEMBER 14, 2018

It did my 🤍 good today. I found out yesterday that a few of Logan's friends were graduating from UCCS, including his best friend, Jared. As the group of friends that were going to attend grew, I knew Logan would have been there and felt very compelled to be there in his place.

He might have laughed at this thought or maybe loved the idea. I really feel like it would make him so happy, though, to know how much his friends mean to me, and hopefully I to them 🖤 . We are "pieces" of a puzzle that can somehow be connected even if the edges are jagged (because there is something still very much absent).

At times it was hard to think about how Logan should have been there as a graduate and not just a sideline cheerleader. He spent 3 years at UCCS.

But I wasn't there to dwell on sadness. I was there to celebrate and enjoyed being included in Jared's family seats throughout the ceremony. I was surprised at how many other names I recognized. Also so exciting to think I will get to do this in only a few short months with my Savannah.

On this eve day of such significance in our lives now, I can think of no better place to be than surrounded by people that remind me so much of Logan. In celebration of their accomplishments. I hope these friends and families can grasp just how much they mean to me.

Congrats to all of you! 🎉

#UCCS2018 #findingjoy #heshouldbehere

## DECEMBER 15, 2018

As you all know by now, I'm NOT a human of few words...but reflecting on what I wrote a year ago, those few words still sum up how I feel.

We did love Logan the best we knew how.

We have been carried through this year of unbearable pain, only because of our HOPE in things eternally. God can make all bad things turn into something good and has been the only way we can imagine getting through the worst circumstance that could ever happen to us.

Love and many thanks to all of you who have prayed, reached out, encouraged, cried, left gifts, hugged, made meals, and most important-ly...change the way you live life in remembrance of Logan.

#suicideawareness #oneyeargone

## DECEMBER 16, 2018

Yesterday was 1 year since we lost our Logan. Wow. I can't explain time. I mean, in some ways it seems like 3 years and in other ways, it's been 3 weeks. I'm somewhere in between trying to find when and where the tide is.

I've read a couple of good books that have helped me, but the theme on any grief info is: everyone in their own time, grief is different for each person at different times, it comes in waves, and you can't predict it.

Yup. I can attest that it's all true and it makes for trying family dynamics at times.

One more thing...sometimes the anticipation of a day or date can be way worse than the actual moment/day.

I think this happened to me yesterday. I was so worried. I mean, I know we all had ideas of what that day would be like: awful, painful, crying all day, negative, sad, reliving every moment, etc.

Well, it wasn't. We had a mostly joyful day. I think I cried less than I had any day at least 2 weeks before.

We saw beauty in the mountains. We got to spend time together talking about the future (our house, meeting new neighbors).

And we got to spend time with so many people that loved Logan and us. I loved seeing how many of his friends came out to have a burger at the same spot they often did when he was present. This group, they are family. It made my heart so comforted once again that he had that family. They loved him and he loved them. This wasn't about lonely.

And so many other dear friends and family cared to celebrate making it through the year.

Celebrate—that's what we did. We chose JOY. Prayers are powerful and we are continuing to feel them. I genuinely felt warm fuzzies and enjoyed smiling. Yes, I had my times this week. (Logan's birthday hit me way harder than I imagined and way harder than yesterday.) Other events this week caused my mind to feel vulnerable, and fragile, but I made it through. And sometimes you can run out of tears...I believe that to be true.

But yesterday? No big sobbing mess. There has been a time and place for that, but peace carried us through so that we could be present.

Thanks for all who came, who wanted to come, who reached out via text/message, who prayed, and who remembered. Each of you made a difference.

Thank you from all the Boarman's. 🩶

#choosejoy          #suicideawareness          #mentalhealthawareness
#misshimsomuch

#itsbeenayearsincemylifechangedforever

## DECEMBER 17, 2018

Logan was known to be an amazing big brother, playing all sorts of things to keep Savannah happy. 🩶

He was so sweet at 8 years old to write to Santa on behalf of his sister (did he secretly want one, too 🙄😄).

#misshimsomuch

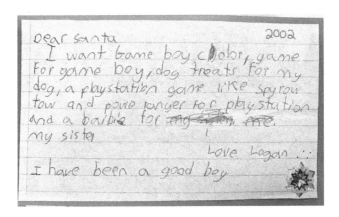

## DECEMBER 18, 2018

What does this look like to you?

Is it *just* a humidifier? What if I told you it's a super special emblem?

You see...when I finally decided to go into Logan's room, I saw it plugged in, sitting on the floor at the end of his bed. I reached and grabbed it and actually hugged it like it was a treasure worth hundreds of dollars. For me it was way more than just a humidifier, it was a symbol of my efforts to be a loving, caring mom.

Logan had complained of various ailments, which I mostly attributed to remaining in his cold, dark room for hours fixated on his computer screen. Regardless, always wanting to help I would offer suggestions and so when he approached me about his dry nose and throat, I bought him this humidifier. A need expressed, a need fulfilled. My motherhood mind is always crossing things off the list. But as a mom surviving the suicide of her son, we think we failed them and instinctively reject that we did all we could do and think of all those more things we could have done.

What ifs.

They flood everyone's mind after a suicide, even those that hardly knew Logan have reached out in apologies. But as a mom, we inflate our role in their death and want to stand firmly that our last parental act is remorse. Somehow that makes us think we are continuing to show our love and furnishing their needs, but of course, it's only in our heads and acting on those wishes will do no good, our children are dead and there are no more chances. Maybe we feel connected to them in this way, that we are still trying to be a mom by attempting to figure out what we failed to provide.

So with this struggle, it is advised to make a list of the great things you did for your child. Of course, this is helpful, but it does feel like we are putting ourselves on trial and submitting all the evidence. But I also know it has to be a fair trial. So I can submit evidence all day long, but I'm not deity and recognize there are limits to what I could change. When evil forces its way in, and we allow it, it can take over and deprive one of *hope*, which is exactly what happened in Logan's case.

"I'm sorry my hope has run out," he wrote in a letter he left. So I remind myself I offered that hope.

I remember the first and only day he asked me to leave his room. When I verbalized that ever since he had rejected his faith, his life had turned dark. I continued to invite him to church and promised to be patient.

We purchased a gym membership to take the burden off trying to figure out where and when to work out.

I used my network and worked behind the scenes to get him transferred from School of Mines to UCCS after he struggled his freshman fall semester.

I mapped out what it would look like if he changed his degree. I told him I would accompany him to a visit with the dean.

I went with him to the doctor when he wanted to figure out why he struggled to eat.

I begged him to see another counselor after he didn't like the one we had a couple of appointments with.

I sat through a second viewing of a 20/20 special on video game addiction I had watched and begged him to dissect.

I invited him numerous times to play indoor soccer with us.

I prayed during a movie he agreed to attend with us ("A Case for Christ") in the last few months.

I paid for expensive running shoes in hopes his feet wouldn't hurt.

I did this and that and more...

...and I bought him a humidifier.

I have since moved that humidifier next to my bed. My bed is a commonplace of disorientation, guilt, regrets, and what-ifs, so I am using it as reconciliation and resuscitation of motherhood views of myself; it's positive evidence. You may see it as a humidifier, to me it's an emblem.

#hope #suicideawareness #mentalhealthawareness #misshimsomuch #whatifs

## DECEMBER 19, 2018

It took a few weeks to even begin to regain my thoughts and composer, but my momma always taught me to make sure and let people know they are appreciated. So I finally started writing thank you notes and trying to figure out how the heck I would be able to express gratitude to those that had truly stepped in and also wrapped us in major shields of protection. I really desired a tangible way to offer a piece of thankfulness to my 'angels,' and not just some generic gift card. Despite my obsessive personality, I don't always find the perfect gift, but in this case and to my already tattered heart's relief, I stumbled upon these precious angel tree ornaments.

With Logan's death knocking on Christmas door, everyone would have their trees up when this date circulated every year. Wanting these exceptional people to be reminded of the peace and hope and love they had offered, what better than an angel itself? And these angels have 2017 inscribed to easily recall the year, placed perfectly on what I believe could be a symbol: Logan's book of life. They even offered a token where I could personalize them by carving Logan's name in remembrance. Ironic maybe, but they are the same willow tree brand that our 'Logan angel' is that we found in Estes Park.

You know the warmth and joy when you feel you've discovered that perfect gift? #findingjoy

It truly soothed my soul to hand them out. #bettertogivethanreceive

Thank you to a few of you that have sent me pictures of your angels displayed. #grateful

## DECEMBER 20, 2018

One of the very hardest things about Logan's death has been experiencing this grief journey parallel but incongruently. I'm talking about my immediate family here: Glenn, Bryce, Savannah, and Amaya. The cries of suicide are brutal, and they are often without tears or sound. Only you know what's going on inside.

While Glenn went to work only a week later, I took off 6 months. He needed something to fill the space and time in his head, while I needed to have time and space to be able to find the info to fill it.

My family didn't want more information while I couldn't help but dive into every aspect of every detail I could find. I searched Logan's computer, I read the police report, I met with his co-workers, I even listened to his dispatch call. It's like I was performing a psychiatric autopsy. I wanted any answer or clue or peace or piece that I could find, while they couldn't bear hearing anything surrounding details. It's like I felt obligated to accompany him through the end.

I needed to see what was left of Logan's physical presence and have that one last touch, while Glenn and the kids all stayed home.

I needed (and let's be real, still do) to talk out what happened, what the past was and how it weaved its way into our new future. That appeared to be something Savannah needed for about 24 hours and then she didn't want to talk about it anymore. I don't think today she still has had but only a very few private conversations regarding the how and potential why.

I became immersed in writing and sharing publicly my thoughts on suicide and the effects it was having on us, while I rarely hear anything regarding them (from family) despite the Facebook world reaching out to me faithfully.

I needed to make people remember it had been a year. I wanted to get together with friends in the hopes of hearing lasting memories accidentally omitted to be shared previously. I didn't want anyone to forget Logan already. My family grumbled at my efforts to bring everyone together on his one year death anniversary; they didn't want to be around "a crying fest." I had all these great ideas like everyone bring an ornament that says something about you or your relationship with Logan and we'll have a special tree up every year with them displayed. But all I heard from my group texts for input and agreement were crickets. I'm glad I moved forward with the day anyway. We didn't do anything special except to meet at Logan's favorite restaurant, but it was a day of sharing and smiles (at least on the outside) and not of sobbing and sorrow. Maybe what we fear is what we most need? Or maybe they just faked it really good that day.

And while early on the tears and moods are predictable and expected, after some time, just like the outside world, it's easy to be less forgiving and remember to attribute anger, depression, and coldness to grief. You make assumptions on others, despite knowing your grief is front and center to every character trait you have.

And then there are moments where you gradually have a decent day, and you expect your family to be right at the same tier. Oftentimes they can be, but not necessarily in the same minutes, hour, or days. Or even weeks. It's hard to have your glimpses of joy be crushed because of others temporarily drowning. And then other times you are the one hit by lightening tumbling down that mountain while another is smiling at the sun peeking from behind those same clouds. And I don't even know what's better?? If we were all equal emotionally, it would be certain double hell. Maybe it was meant to be this way so we could always see the hope others are experiencing in those moments?

Some of the things that seemed 'easier' initially, like comforting, became much more difficult as the waves and certain emotions settled in. We seemed more focused and attentive in the first months, and now the blur of reality and grief depression makes it hard to see what another is going through. And even if you see it, how do you comfort someone on something you're struggling so intensely as well?

It seems there has been a gap created in being able to talk about him. It was 'the obvious' the first few months, but now I worry about reactions so I often resist saying his name; I can't take that risk. I long for the day I can bring up anything to do with Logan and not worry that someone is not ready to hear about it. But then I fear the longer it goes, the more unnatural it will be to mention him and will cause a suppressed reaction. There is no winning here. These thoughts crush me and cause physical pain.

I wish I felt like we knew each other better for being on the same path, but there is still so much inside that never comes out, I often still feel lonely. The fear of causing a trigger with someone else usually gives way to silence. I often cry alone and feel so depleted. I know I don't have the energy to give back to them what they would give in comfort. And while I know my family would sympathize in those moments, I don't want them to have to.

My family loves each other deeply and with our faith as a foundation, I'm confident we will stay intact throughout the journey. But we each have very different personalities, and even if we didn't... this is grief life. And it right now it really sucks.

#mentalhealthawareness #suicideawareness #grief

*Taken at Logan's memorial service*

## DECEMBER 21, 2018

One year ago today....we celebrated Logan Ray Boarman's life in a formal service at a church he was (practically) born and then raised in.

I'm not sure I can accurately really depict what goes through your mind. I feel like we all probably think about our own memorial services (wow, I just hate the word funeral...so hard for me to say and even write), but I had honestly never pictured my kids dying before me. Everyone says, "You should never have to bury a child", but people do it every day. I guess I was naive to think that couldn't happen to me.

Hey.....people, it could happen to you.

I'm not saying we are perfect. I'm not saying we never made mistakes. But Logan was raised in a middle-class family, in a great Jesus loving (and not religion-focused) church, in a great school, with lots of friends, with lots of extended family, with lots of resources, and lots of "unconditional" love. If you think suicide or death can't happen to your family, you're wrong. And I'm not saying we were "too good" to consider it could happen to us, I just don't think we ever really thought about it. Or thought about it seriously.

Back to the day...I remember this day, this week, as surreal. I mean, really...did that happen? Did we write an obituary, somehow trying to depict our child's life in a few paragraphs? Did we have to choose to cremate or bury? And wow are there a million urn decisions....wood, carvings, pictures, phrases...Glenn kept telling me money wasn't an issue but did this urn really even mean anything to me now? His spirit is in heaven—that's what mattered. I more was concerned about which parking spot he last took a breath. I wanted to leave his urn there, but of course, that's not an option.

Were we really asked about purchasing fingerprint souvenirs as if we had traveled to a place without a time?

Did we really have to choose if we were going to keep his clothes or not? At the time I thought, no way. Then a day later I regretted that and wanted his cream zip-up jacket I had seen him wear a million times plus. I didn't care the condition, I just wanted to see it. To smell it. To hold it. It was too late when I asked again, it's in the urn now. I feel like there are so many thoughts and emotions I could expand on (like the clothing thing), but probably not here as I make these posts longer than planned already. All of these decisions and questions continued to play out in my mind that day...and I already had seen regrets so I needed to make sure everything was perfect.

I know I didn't get much sleep the night before (or all week for that matter). I was making Logan's life video and picture slide show. Show...that word sounds like this was a show...ugh...again, I want to expand on words but won't...

With Savannah's help, we had muddled through probably 20,000 pictures, and enough hours of home movie videos that we could have made a couple hour long documentary. (I'm so thankful for all the times I've forced my kids to be on camera, no regrets there). I was still finishing getting it to Randy at the church by early morning. I remember then going through Logan's "tub" of memories and choosing a few to display when people walked in. Hoping, they would see something that connected them to my baby. Would Connie and Angela be there and see the Tickle Me Elmo they had managed to scrape away from the other 100s of people trying to purchase one that Christmas? Would Logan's Boy Scout leaders be there and see his uniform and belt with all the buckles he earned? Would they remember how hard he worked to have the best pinewood derby car? Would anyone who knew him as a young boy smile so big when they saw his stuffed Barney with the worn and torn books to go along with it? Would his teachers be there and recognize all his Science Olympiad medals, remembering how well he represented his school at even the national level...wait, I couldn't find those. It's still a mystery where they are and so now I seem to want them more than anything. (Want what you don't have? For me, it's a teen boy's medals he was so proud of.) I could have placed a million memories that day but had to choose among a few, hoping as people saw them they would be reminded of my precious son and how he had impacted them. It was like taking pieces of my heart and putting them on display. Still trying to decide if that's comforting or not.

Lastly, I remember how physically hard that day was. I felt like I was hyperventilating all day and at one point, when Savannah was in my room helping me get dressed, I turned to her and said, "I know now what they mean when they say they couldn't catch a breath". It's really not just a saying, I felt so heavy chested that it was difficult to breathe. Each breath was strained and exhausting. She agreed. There are other ways the body reacts, but this was by far the most significant as I can remember.

And then, we made our first trip as a family of 5 to the church. I can only imagine what everyone in that car was thinking, but I looked out the window only to be so jealous of all the people I saw. After all, it was a typical Thursday afternoon just before 3:00. Were they hurrying to get that last present? Out buying ingredients for dinner? Were they on their way to pick up their babies from school?

Whatever they were doing, I wanted to be them. I pictured all the services I had seen on TV, staged and real. The views of the families traveling with the tear-jerking music playing in the background and the cameras capturing them with their somber faces and tissues.

This was us.

Only people didn't know where we were headed.

#suicideawareness     #suicidesucks     #mentalhealthawareness
#misshimsomuch

## DECEMBER 25, 2018

Hardest parts in the last 24 hours:

As I walked the dogs, the air, trees, cold...scenery...all "senses" are the same as exactly one year ago...

Heading to celebrate the birth of our Christ; similarly dressed up, at about the same time of day, and the same place we celebrated Logan's life's end.

Sending the candlelight down the row of family...knowing one light will never be lit again.

Taking family pictures. Without our entire family.

Watching "A Christmas Story" without him. Oh, how excited he was to watch that movie year after year. I especially remember him laughing at those stupid jokes.

Stuffing the stockings...leaving his hanging empty.

Going to bed, knowing I didn't have to think about what to purchase for him this year. I so wish I had that struggle.

Waking up seeing his ornaments staring at me as we gathered around the tree.

Receiving so many sweet messages from people that care, but a constant reminder that we are hurting.

Missing our main distributor of the presents. Logan loved to figure out the owner of each one, and always handed them over with such joy.

Holding hands as we thanked the Lord for our food. Why is it times like this just burn the core...knowing the circle is not complete? Nor will it ever be. again.

*Christmas Eve 2016*

#misshimsomuch       #mental-healthawareness #suicideawareness

## DECEMBER 28, 2018

I can't help but share this again. Please don't stop talking about my Logan to me. As a parent, your worst fear is people forgetting and not talking about your baby anymore.

#misshimsomuch

## DECEMBER 28, 2018

Most everyone is excited to jump into the new year; goals and wishes for what's to come. Some of you had an awful 2018 and can't wait to get a start on something you're hoping will be better. I read your posts...bad things happened...and there is something about the numbers changing to a higher one that gives us a renewed excitement that things can be different.

As far as the numbers changing in my house, they will not increase. We will be a family that still has a room empty that another digit change cannot fill. I have some hope in new things to come, but nothing will satisfy me like my son coming back, which he won't.

I am not excited for the new year because it's one more year that all of our memories of Logan will be more tucked away.

Time. There is the time when Logan was here, and now the time that he is not. I'm desperate for healing and not to feel this way forever, and yet I don't want time to move forward. It scares me to know his existence will be that much more forgotten. One day I will be the mom that lost her son __ years ago. Somehow it seems like I will lose my credibility to know what it's like because it will be another year's number scrolled by from the past and I should be better and fine like before.

The calendar filling up without his name anywhere on it...the calendar filling up without grief work scheduled in...the calendar filling up like life is just getting back to normal...

But it's really only on paper, right?

It's really only a number: 2019.

It's really NOT just a number...It's the world dreaming, hoping, planning.

And it's me...sitting here wishing the numbers would just scroll the other way.

#choosingjoy    #notsohappynewyear
#mentalhealthawareness

## DECEMBER 30, 2018

Like many myths, the high divorce rate following the death of a child is one that snowballed out of proportion. One researcher back in 1977 said 90% of couples were in serious danger within months. No one challenged sources or questioned, and so like many others, someone's statement became a fact. Grief experts are now disputing this. New stats are showing numbers like this: only 16 percent of the parents divorce after the death of a child and only 4 percent said it was because of the death...that there were problems in the marriage way before the child died.

So many people were quick to warn us following Logan's death, also assuming those ugly stats of 90% were true. Although I had a peace about it and confidence in our relationship, it was still unnerving. Once my counselor told me it wasn't true...that couples that divorce was in all likelihood going to anyway, it just speeds it up...I had renewed hope and comfort. Amazing how your mind goes down certain pathways when you are lead there.

Has it been easy? In all honesty, mostly.

Not the answer you were expecting, right?

But our many years of marriage, and work at it, has produced thick layers of trust, selfishness, love, and respect. Nerves that were raw and unprotected were revealed, but a substantial digging has only hit clay, capable of being molded, or even better, rock.

The feeling of isolation in grief is more devastating if your belief is that you are going through it alone. I never felt this way. It's liberating to know there is someone that relates, but what about someone that is feeling so many of the same emotions, thoughts, and agonizing questions?...maybe not always exactly, but someone that knows how I got here...

...knows the pains I've endured to shape me up to this point and happy moments that also made me the person I am today. And then there is the awareness, personally within these walls, of the trials, attempts of restoration, time, energy, celebrations, tears, and hugs that were given directly relating to Logan.

To be able to be comforted by that person that transcends my thoughts and struggles makes me almost whole...if it weren't for missing one 'hole'.

One struggle for us comes from the unfamiliarity of the situation. Nothing had happened before where we could use lessons learned....oh this is how we handled that last time...

No point of reference. All we can do is take it one day at a time, well because as common as days will be, is there a norm?

Another big struggle is navigating this as unique individuals. We all grieve differently (a myth that it's a process of straight lines and order) and we are often in different places of the complex journey. Sometimes even meandering within the varied stages throughout a single hour.

How are we surviving? Not individually, but together? As our anniversary approached, I started reflecting.

- Seeking counseling. Helped us learn to understand where we are and where we want to be.
- Openness and communication. Sometimes calling out the other, simply stops the behavior and produces waves of tears and leads to hugs. Usually what we are expressing or how we are acting, has nothing to do with anything, but grief; sadness.
- Being self-aware. "I'm sorry." Realizing what moment you are actually in...the truth about what is bothering you...those 2 words wipe away so many marks on the heart.
- Kinda the same as being self-aware, but recognizing that emotions are so close to the surface. They are, more often than not, exaggerated one way or another.
- No expectations. We are both pretty productive and motivated people, but more often than not in the last year, we have been tired. Mentally exhausted. Physically exhausted. Allowing the "no's" to events and days of accomplishing nothing have been soothing and respectful.

- Physical touch. Sometimes that's all it takes to get the tears flowing, but also to then, a few minutes later, have a significantly improved mood. It's innate for us to want to feel secure. I love being held, it gives me peace. Even when there is nothing to say, which is often, just the touch is the acknowledgment and validation we need.
- Not judging. We have both said and done things that were not our typical selves. Allowing these moments to happen and remembering where they stem from, helps move forward in optimism instead of dwelling on the evil that takes hold at times.
- Allowing our tears to flow. I believe one of the top 2 things that have brought us forward together (faith together being the other), has been my man's owning of his heart. He has stepped forward in ways I never imagined simply by allowing his love to show through the pain on his face, the crumbling of his body, and the weeping of his eyes. There is more strength in allowing, then withholding.
- The body of Christ. The hundreds of people that have prayed for us have no doubt given us so much peace and turned days and moments to light instead of dark.
- Friendships. The cards, gifts, notes, meals, and hugs have kept both of us very afloat. No doubt it lifts our spirits. People will never know the effect we've had because of them. You.
- Family. All of them.
- Faith. Having HOPE. Together. Is the single most effective aspect of us surviving. Knowing we will see our Logan again makes all the difference. Spending time together doing daily devotions, and leaning on Jesus is no doubt kept us from living in a pit. Intentional choices of joy, love, and hope all come from feeling secure in where we are going.

As tragic as it can be, we have learned more about ourselves and life in general- together. We have a long way to go, but I am confident the corners, and edges of the puzzle are nailed in place and cannot be torn apart or lost.

When people say they can't imagine, it always brings me to the thoughts of, "I can't imagine doing this without faith and a Glenn".

Glenn, I love you so much and thank you for choosing me.

#wearemakingit #suicideprevention #suicideawareness #mentalhealthawareness #misshimsomuch

Happy 28 to us 🙌 🎉

#wemadeit #lovehimsomuch

**DECEMBER 31, 2018**

Hi Mrs. Boarman,

You don't know me but I'm friends ▮▮▮▮▮▮▮ ▮▮▮▮

I found your FB page through Bryce; you had tagged him in a post after Logan took his life. I've found myself reading every single one of your posts on his death ever since.

I want to thank you for your honesty and vulnerability. If it weren't for your words about Logan and the seriousness of depression I wouldn't have ever gone to seek help myself. I've struggled with depression for a long time and in the past year it's gotten very bad. I was driving home from workout one day and almost crashed my car into the side of the highway. I was ready to do it and decided the next time I was driving I would do it. Later that day I read a post of yours about how you wished Logan had said something to you or someone else because it could've saved his life. I'm not sure how or why but right after that I told my mom about my suicidal thoughts. I've been on medication and in therapy for the last six months. It's a very long and often dark road but praise God I'm still here and finding restoration in His mighty love and grace. I'm telling you all this because I want you to know, you saved my life Mrs. Boarman. You're boldness to talk about Logan's depression so openly made the emptiness in my soul ache and it encouraged me to seek help. It was such a God thing how I found you on FB but it was all in His will. I pray everyday for you and your family. Logan is in heaven, resting in God's arms and feeling no pain anymore. One day I'll be there too, but for now I'm fighting to stay here until the Lord calls me home. I have you to thank for that.

Mental health has such a negative stigma, but I'm so grateful you've helped to change that. You're words are reaching more people than you know.

I can't wait for your book; I'll be one of the first people in line to read it.

God bless you.

**DECEMBER 31, 2018**

A huge pet peeve of mine is when something great happens to people and they follow it with, "God is so good."

They got the job, "God is good."

Their day twisted from bad into something not expected, "God is good."

Their cancer is gone, "God is so good!"

While I believe that He IS good, I feel like by saying these things we portray Him as only being good when things are great and life is going well. This makes people feel estranged and it also makes it easier for them to turn away from faith.

What I want people to hear, is that God is good ALL THE TIME. God isn't good just because we get that job. And...I'm not saying we have to go around being excited when things go bad (like we didn't get the job) either.

But, He's good because He grieves and mourns with us and carries us as He's redeeming our pain and healing our hearts. I think he is super sad for the things that we struggle with, and never plans or wants an unfortunate event to happen.

I've had to continue to navigate through life figuring out why God is good when you get to celebrate holidays with your son, while mine is dead of his own hand. 💔

But, I continue to be confirmed that He can ALWAYS make something good come from what we perceive as bad (or even life-ending). When we trust that we don't know the whole story and give Him the control, we allow Him to navigate the journey and have that HOPE that He'll take care of the things along the way.

This isn't it...this isn't the whole story.

Unfortunately, it's not always revealed to us the seeds we plant, but this morning I found this message in my FB inbox. I hope you cry with me as you read it and celebrate that Logan's life-ending story made a difference for another mom's precious daughter. 💚

Something really, really, good came from something unimaginable.

#grateful #hope #Godisgoodallthetime #suicideawareness #mental-healthawareness

## DECEMBER 31, 2018

*Dear Logan,*

*I have been thinking I would write a letter to you at one year. I've thought about it over the months many times and what it would contain. Only, it's one year later and I'm still not even sure what to say. I want to put so much into words, but they don't come to me.*

*Of course, there is the typical plea that you know how much I loved you, how much I do love you, and how much I will always love you. But it still seems inconceivable that you are not here and that it's a letter I have to convey my feelings through. Written words rather than just being able to hold you and look you in the eye. And the reality that you won't even be reading this, it's really just for me because it's supposed to help my pain. And many people think you will hear it, but I don't. My hope is that you are in Heaven and I know there is no sorrow or pain in that great place so no way you know what's going on down here!*

*Every time I think about what to say, my mind flutters away to thoughts about the events, and then on to what I could have done, and then I just see your face as you walked upstairs that last time I saw you and hurts in a way I can't articulate. It's just all hurt for me right now. What if time doesn't do what it's supposed to do? What if these moments are always only remembered as heartache? Logan, I will work hard at remembering you with compassion and not letting suicide define you.*

*Time is such a dimension, a weird phenomenon I'm trying to understand. In so many ways, it seems like the events happened just a few weeks ago, and in that same stream of thoughts, it feels like it's been so many years. How do you have both? Logan, I've never experienced so many emotions that clash and seem so opposite, how can one experience things on such conflicting spectrums, at the same time or in the same minutes, hours or days. This is the confusing part of grief. Logan, we are surviving but what does that really even mean? Because we get out of bed and put on clothes and shop for food? We might do those things but we don't like it. In fact, we hate it. This has completely defined our lives now in every way. I don't say that to make you feel guilty or bad, I say it as my way of expressing how much you meant to us. You acknowledged you knew you were loved in your letter, but I still don't think you had any idea. Saying you hoped our lives would get better?*

*Still, one thing I hold on to is that we can't blame you. In the end, you weren't yourself and so you can't be held accountable. I wished early on you would have realized you had the support system and then learned coping skills and your pain threshold…but that didn't happen…Your clothes were in the dryer… I don't think you planned it that day, except that you couldn't get out of that dark moment like you had potentially before. I can't understand why that didn't happen for you. I just can't.*

*There are the times we've been able to function (on the outside) through routines and days and events like before, only it takes so much effort. I literally can't do anything without embodying you; your face, what you would think or do. Would you be on this trip with me? Where would you be living? Would you eat this rare meal I prepared? Would you buy me a birthday card this year? Would you be excited about this or that, or would depression still have a hold on you? I usually think happy things, because I always had hope for you. I always thought the next day, the next event, would be the new beginning for you. I never saw it being over before it starting new.*

*After a year of analyzing over and over, my biggest regret? Is that I didn't ask you, Logan. "Are you thinking of taking your life?"*

*In the last days, I felt your pain somehow, it's like your questions of life ran through my soul like they were mine. I predicted your thoughts and even verbalized some of them to my good friend from work on the day you ended them. I didn't understand completely at the time my worry and wasn't sure if what I was feeling was real or just another mother's overanalyzing. But somehow I still knew, it wasn't a typical worry for me, but I guess I didn't know how to respond to it. At work, I always teach parents to go with their gut, but I didn't go with mine. I pride myself on communicating, but I failed you. I failed my own son. I know your refusal to get help limited us from giving it, but now I am trying to cope and turn from saying how guilty I feel, to calling them regrets. Because that's what the books and therapists say to do.*

*It works some of the time. All I keep asking for is enough peace to get me through until the next day.*

*I say I can't find the words, and then all the things that are different come rushing in, crushing my heart to where it actually hurts like physical pain. I think I thought this letter would contain all those things you needed to know that are different now; the missing pieces, updates on specific aspects of our life and maybe even how I see life differently. But honestly, that letter would never end. The list is not only already too long, but things get added daily. There's no room outside my brain for sharing all the loss, so I just shared a few things floating around.*

*I remember the many talks we had when your dad and I were concerned about you. We always ended with a hug and "I love you." I want to end this that way again, only I can't hug you. Suicide is an unfinished conversation. But I'm going to finish it by telling your story because the needs of the living take precedence. You learn a lot about someone when they're gone and I can imagine you would be okay with that; you wanted to help people. I'm still trying to figure out what is left, knowing what is gone, but I'm hanging on to what is to come…what of your story is possible to save others.*

*I love you so so much,*

*Mom*

# JANUARY 2019

## JANUARY 1, 2019

When Logan died (yes, I hate that word but it *is* what happened), so many friends—best friends, church friends, family friends, co-worker friends, and even distant friends, stepped into a world of unknown. MY world of unknown. A world often absent of words, where scars can become obvious again, where their own scabs might be ripped to bleed anew, where there are no manuals or guidebooks, and where emotions can float on the surface.

But I have received a lot of my strength from these friends. That they are willing to be vulnerable with me is such a gift. Really one of the best gifts you could give someone going through a tragedy. To not be afraid to walk alongside uncharted territory—that's love. And I sure do feel loved.

But sometimes people want to share a tangible gift. One that when they walk away or aren't in reach, can be felt, or seen. More than just cards and words of goodwill. My co-workers were one of these groups of friends that wanted to leave me with something I could reach my emotions with, in a physical way.

What's frightening about this you wonder? When you are entering the realm of a mother/son bond, it's a scary place to fall short in...

...what if the color isn't right

...what if it's not aligned correctly

...what if the quality seems only fair

...what if the end result is not what is expected or desired

...what if a precious valuable gets destroyed or ruined in the production

...what if the timing isn't right? What if the expected finish date gets altered?

...what if it brings up unwanted emotion in the creator...can they finish? Will they be able to push through their own tears?

So many what-ifs when friends don't want to let each other down.

And so I am grateful I have friends that are willing to initiate and undertake such a special and important endeavor.

Most of you know it took me a year to venture into Logan's room and expose my heart to those intense feelings and emotions. But, that is where the t-shirts remained. So the project duration had to be extended. While sometimes it seemed ridiculous that I couldn't just walk down there, I prayed that I would know when the timing was right. I'm thankful I allowed myself to not worry about what others thought or conformed to what I and others might think is "normal." There is nothing normal about this and I continue reaching for every confirmation that these words are true. It's really hard sometimes. And I'm really hard on yours truly. Trying to be self-aware at the beating I bestow. But that's really another post.

I wish I could put into words what Logan's t-shirts mean to me. They symbolize so much.

T-shirts were his attire of choice; From the time he could choose until age 23. I thought he would surely choose to get married in one.

These shirts express passions of his, ventures of his, and even aspirations.

Looking at the vast topics, these pieces of cloth, sum up so much of my Logan.

Logans shirts—my memories—were stitched together with the utmost love and created into new joy; an amazing quilt. This week, with an emotional exchange of hands, it came back to reside forever in our home and our hearts.

While there are others to be thanked and hugged (I so appreciate each and every one of you), I am beyond grateful for the creative mind, intuitive thoughts, and talented results that Sprout Hunt made into one of the best gifts I have ever received. It's truly perfect and I wouldn't trade anything about it. (Well, unless you can put laminate on it to preserve forever!)

Thank you for being vulnerable.

It has touched our family...forever. 🥹
♥️🙏

#findingjoy  #mentalhealthawareness
#Suicideawareness

#griefsucks          #lovemyfriends
#thankful

## DECEMBER 10, 2019

This week is nearly two years to the day our lives changed forever. I'd like to say for the better, and while there *is some* better, I still feel it's for the worse. "I hope your lives improve and you find and keep happiness," is what Logan concluded his letter to us with. I wished I could honor his wishes, but we can never be complete again and so there is nothing that can make it *better*. As good as it might get, it will always be shy of *better*.

I'll admit, time does heal some, meaning I don't walk around unable to control my emotions in every situation. I find myself preserving my tears (and being able to) more and more for quiet time and away from disrupting the rest of the world. The summer was hard, I feel both Glenn and I were in a depression. Still doing life but not a lot of happy moments and emotions running high. But seasons change; we are doing much better. I am really living just one day at a time, so much like they say to. Trying to be in the moment and not pressuring myself with too many goals.

I continue to hear, "I can't imagine" and for that, I respond, "I can't either." You see, it's 'unimaginable.' If you look up the definition for that you get: impossible to comprehend. I still can't realize, grasp, understand what happened and therefore still really can't believe it; just like you think. So when I feel numb, I'm still unsure if it's denial to survive or I simply am unable to perceive reality. By definition, you can't understand the unimaginable. I have to repeat back these words to you. I can tell you about some bad days, some terrible triggers, some hard moments and even give you a glimpse of what it's like when you want to give up. But I think it's preservation of the body to not be able to stay in that state and therefore I end up...

Everything is now in relation to before Logan died, or after Logan died.

Bryce has been working for the Olympic Committee and recently just got a new job within the walls of the same building/entity downtown. He's been traveling the world and I was able to join him on a trip to Italy recently. It's hard to continue to do memories with my children and not constantly think about the ones I won't be doing with Logan.

Savannah graduated from college in May with her BSN. She moved into an apartment with a schoolmate across town and got hired in my department at the hospital. So we are now both NICU RN's and I'm loving that I get to see her, if not just in passing since she works nights and me days, a few more times a week. Extra hugs are always so good for my mental state.

Amaya is in 7th grade at the Junior High. She is playing on the top club soccer team in Colorado Springs and travels quite frequently. She is very mature for her age and is the only one requesting and attending counseling.

Glenn continues to work for the Sheriff's Department and is spending many weekends tearing apart some logs that resided on our property we hope to build on soon. He's continued to be open about showing his emotions. It's been such a blessing to me and a great example to all the kids.

I am still working part-time as a NICU RN. As I've said before, I would rather not be in a job with a schedule, but I do so love what I do. My

Plexus (side gig) continues to pay the property mortgage, but I have found little motivation to work it actively. My time has been focused elsewhere and as much as I love and believe in the products, I find myself much more introverted these days and just keeping to myself. I've really become a homebody enjoying dogs.

Speaking of dogs, our beloved Mowgli had to be put down in May after the meds and seizures wore on him. It was incredibly hard as he will always be our 'heart dog.' In an effort to keep my brain filled to the max and keep time from slipping in and giving way to free-flowing anguish thoughts (Glenn says I always create my own stress), we have decided to show and breed St. Bernards. We've been in love with the breed for quite some time and they have helped fill horrendous voids. Marlo and Lolly made the 2nd and 3rd girls joining Mia. We still have 2 cats and Puppers, our Yorkie who of course thinks he is the boss of all. My favorite part of the day is any part with my dogs. They are so intuitive giving hugs, and my walks with them viewing our amazing Colorado mountains always gives me a tad more peace and smiles. When I'm talking to my puppies as I often do, I want to mention things they would remember about Logan and have to remind myself Mia was only 6 months old, and the other two Saints never met him. They were robbed of his love; life without Logan is moving faster than I want.

Logan's room remains intact just as he left it. I have been unable to get rid of anything except for some games and t-shirts that were offered to his friends. As we move towards getting the house ready to sell, determining what to keep surely will be the most difficult task.

Logan's friends have thankfully kept in touch and I have hope we will be a part of their lives forever. They truly are a connection I am most thankful for; such a huge piece of Logan I can physically hang on to.

We have decided to celebrate Logan's birthday this year, and not the day of his death. His ashes remain in his urn in a curio cabinet in the dining room, along with some favorite memorabilia. We still haven't discussed what, if anything, we will do with them. They honestly don't do that much for me, for it is our spirits that live on.

Putting Logan's death aside, we have faced more tragedy/devastation in the last 2 years than all our years put together. But we still have so much to be thankful, grateful for and continue to focus on all the positives our lives. I have learned so much and still know that God is good no matter what.

# FAKE

Fake. That's how I sum up this last year of grieving.

I was thinking about it last night...brushing my teeth I was very much in my head and was feeling bad. I had been at my work Christmas party trying so hard to have fun. And I really do enjoy these people and did *mostly* have fun. But underneath that was me constantly thinking about the day. And then expressing my pain later in a post, a co-worker apologizes for not realizing. Welp that's not her fault, it's me being fake.

While I can genuinely have fun, its not without an internal awareness. Me thinking things like:

Wow, I'm having fun despite. You seem to be having a little fun Lori, did you forget already? Lori, enjoy this moment because it won't last. Do you think people think I'm doing great because I'm having fun this moment?

At first, it's the obvious thing that everyone is thinking so it's evident in every touch, tone and content of conversations. Sure there are a few that leave the elephant in the room, but overall, people know. But after a while people assume you aren't thinking about it all the time. And you hope they don't just identify you with the death of your son, but yet secretly you are screaming for them not to forget.

Logan dying still hasn't escaped my thoughts enough. Yesterday was me thinking about it being the eve of December 15th...the whole dang day. Today is the 15th and how do you escape that even if it's just a day on the calendar? Last week it was me thinking about the 15th being only a week away. And tomorrow my thoughts will be on the day before. And in 6 months it will be 6 more months until the next December 15th. It's always something. And I know everyone knows this about greif and I don't need to be told it's okay to feel this way. I know that too. And of course it's heavier on my heart right now, dah...but still, nearly everywhere I go, I'm being fake. I'm pretending like it's not bothering me. I'm pretending like I'm not aware of dates or that they won't effect my thoughts like they do.

Instead of me listening to conversations, I'm being fake and wondering...do they know the day is coming up? Do they know I'm hurting as we are laughing? Do they know I'm trying to figure out if they know I've lost a child? Do they realize I cried for 10 min before our conversation? Do they know 'I know' they are watching to see my reaction to a certain comment? Do they know 'I know' they are looking at me to see my reaction to a certain song? Do they know when I make a sniffle I realize they turn to make sure I'm okay? Do they know I'm struggling despite clicking a happy face 'like' and making a sweet comment? Do they know that 'I love you' won't leave my mind for while? Do they know I really want to help, but fear I don't have the answers for their mental health questions? Do they know how much I appreciate their cards or messages...but that it does often trigger more emotions...but that they mean so much I keep every single one and anticipate the next one? A doctor approaches me with a simple conversation...does he know I am still thinking how appreciative I am that he came to Logan's service? When someone hasn't seen my husband for a while...do they know I'm wondering if they told their spouse, there they are...there he is the one that lost his son? Do they know I go to a bazaar with my dogs to get a Santa picture and leave thinking only about suicide because of a booth that was promoting mental health? Do they know when they give me a meaningful hug and ask how I'm doing and I answer vaguely that I really have so much more to say...but just don't want to say it. Do they know, do they know, do they know...?

Even if I make it through an hour not recognizing my inner thoughts, they seep in somehow. Often it's not a conscious awareness, but weird how every aspect of my life finds relation with my sons death when I contemplate them. It's like it's so consumed in all that I am, it's impossible to escape.

So, I can be a little fake, and I can be a lot fake. Although it's been much easier to hold off my tears, sometimes I'm working incredibly hard to do it, and other times I'm able to just redirect my thoughts. But I do it because you can't be a spectacle all day long. I don't need people feeling sorry for me all the time. I don't 'want' people doing that either. Most of the time I don't want comfort. And it gets old to have it be a a part of every interaction.

It's how you move through the process. Fake it till you make it. You begin pretending and not bringing it to the forefront of the conversation. Others stop asking because for one, 'they' don't want to keep bringing it up. And two, they know 'you' don't want to keep addressing it.

So if I'm being honest, I'm still faking it a lot. And even though I don't like to be fake (in fact I hate it), it's too exhausting for everyone, including myself, not too.

It's just the way it is.

I KNOW IT MAKES YOU UNCOMFORTABLE. IT MAKES ME UNCOMFORTABLE TOO.

#suicidesucks #suicideawareness #mentalhealthawareness#misshimsomuch #twoyears

# MEETING LOGAN'S CALL TAKER

The next time you're at Starbucks, look around and imagine why some of those people are there.

There just might be a two people meeting for the first time, and when you see them hug for an extended heavy embrace, smile. This encounter might be nearly 2 years coming and it might be like one of those feel good 20/20 stories where the 911 call taker gets to meet the mom whose son she saved.

But what if the son didn't live? How would that change things? Would they still even want to meet?

When I got a friend request last week from Christiina, I saw we only had one random friend in common. I checked her out and although I could see at best a few things, I did see she had just lost her brother...assuming she found me because of my grief posts, I accepted.

Only a few minutes later I was shaking, reading the words... "Hello Lori. I have wanted to reach out to you almost two years now. I had asked for advice, and was told to wait so I've hesitated for quite a while now. I think about Logan pretty much every day, and this morning when I saw a similar car to his, I just thought I couldn't wait any longer. I've always wanted to share my part of the story with you, only if you would like to hear it."

Did Logan have a girlfriend I know nothing about? Those thoughts filled my mind as I quickly wrote back saying, "please, please!"

She returned the message by sharing some memories of Logan... "instantly I knew he was a character...He made me lift my head and just smile...He would joke...he was amazing...Well Lori...I was the one who took the call that night."

Oh...wow...I didn't realize she 'knew' him.

Logan had began working as a 911 call taker just a couple months before, so his call to the line to give a location of his car as he was about to take his life was unique. I knew it was a female that night, and although my devoted mind always wants every last piece of data, I had never pursued more about 'this' lady because my understanding was that she did not really know him. I 'had' been thankful for that.

But that wasn't the case. The environment was fairly small and he worked her shift for an amount of time...and had taken a liking for him.

So on that night, it was a call that would forever change her. She says, "the most important call I will ever take." These are never easy or 'normal' calls, but this time she just sensed 'something'... and now is beating herself up for it. I should have recognized his voice, I should have told him he was special, I should have...I should have...I should have...

(This is one of the devastating patterns of suicide. It leaves so many questioning and wondering and regretting that a number of those effected is impossible to predict or measure)

But...what Christiina didn't know, was that I had listened to that call.

In my efforts to gather any and all knowledge to add to my summarization of the events, 'I had to.' It wasn't about judging the call taker, it was about knowing what my babies last words were.

And... 'I needed to' listen. I longed to know his demeanor. Was he scared? nervous? somber? sobbing? or just nonchalant... just like a typical Logan call would be?

But what would turn out to be the most important reason I listened to it, was so that I could ascertain to this amazing woman, that she did not fail us or Logan in that night. While she has been feeling like she "flunked her most important call-ever," and just plain "didn't do a good enough job," I was able to praise her efforts and tell her in all honesty that she did everything she should have done, could have done, and that I wished was done. And although no other Boar-

mans have listened to the call, I was sure that they all would agree and tell her the same.

But I needed to give her a hug. So...YES! We did meet and I was able to tell her these things in person, receive a much needed hug myself, and all of it, despite some tears, was so, so fulfilling. 💜

I am so saddened she hesitated until now, and lived so long with extensive anguish, but I'm so thankful she finally did reach out and we were each able to experience some closure. Information she offered utters there is still so much to be done regarding mental health aware-ness and the recognition of services available and training that should be done with those in the 911 world of Colorado Springs. Maybe we can somehow come together and make a difference?

Peace.

We were both able to get some of that good stuff. I gave her one of Logan's ornament angels I offered to those who had been angels to me.

No coincidence I had one left. 😇 She was reaching out to apologize, and instead I was able to hug her, thank her, and give her a tranquility she hasn't felt in nearly 2 years...and for me I was able to have just one more connection to my son. 🤍💔🤍

#suicideawareness #mentalhealthawareness

#findingsomepeace #misshimsomuch

Christiina Hannum
Yesterday at 1:29 PM · 🌐

I met with someone so dear to me, FINALLY. Almost 2 years have gone by since I got that call. Logan's call. For almost 2 years I have blamed myself for being the one who couldn't save him. And for almost two years I have waited and waited to reach out to his family. I finally did it. I met with his beautiful mother **Lori Logan Boarman**, and it was amazing. I finally have a sense of closure. I was able to share my piece to the puzzle and learn so much about his. It reminded me so much of my brother, so many similarities.. Logan was so special, I knew it right away from the first moment I heard him speak. Lori gave me this very special ornament, which is so perfect because I have an all year tree in my room. I now have a special piece to remind me of him every day, my 3rd guardian angel 🤍🤍
Logan, you hold such a special place in my heart. I love you forever buddy.

# ACKNOWLEDGMENTS

Grateful, thankful? There are no words for how much I have appreciated those who have embraced us and been brave enough to be by our
sides throughout, whether it was in person, through cards or gifts,
words, voice messages, or the best way possible—in prayer. While I
can't record all the names here, because for one it's a continuing list,
please know I cherish each and every one of you. I really do take time
to read back, reflect, and consider all the time and efforts of others. I
consider ourselves abundantly gifted.

Foremost, I want to thank my husband, Glenn, who knows my pain
best and has a shared love for Logan like no other. Thanks for
enduring my emotions, especially the darkest ones. There is no other I
would want to be by my side with on this journey. I admire your
candidness to grief and visible pain displayed openly to teach all those
around you what it's like to really hurt, and to do it with so much
integrity. Your closeness and continued trust in the Lord have made a
difference for me and your hugs and positive words towards me have
truly kept me alive. To Bryce, Savannah, and Amaya who I hurt for,
knowing the pain you've endured and will continue to. As you all
manage to read through many of the parts of this book, know I am
forever grateful for your private selves to allow our interpersonal

stories to be used to help others. Never doubt you have a great purpose, and my prayers are that you pursue it and find peace from all your trials. Thank you for playing such a significant role in Logan knowing, even in his hopelessness, that he was loved. I love you all.

To the rest of my family, who understand the enormity of this loss and have been a constant presence. In my own self-care, I have neglected to perceive your suffering and respond to it, but I thank you for tender care in ours. Heidi, your renewed friendship is at the top of the good that has come from ashes. Taylor, we have a special connection I cherish always. Auntie Marti, your faith and physical presence, especially for Amaya to witness consistently, is so admired and appreciated. Collin, you mean so much to me. The best words to summarize: the noun Angel, with the very important adverb "my" preceding it.

To Logan's friends for embracing me and sharing your grief and memories along the way. Your presence not only at the Service but how you have continued to keep his spirit alive, gives me so much peace in how my son was loved by you all. I'm most thankful for allowing me to experience an amazing connection to your friend, my son. Jared, I treasure your compassion towards me and maturity through losing a best friend. Thank you that Logan knew you were there for him.

Thank you to all in "the village":

My church family has been so valuable; a solid foundation, especially Pastor Stewart and Randy. Randy, you loved my son like no other, an incredible mentor and certainly one of the most important people in his entire life.

My co-workers, who have gone the extra mile to support, recognize, and offer patience. Carmen, well...you know. Michelle and Janice, thank you for that last extra push to compose this book and connection to my amazing publisher.

Christian music and our local radio station WAY-FM. Your words softened my struggles, offered hope and kept me afloat daily.

My neighbors, your random and timing of hugs will never be forgotten.

Kim, you raised an amazing young man in Jared. Your passion for suicide awareness massively warms my heart and I'm so excited to see what you do for it in the future.

Maxwell, you did all the dirty work. Your advocating and assertiveness helped us move through this so much easier. Glenn is a better man because of you.

Kelly, Leigh, Nancy, Ann, Deb, Gerri, Jill, Cindy, Carolyn, Christine, Crystal, Susan, and Christina, your friendship means the world to me. You have all played such important roles at some of the most perfect times.

My fellow moms that reside in my club who I have grown close to: Heather, Lori, Kristyn, and Melody. You each have helped me grow, grieve, and breathe.

Kirsten, Linda, LeeAnn, Connie, Angela, Carol, Maggie and Wendy. Forever friends, you all give me so much courage with your consistent flow of love, gifts, messages, and visits. You take the extra step to let me know you're there, and in tragedy, you all came through in mighty ways. Audrey, you have cried with me more than anyone. Your struggles are mine and mine yours.

Kristi, you hold such a special place in my broken heart. Thank you for being there that day, and in one of the most profound moments I will ever experience. You were comfort when I doubted I could have any.

Angie, your presence is peace. You go above every time and capture the details. Thank you for being on the other end when all I could do was cry. I know you're always the first one to offer presence, love, and offerings, expecting nothing in return. Lighting candles all around the world you are helping keep Logan's memory alive!

My besties, Julie, Elisa, Erin, and Julie, I love you more than you will ever know. You have been there from the beginning and perceive my needs and thoughts before I say them. The extensive history of our friendship is something most will only ever read about; it's truly so special. You have been present when it counted the most and somehow always find a way to comfort me and help me love myself again. When I ramble and overanalyze...you care. I really can't say enough about how amazing you women all are. Julie L., you especially helped me see my strength and remind me heaven is cheering me on. Thanks for showing up so many times unannounced when I didn't know what I needed; especially that first night.

My fur best friends, especially the late Mowgli. Their unconditional love is such a sense of peace that I can't get from anywhere else. The intuitive offering of hugs has given way to fur-filled tears more than anyone can imagine. They bring joy and distraction when often little else can.

And finally to Jesus Christ who without his love, I would be without the *HOPE* to continue the journey. This book was written by Him, through me.

I am especially grateful for all of those that allowed me to include them in our journey, and then again in my journaling. I know it will be hard to walk this painful process again, but your struggle and broken hearts will surely allow others to not feel alone. I've found support in unlikely places  through my "grief work" and by allowing myself to be vulnerable. I encourage each of you to do a little more of that; you never know who will be blessed.

# THANK YOU

With great thanks to all who supported this project:

*In honor of Logan. Elizabeth Kirkman*

*Lori and Glenn Boarman*

*Scott and Angie Geiger*

*In loving memory of Logan Ray Boarman and all those we have lost. Love, Elizabeth and Joseph Rathbun*

*Bryce Boarman*

*Kathy Wood*

*In honor of all families struggling with mental health issues and loss.*

*Julianne Margurite*

*Gina Fitzpatrick*

*In honor of Tony Digirolamo. Erin Digirolamo*

*Milana Root*

*Alysia Woods*

*In honor of all of us who suffer on the inside and cannot find the words to express. This is for you. Trish Bernal*

*Zack and Julianne Margurite*

*Carlos and Vivette Cardenas*

*In honor of our loved ones who have gone before us. The love we have never goes away and the day we meet again will be filled with only joy. Vivette Cardenas*

*Brittney Perea*

*In remembrance of Jack Gar and Eddie Dolan. Gone, but never forgotten. Janice Moran*

*In honor of Bill Barksdale lll. Martha Barksdale*

*Steve & Carol White*

# ABOUT THE AUTHOR

Lori, wife and mother of four, lost her 23-year-old son Logan to suicide in December of 2017 and instantly began sharing her story through social media; being raw and vulnerable, she opened her mind and heart for all to see. She resides in Colorado Springs and is a family devoted, faith professing, health and outdoor enthusiast, NICU RN, entrepreneur, slobber-loving woman just trying to make it one day at a time.

CPSIA information can be obtained
at www.ICGtesting.com
Printed in the USA
JSHW010759020620
5982JS00006B/73